Ecological Nostalgias

Studies in Environmental Anthropology and Ethnobiology

General Editor: **Roy Ellen**, FBA

Emeritus Professor of Anthropology and Human Ecology, University of Kent at Canterbury

Interest in environmental anthropology has grown steadily in recent years, reflecting national and international concern about the environment and developing research priorities. This major international series, which continues a series first published by Harwood and Routledge, is a vehicle for publishing up-to-date monographs and edited works on particular issues, themes, places or peoples which focus on the interrelationship between society, culture and environment. Relevant areas include human ecology, the perception and representation of the environment, ethno-ecological knowledge, the human dimension of biodiversity conservation and the ethnography of environmental problems. While the underlying ethos of the series will be anthropological, the approach is interdisciplinary.

Recent volumes:

For a full volume listing, please see the series page on our website:
http://berghahnbooks.com/series/environmental-anthropology-and-ethnobiology

Ecological Nostalgias

Memory, Affect and Creativity in Times of Ecological Upheavals

Edited by Olivia Angé and David Berliner

berghahn
NEW YORK · OXFORD
www.berghahnbooks.com

First published in 2021 by

Berghahn Books

www.berghahnbooks.com

© 2021, 2023 Olivia Angé and David Berliner
First paperback edition published in 2023

Library of Congress Cataloging-in-Publication Data

Names: Angé, Olivia, editor. | Berliner, David, editor.
Title: Ecological nostalgias : memory, affect and creativity in times of
    ecological upheavals / edited by Olivia Angé and David Berliner.
Description: New York : Berghahn Books, 2021. | Series: Studies in
    environmental anthropology and ethnobiology ; volume 26 |
    Includes bibliographical references and index.
Identifiers: LCCN 2020017989 (print) | LCCN 2020017990 (ebook) |
    ISBN 9781789208931 (hardback) | ISBN 9781789208948 (ebook)
Subjects: LCSH: Human ecology—Case studies. | Ethnoecology—
    Case studies. | Global environmental change—Social aspects—
    Case studies. | Nostalgia—Social aspects—Case studies.
Classification: LCC GF51 .E25 2021 (print) | LCC GF51 (ebook) |
    DDC 304.2—dc23
LC record available at https://lccn.loc.gov/2020017989
LC ebook record available at https://lccn.loc.gov/2020017990

British Library Cataloguing in Publication Data

A catalogue record for this book is available from the British Library

ISBN 978-1-78920-893-1 hardback
ISBN 978-1-80073-908-6 paperback
ISBN 978-1-78920-894-8 ebook

https://doi.org/10.3167/9781789208931

Contents

Figures and Maps

Figures

Maps

Acknowledgements

We would like to express our gratitude to the authors of the present book. We are grateful to Dominic Boyer who later accepted to write an afterword. We very much appreciated the rich insight provided by two anonymous reviewers and we are indebted to them for thoroughly reading and commenting the manuscript. The cover picture is a courtesy from Alexander Sigutin, we thank him warmly for giving us the permission to use his art. We have also been fortunate to receive the editorial support of Aron Ponce. Finally, we address our sincere thanks to Marion Berghahn for her interest in our work and for making this book happen.

Introduction

Olivia Angé and David Berliner

This book furthers reflections engaged in a previous collection on the anthropology of nostalgia (Angé and Berliner 2014), by specifically addressing longings for past forms of life in earthly environments. Ecological nostalgias, or as we call them, 'eco-nostalgias', are so pervasive in contemporary societies upset by climate change and the devastation of ecosystems that we believe it deserves to be approached as a singular ethnographic object. Within a modern temporality made of radical revolutions and patrimonial desires for the repetition of the past (Latour 1991: 103), it is no surprise that the major ecological destruction that humans are facing nowadays triggers all sorts of attachments to living organisms that are jeopardised, or already gone.

Let us begin with an example which encapsulates the questions this book explores: agrobiodiversity conservation. All over the globe, a substantial amount of resources and energy is currently being devoted by farmers, scientists and bureaucrats from institutions at all levels, from local NGOs to multinational stakeholders, to curate germplasm from crop plants and their wild relatives. Since the 1970s, Western consortia have started to support gene banks where genetic and phenotypic material is examined and hoarded to ensure their protection. Intended to overcome human hunger in a context of population growth and environmental destruction, the practices involved in seed banking are based on the predicate of 'genetic erosion' (Plucknett and Smith 1987).

The emergence of scientific plant breeding in the 1920s provoked germplasm simplification in many parts of the world (Plucknett and Smith 1987: 8), including centres of domestication. It is ascertained that agricultural intensification in Europe and North America has produced significant genetic erosion from the beginning. In these regions pioneering the industrialization of agriculture, maize production instantiates the devastating effect of crop genetic manipulation in the twentieth century. The diffusion of hybrid seeds in the USA is infamous in this regard: it is estimated that, two decades after their introduction, hybrid varieties covered 90 per cent of the maize fields across the country (Bonneuil and Thomas 2012: 77). In Asia, it is rice that epitomizes the genetic erosion process. In some places, the so-called green revolution[1] expanded on such a massive scale that it may have wiped out heterogeneity in paddies (Brush 2004: 155).

While scientists had been warning about the dangers of monoculture since the 1930s, it was only during the 1960s that concerns about genetic erosion started to grow. The proceedings of a FAO meeting, released in 1970, was the first substantive publication by plant experts to convey anxiety about crops' biological disappearance. In their introduction, Otto Frankel and Erna Bennett assert that 'it is now generally recognized [that] many of the ancient genetic reservoirs are rapidly disappearing' (1970: 2, quoted in Brush 2004: 156). By 1985, a decade after the media had started to broadcast concerns on biodiversity loss, about half of the world's nations had germplasm conservation infrastructure established or underway (Plucknett and Smith 1987: 138).

Genetic conservation in this context is not past-oriented, however. To many curators, the purpose of safeguarding biological material is guided by the hope of creating new varieties in the future.[2] Breeders want to keep the material available to develop grains able to cope with the future food shortage that humanity will face. The strategy is enmeshed in a horizon of catastrophe yet to come. It is cast in apocalyptic times, when climate change will have resulted in severe drought and higher temperatures; or when people will be evicted from their land, obliged to cultivate unfertile plots in new, unexpected ecosystems.

In this vein, genetic erosion is regarded as a systematic consequence of the integration of high-yielding varieties. These would gradually replace the landraces, despised as less productive according to the criteria of agro-industries (Bonneuil and Thomas 2012). In a report published by the FAO in 1999, ethnobotanist Stephen Brush refuted the universality of the genetic erosion predicate, contending that 'historical experience and fieldwork in different cropping systems seem to suggest that there is no definitive pattern of loss. Replacement has occurred in some areas but not in others'. For instance, Andean potato fields feature an outstanding agrobiodiversity,[3] although improved varieties have been widely introduced in the cordillera. The genetic erosion paradigm thus generalizes the homogenization of seeds as an inevitable outcome of the modernization of cultivation. This model supposes that 'primitive agricultures' were stable before development programmes came to disturb ancient patterns of crop distribution by promoting high-yielding varieties. Seed replacement, however, has been proven for centuries and so-called traditional agriculture is in fact extremely dynamic (Louette, Charrier and Berthaud 1997; Zeven 1999). American botanist Jack Harlan praised landraces as 'balanced populations – variable, in equilibrium with both environment and pathogens and genetically dynamic – ... our heritage from past generations of cultivators. They are the result of millennia of natural and artificial selections' (1975: 618). The product of continual selections, landraces, are thus anything but frozen in the past.

Considering the conservation of heirloom varieties as an icon of the intertwined construction of global nature and global culture, Franklin stressed that the purity of lines sought in seeds is not a strictly biological project; heirloom varieties are also appreciated as a source of cultural authenticity. As she unravelled the genealogical tropes permeating seed saving in the global nature-culture, she noted that the 'oldest and most traditional cultural values' are used to instantiate change and transformation (2000b: 84). Longings for past forms of life are enmeshed in complex and ever-changing spatio-temporalities that the concept of eco-nostalgia is intended to explore.

Seed conservation is only one among a series of contemporary actions meant to resuscitate past ecological connections against experiences of degeneration. Practices as diverse as 'forgotten vegetables' revival, herbal medicine, survival camps, rewilding initiatives, lightweight dwellings, ecotourism, urban hives, permaculture or collective gardens are nurtured by representations of a bygone equilibrium. The longings instantiated in these practices rest on the perception of environmental changes that can be gradual or abrupt, dramatic or subtle, wide in scope or locally circumscribed. They engage micro as well as bigger organisms, ecosystems and regions, the whole earth, or even the cosmos. Drawing on an array of ethnographies in the Arctic, Iceland, Mexico, Peru, Malaysia and Mongolia, the contributions to this volume examine the deployment of such eco-nostalgias across continents. We shall see that it is not only multiple life forms that are at stake in these yearnings, but forms of life[4] unfolding in tuber, maize, ice, rock or oil fields.

Above all, this book argues that a notion covering ecological longings is useful to think with. This is justified by the empirical mushrooming of environmental anxieties and the crucial political stakes that lie behind related initiatives. But as much as the concept is accepted as a non-essentialist heuristic device with blurred boundaries, it will also enrich theoretical discussions about nostalgia. In a pioneering text, Dominic Boyer pinned down five necessary ingredients of nostalgia in Eastern Europe. He suggested that it is heteroglossic, indexical, allochronic, symptomal and oriented toward the future (2010). Following his effort, our own exploration of yearning for earthly flourishing aims at singularizing eco-nostalgias as compared to other types of longings. In particular, this introduction puts forward four propositions. First, eco-nostalgias are spatial and temporal at the same time. Second, they unfold in natures-cultures. Third, they are critical and creative; or else, and fourthly, they exude imperialist impetus.

First Proposition: Eco-nostalgias Are Spatial and Temporal at the Same Time

Eco-nostalgias help us rethink the links between time and space. The etymology of nostalgia as a regret for a lost home,[5] conveying the sense of a spatial impossibility to return, is well-known. Beside military displacements, traumatic professional migrations were reported by Doctor Hofer in his thesis introducing the neologism in the seventeenth century. During the nineteenth century, however, the spatial dimension was replaced by a temporal one, in line with the celebration of a modernist ideology articulated on a temporality of acceleration, progress and rupture.[6] This semantic shift contrasts with the historical context, since this was a time of major spatial disjunction triggered by the intensification of capitalist economies of exchange and extraction. Previous agricultural enclosures stood out as a turning point in the European peasants' history when attachment to usurped land caused massive riots and social protests. While claims for communal land tenure were despised by elites as 'nostalgia for the past' (Federici 2014: 70), these very same elites favoured other instantiations of conservative eco-nostalgia.[7] Despite such important geographical transfigurations and related affective effusions, the spatial meaning of nostalgia was substituted by a metaphorical one hinging upon temporality: more than a yearning for a lost place, nostalgia began to refer to a vanished time. Thus, addressing eco-nostalgia brings its spatial dimension back to the fore.

Whist eco-nostalgic experiences existed long before an international awareness about massive environmental disasters was raised, human displacements are taking on an unprecedented scope in the twenty-first century. Recent catastrophes have forced populations to flee areas that have become inhospitable, described as 'sacrifice zones' by Naomi Klein (2016). First coined in a 1973 report by the US National Academy of Science in reference to zones where intensive mining eliminates any prospect of productive rehabilitation, this expression was subsequently generalized to designate territories that have been given up in the name of profit and technological progress. Today, these areas extend beyond sites of extraction, through the effect of ubiquitous ecological upheavals. The multiplication of climate refugees raises major concerns and international tensions, and the expulsion of communities as a result of global warming will certainly generate many nostalgists in the future.[8]

Furthermore, eco-nostalgias encompass significantly more traumatic experiences that do not necessarily imply embodied displacement. Under capitalism, intense and widespread ecosystemic transfiguration operates in our surroundings within very short duration. People lose their place without going away from it physically. Mining extraction, nuclear accidents, logging, water contamination, temperature increase or species extinction and invasion transform familiar environments into estranged locations. In this case, the passing of time entails spatial disjunctions that are not related to the endless journeys with which nostalgia has been associated since Homer's Odysseus. As Glenn Albrecht put it, 'environmental damage has made it possible to be homesick without leaving home' (2006). This is corroborated by our stories about Andean potato growers, ice dwellers in the Arctic and Iceland, rainforest inhabitants in Ecuador and in Malaysia alike. This book asks what it means to occupy a place that is shared with jeopardized organisms, haunted by the absence of former non-human life, a biotope experiencing what Ann Stoler lucidly calls 'ruination'.

Second Proposition:
Eco-nostalgias Unfold in Natures-Cultures

The core themes addressed by existing anthropological scholarship on nostalgia hover around the formation of social and cultural identities. In this book, however, we argue that a strictly human-centred perspective cannot account for the importance of these yearnings, even less in the ongoing context of climate change and ecological disasters. As our contributors demonstrate, in damaged environments, longings bring together humans, plants, animals, ancestors and a wide array of earthly organisms connected through bodily communication. To many people around the globe, the world is not experienced as a 'nature' ontologically distinct from anthropic sociality, but rather as a configuration of heterogeneous relations involving an array of living creatures (de la Cadena 2015; Descola 2005; Ingold 2000; Strathern 1980). Hence, we think that investigating eco-nostalgias requires delving into nature-cultures (Latour 1991) across multiple settings. Therefore, the exploration of eco-nostalgias demands that we take a multispecies approach encompassing 'the host of organisms whose lives and deaths are linked to human social worlds' (Kirksey and Helmreich 2010: 545; see also Ogden et al. 2013; and Van Dooren et. al. 2016). Latourian and Harawayan in its premises, this perspective examines the participation of ontologically diverse actors in the fabric of existence, focusing on embodied experiences and affective engagements within more-than-human assemblages.

In her seminal analysis of dog-human complicity, Donna Haraway scrutinized encounters between 'companion species', these cross-species intimate partners tied by an enduring relation that is both instrumental and careful (2008). In the same vein, the intertwining of emotional and instrumental dimensions is beautifully captured by Vinciane Despret and Michel Meuret's study of cosmo-ecological sheep breeding. They describe how young urbanites in Southern France become shepherds by learning herding practices, such as transhumance, abandoned by most farmers in the quest for agricultural modernization. In this process, humans and sheep jointly discover how to behave in unfamiliar pastures; together they discover how to dwell in unknown mountainous ecosystems. As the authors explain, what is at stake here is not only a matter of producing more and better meat for consumption. 'These practices cannot be reduced to a livestock economy: shepherds consider herding a work of transformation and ecological recuperation – of the land, of the sheep, of ways of being together' (2016b: 24). The ethnographic accounts gathered in this volume document nostalgic attachments emerging in interspecies encounters that are also instrumental and careful. Yearning for merry cassava beer festivals (High), pigs and deer proximity (Ellen), collective mountainous journeys (Pitrou), fresh water to bathe in the river bed (Irvine), uncontaminated narwhal meat (Hastrup), or freshly harvested smoked potato (Angé), they all convey a sense of regret for past enjoyments.

Yet they also manifest concerns for others' discomfort, shedding light on non-humans' experiences when homes are destroyed, estranged or unreachable.[9] In Thom Van Dooren's poignant book (2014), we meet little penguins dwelling at the shorelines of the Sydney Harbour, members of the last colony on the Australian mainland. Van Dooren highlights these birds' perseverance in returning to the same spot to engage in their reproduction work, year after year. His examination of penguins' forms of life shows that 'these are specific places, not all interchangeable, but deeply storied, carrying the past experiences of individuals and the generations before them' (2014: 64). However, an increasing population of pets and their human partners building houses, seawalls and swimming pools has made the shorelines inhospitable for the penguins who now survive at the edge of extinction. They are 'fatally tied to disappearing or lost places' (Van Dooren et al. 2016: 66), like many other philopatric[10] animals all over the globe. Their *Umwelt*[11] is becoming uncomfortable, unlivable. In the same vein, Howe's description of bears' lethal disorientation, Irvine's account of weakening trees, and Angé's study of potato discontent in dried fields are stories of non-human suffering in rapidly changing worlds.

Within interspecies companionships, partners are enmeshed through multiple sensorial captors, allowing for increased 'attentiveness' (Van

Dooren et al. 2016) to possible transformations in their respective state of being, thus providing a relational intimacy prone to the emergence of eco-nostalgias. Such expressions of nostalgia are always contingent and evanescent: they yearn for the presence of an animal or a plant, for biological symbiosis, for interspecies mode of connection, for an assemblage inside a given ecosystem. In her account of matsutake mushroom love in the Japanese society, Anna Tsing eloquently highlighted smell as a powerful conveyor of fungi affect. While Europeans qualified it as nauseating, Japanese aficionados say matsutake 'smells like village life and a childhood visiting grandparents and chasing dragonflies. It recalls open pinewoods, now crowded out and dying' (2015: 48).

The following chapters corroborate the importance of olfaction for triggering memories of interspecies constellations; they also acknowledge the potential of other kinds of sensorial communication to conjure up former ecological entanglements. Waiting for the 'Devil's Symphony' in an icy world (Howe), watching the horizon of empty hunting grounds (Hastrup), smelling the acrid odour of animals killed in a poaching massacre (High), missing the taste of smoked potato at harvest time (Angé), searching for chestnuts in thorny brambles (Sallustio) or muscular tensions in maize fields (Pitrou) all constitute transient instants of bodily perception likely to induce nostalgia.

Interestingly, such encounters condense memories that are simultaneously biographical and historical. Collisions between childhood remembrance and the current situation bring out decaying colours, scents, rustles, streams or flavours subdued by environmental deterioration. Conveying a sense of temps perdu like the Proustian madeleines, eco-nostalgia departs from mere recollections of pastry, to being more than reminiscences of personal experience: here, lived stories are concatenated with tales of devastation. To Tsing's matsutake lovers, the village life encapsulated in smell 'was an easier time, before nature became degraded and poisonous' (ibid.). It is in such a diachronic perception combining historical and subjective spatio-temporalities that the critical and creative potential of eco-nostalgias emerges.

Third Proposition:
Eco-nostalgias Are Critical and Creative

Whilst being seen as a conservative affect by some (Albrecht 2006), we argue that eco-nostalgias can encourage for innovative action and 'reclaim'of devastated zones (Stengers 2012). Furthering Tsing's exploration of 'blasted landscapes' (2015: 181), Kirksey et al. delved into desolated places of New Orleans in the aftermath of Hurricane Katarina to highlight the emergence of new forms of interspecies intimacies and responsibilities that brought forth 'biocultural hope' (2013: 229). Sometimes, complicities arise taking the shape of a 'radical solidarity project' (Myers 2017: 299). Despret and Meuret's above-mentioned description encapsulates the subversive potential nested in past inspiration. The authors specify that this is not 'the vague nostalgia of a harmony that would have been lost' (2016a: 27, our translation), in the Proustian vein. Theirs is a political and aesthetic decision to 'invent ways of inhabiting a world that is being destroyed while resisting, locally and actively, this destruction' (2016b: 30). Similarly, in Kyoto, Tsing met with a professor who sublimated his yearning into practice by revitalizing an abandoned woodland with his students. Learning the arts of multispecies care, they engaged in a 'labor of love' (2015: 183) intended to create propitious conditions for a thriving forest.

Another illustration of such creative potential is provided by the Latvian 'tomato rebellion' reported by Guntra Aistara (2014). In this region, newly integrated into the European Union, attachments to seeds as carriers of the taste of childhood and the Soviet years incentivize political activism. Gardeners grow a diversity of tomatoes embodying biographical and historical pasts, as forms of resistance to the implementation of the European Union seed law encouraging standardization and registration. Studying the use of seeds by Vietnamese migrants in the US to forge a sense of homeland, Virginia Nazarea points out the disruptive potential of activities triggered by nostalgia: '[Heirloom plants'] persistence against the hegemony of modernity sustains stirrings of nostalgia, making the desire to journey back, or to re-create a place, less of a romantic anachronism and more of a real possibility' (2005: 114–15).

In her examination of migrants' suffering, Sara Ahmed drew on the Freudian theory which understands melancholia as a sad longing for a lost object that is not identified (2010: 140). In contrast to such death wishes, she acknowledged that 'the recognition of loss does not involve the pathos of realizing that something has gone that cannot be retrieved but rather the excitement of recognizing what can be retrieved, of what is still possible, even if not available at present' (2010: 153). Then, yearning for the past entails hope, even if what is retrieved is not identical to the lost object. As a matter of fact, the regret for lost lifeforms can produce 'concrete objects of desires' (Kirksey et al. 2013: 241). Nadia Seremetakis' (1994) story about a peach known as the 'the breast of Aphrodite' is an emblematic case in this regard. Longings for the precious fruit that she ate during her childhood in Greece engaged her in the search for a variety of tree she wished to plant in her yard.

Eco-nostalgias are very much expressed through 'acts' that materialize what is said to be vanished: cooking 'forgotten vegetables' brings them to existence. Such a performative dimension has been famously encapsulated in Svetlana Boym's notion of restorative nostalgia, as an attempt at 'a transhistorical reconstruction of the lost home'.[12] When driving to their ranchos to cultivate maize plots, the Mexican villagers studied by Pitrou enact agricultural and food practices they would not want to see lost because of urbanization. Likewise, in France, Sallustio documents the creation of original ways of life by recent rural settlers who take inspiration from pre-industrial farming to cope with present-day ecological challenges. Young adults planning to build new camps in the Amazonian rainforest (High), potato growers experimenting with native varieties better suited to changing climates (Angé), Icelandic artists releasing 15,000-year-old air encapsulated in ice-blocks during the COP21 (Howe), or arctic trackers using their dog sledges to hunt and transport film crews in search of the 'last Eskimo' also illustrate the valorization and reconfiguration of ancient techniques to navigate troubled times and spaces. In that sense, studying ecological nostalgias opens up avenues for understanding the forces that bring people to produce critical tropes and alternative acts in their quest for a liveable future.

Be that as it may, let us not be too romantic. Some are equally inclined to deviate from the subversive potential of nostalgic attachments and instrumentalize them according to their own political or commercial agenda, as our fourth point shall suggest.

Fourth Proposition:
Or Else They Are Imperialist

Contemporary eco-nostalgias are a nexus where visceral yearnings for past forms of life and institutional tropes of nostalgias meet. Ethnographic accounts in this book represent scientists, government officers, schoolteachers, development stakeholders and conservationists who convey, often vicariously, nostalgic figures of environmental loss. Ironically, these outsiders are sometime complicit, however inadvertently, in the very changes they lament, turning eco-nostalgias into 'imperialist' ones 'where people mourn the passing of what they themselves have transformed' (Rosaldo 1989: 108). In his groundbreaking article, Rosaldo mentioned the paradoxical dimension of eco-nostalgias: 'at one more remove, people destroy their environment and then worship nature' (1989: 108). Eco-nostalgias not only hint at 'mourning for what one has destroyed', but also involve lamenting for what one will annihilate in the future (Howe, this volume).

Take for example the implementation of Protected Areas which is justified as safeguarding wildlife against the damage caused by human livelihood. Geographer Roderick Neumann drew the historical continuity between the circumscription of safeguarded areas in Great Britain (hinged upon agricultural enclosures) and the establishment of national parks in post-colonial Africa. He argued that 'Africa, for some Europeans, represented a lost Eden in need of protection and preservation, and that this sentiment was a major motivation behind the conservation laws and national parks' (1996: 80). At the same time, it is well documented how national parks served to legitimize the displacement of some of its dwellers for the benefit of others, while extractive devastation continued in the surrounding areas (Adams and Hutton 2007; Meskell 2018; West, Igoe and Brockington 2002).

Similarly, Dustin Greenwalt and Brian Creech have analysed the strategic use of nostalgia by a state institution through the case of the Documerica project, a photographic campaign launched by the US Environmental Protection Agency. Comparing pictures of polluted landscapes, massive extraction and industrial towns with those of apparently uncontaminated wildlife, they show how nostalgia for both wilderness and unlimited industrial extraction is displayed to promote economies of sustainability, intended for the perpetuation of a capitalist mode of exploitation and consumption. Such instrumentalization of eco-nostalgias can also serve marketing purposes. Olivia Angé (2015) has described the extent to which attachments for lost rurality, related to artisanal craft and a sense of solidarity, are utilized as commercial devices by an international bakery chain based on capitalist manufacturing. In his afterword, Dominic Boyer affirms that ecological yearnings often glorify a politics of the future, avoiding any substantial changes. Public campaigns in the Documerica style, sourdough bread or germ plasm hoarding support his claim, as they all 'appear to be about the restoration of imperial splendour (Making the Anthropocene Great Again)'. Such nostalgic tropes, intended to maintain the current state of affairs, have a long history under capitalism.[13]

What our contributors show are the complex entanglements of hegemonic eco-nostalgias with other forms of longings. Often, vicarious nostalgia draws on the affective impetus involved within interspecies companionship to pursue imperialist endeavours.[14] Roy Ellen unravels a clash between rainforest nostalgia held by its inhabitants who bodily engage with it on a daily basis, like the Nuaulu in Indonesia, and eco-nostalgic motives depleted from sensorial density, expressed by government officers, urban citizens, biologists and environmentalists. While the forest is a place of dwelling crafted by the former's care, the latter depict it as a pristine wildland offering a pool of natural resources of global interest. In her chapter, Kirsten Hastrup remarks on outsiders' portrayal of the Thule as 'people from the past', while they keenly engage with all kinds of contemporary opportunities. Although they cooperate with film makers, researchers, tourists and journalists in the search for the 'last Eskimos', their life unfolds in another temporality grappling with the dilemmas of their persistence on the ice, despite climate change and threatening pollution.

Sometimes, institutional tropes find echoes in local communities. Olivia Angé describes the collaborations between Andean cultivators, a local NGO and international agencies to promote in situ conservation of potato landraces, as well as an ethic of more-than-human reciprocities inspired from pre-Columbian philosophies. In the Amazonian forest, the Waorani studied by Casey High have become acquainted with ideas of cultura (culture) and 'environmental conservation'. A new appreciation of the land is put forth where horizons of scarcity and irretrievable loss substitute the tropes of abundance that used to characterize the *wao öme* (Waorani land). Still, to Waorani people what is in danger is not an ancestral culture or a pristine nature, it is *wao öme* as a space-time for enjoyable and fertile relations and the possibility of a good life. Likewise, in the Mongolian steppe, Richard D.G. Irvine documents ecological attachments in a herder village under a post-socialist government. Unpacking another declination of the homeland, the *nutag*, he sheds light on intertwined temporalities materialized in the landscape and explains how kinship stories mingle with nationalist narratives. All such encounters bring into play multilayered perceptions of space and time that are not subsumed within the linear temporality implied by modernist eco-nostalgic tropes.

***

Discourses of loss, whether they address natural or cultural changes, are pandemic today. They tell us something about the world we live in (Berliner 2020): a world under threat in which many humans feel powerlessness and anxiety, where a-good-life-for-all-humans and interspecies relatedness seem unattainable. The anthropologists gathered in this volume bring to light individuals and groups diversely expressing their desires to persist on such a damaged planet, or how they learn from the past to create new ways of inhabiting their homes. Hopefully, as hope and nostalgia walk hand in hand, such voices gain more traction in the public spheres all over the globe. It is, however, a matter of political choice to take these voices seriously.

Olivia Angé is Associate Professor at Université Libre de Bruxelles. She specializes in the study of agricultures and value creation in the Andes. She is the author of *Barter and Social Regeneration in the Argentinean Andes* (Berghahn, 2018).

David Berliner is Professor of Anthropology at Université Libre de Bruxelles. His research interests include social memory and cultural transmission. He is the author of *Losing Culture: Nostalgia, Heritage, and Our Accelerated Times* (Rutgers, 2020).

Notes

1. This expression refers to 'technological change', the spread of high-yielding crop varieties and high-energy inputs such as fertilizer (Brush 1992: 145).
2. Donald Plucknett and Nigel Smith identified the rationale of gene banks as future-geared: 'plant breeding, an outgrowth of genetics, has a central role in the worldwide effort to improve agricultural output, and breeders rely on genetic resources to produce better-adapted and higher-yielding varieties' (1987: 3).
3. While most cultivators have reduced the number of varieties in their plots at the regional level, there seems to be no erosion in the potato gene pool (Brush 1992; de Haan et. al. 2010; Zimmerer 1996).
4. Stefan Helmreich advanced an insightful distinction between lifeforms and forms of life. Lifeforms are organisms entangled in an ecological configuration. The forms of life are 'those cultural, social, symbolic and pragmatic ways of thinking and acting that organize humans' (2009: 6, quoted in Van Dooren 2014, although the latter argues that non-human animals elaborate forms of life as well).
5. Etymologically, nostalgia is a neologism created from the Greek *nostos* (returning home) and *algos* (pain, ache, grief). Originally nostalgia referred to an intense homesickness caused by geographical displacement. While returning to one's homeland is a yearning described in literature as early as in Homer's *Odyssey*, the neologism itself was only coined in the seventeenth century by Johannes Hofer who thereby diagnosed a potentially fatal disease (Bolzinger 2007).
6. As Latour puts it: 'par l'adjectif moderne, on désigne un régime nouveau, une accélération, une rupture, une révolution du temps' ('by the modern adjective, we designate a new regime, an acceleration, a rupture, a revolution of time'; 1991: 20, our translation).
7. Art and literature in the eighteenth and nineteenth centuries contributed to the diffusion of eco-nostalgias at this time. Oliver Goldsmith's *The Deserted Village* provides a striking example. Written at a moment of the dislocation of rural communities under the enclosure legislation, this famous poem is imbued with

nostalgic attachment for an idealized past in the countryside. Whilst Goldsmith longings denounce peasants' dispossession, this nostalgia was not necessarily critical. According to art historian Ann Berminghan, ecological yearnings conveyed by the '[English] picturesque aesthetic muted the problems caused by enclosure and the agricultural revolution and harkened back to a golden age' (1986: 83).

8. In her lecture, Klein emphasizes that these zones are populated by subaltern communities, most of the time cultural minorities, drawing thereby a correlation between environmental destruction and racism (see also Hage 2017a). Studying eco-nostalgias opens a rich vein to shed light on the 'relation between racial and environmental othering' (Hage 2017b) in contemporary societies.

9. Despret and Meuret explain that sheep grazing sites were deserted under breeding modernization initiatives, sometimes becoming inaccessible due to overgrown vegetation. When the new shepherds opened the pen doors, sheep excitedly wandered hills as their 'cradle' (2016a: 120, our translation). The flock articulated on a collective memory embodied and enacted in grazing, which entailed selecting plants as food, thereby regenerating places.

10. This is the term used by biologists to refer to animals' periodic return to their place of birth.

11. *Umwelt* is a key notion in Jackob von Uexkull's (2004) semiotic theory. It refers to an environment as perceived by a given animal, according to the sensorial organs he is endowed with. Sensorial captors enable the perception of certain objects, at the expense of others. Those captured by the senses are imbued with signification and therefore affect the perceiving body.

12. http://monumenttotransformation.org/atlas-of-transformation/html/n/nostalgia/nostalgia-svetlana-boym.html (last accessed 24 June 2020).

13. In her study of the English rustic aesthetic in the eighteenth century, Bermingham deciphers its eco-nostalgic tone as enmeshed in aristocrats' 'strong commitment to the economic order of the present' (1986: 77).

14. Rosaldo already warned us of an 'attempt to use a seemingly harmless mood as a mask of innocence to cover their involvement with processes of domination' (1989: 120).

References

Adams, W. and J. Hutton. 2007. 'People, Parks, and Poverty: Political Ecology and Biodiversity Conservation", *Conservation and Society* 5(2): 147–83.

Ahmed, S. 2010. *The Promise of Happiness*. Durham, NC and London: Duke University Press.

Aistara, G.A. 2014. 'Actually Existing Tomatoes: Politics of Memory, Variety, and Empire in Latvian Struggles over Seeds', *Focaal-Journal of Global and Historical Anthropology* 69: 12–27.

Albrecht, G. 2006. '"Solastalgia": A New Concept in Health and Identity', *PAN: Philosophy, Activism, Nature* 3: 41–55.

Angé, O. 2015. 'Le gout d'autrefois: Pain au levain et attachements nostalgiques dans la société contemporaine', *Terrain* 65: 34–51.

Angé, O. and D. Berliner (eds). 2014. *Anthropology and Nostalgia*. Oxford: Berghahn Books.

Berliner, David. 2020. *Losing Culture. Nostalgia, Heritage, and our Accelerated Times*. New Brunswick: Rutgers University Press.

Bermingham, A. 1986. *Landscape and Ideology: The English Rustic Tradition, 1740–1860*. Berkeley, CA: University of California Press.

Bolzinger, A. 2007. *Histoire de la nostalgie*. Paris: Editions Campagne Première.

Bonneuil, C. and F. Thomas. 2012. *Semences: une histoire politique. Amélioration des plantes, agriculture et alimentation en France depuis la Seconde mondiale*. Paris: Editions Charles Leopold Mayer.

Boyer, D. 2010. 'From Algos to Autonomos: Nostalgic Eastern Europe as Post-imperial Mania', in M. Todorova and Z. Gille (eds), *Post-Communist Nostalgia*. Oxford: Berghahn, pp. 17–28.

Brush, S. 1992. 'Reconsidering the Green Revolution: Diversity and Stability in Cradle Areas of Crop Domestication', *Human Ecology* 20(2): 145–67.

_____. 1999. 'Genetic Erosion of Crop Populations in Centers of Diversity: A Revision', *Food and Agriculture Organization of the United States*, retrieved 28 January 2020, http://agris.fao.org/agris-search/search.do?recordID=CZ2001001045.

_____. 2004. *Farmers' Bounty: Locating Crop Diversity in the Contemporary World*. Ann Arbor, MI: Sheridan Books.

De la Cadena, M. 2015. *Earth Beings: Ecologies of Practice Across Andean Worlds*. Durham, NC: Duke University Press.

Descola, P. 2005. *Par-delà nature et culture*. Paris: Gallimard.

De Haan S, et al. 2010. 'Multilevel Agrobiodiversity and Conservation of Andean Potatoes in Central Peru. Species, Morphological, Genetic, and Spatial Diversity', *Mountain Research and Development* 30(3): 222–31.

Despret, V. and M. Meuret. 2016a. *Composer avec les moutons: Lorsque des brebis apprennent à leurs bergers à leur apprendre*. Paris: Cadere.

_____. 2016b. 'Cosmoecological Sheep and the Arts of Living on a Damaged Planet', *Environmental Humanities* 8(1): 24–36.

Federici, S. 2014 [2004]. *Caliban and the Witch: Women, the Body and Primitive Accumulation*, 2nd edn. New York: Autonomedia.

Frankel, O.H. and E. Bennett. 1970. 'Genetic Conservation in Perspective', in O.H. Frankel and E. Bennett (eds), *Genetic Resources in Plants – Their Exploration and Conservation*. Oxford: Blackwell Scientific Publications, pp. 469–89.

Franklin, S. 2000a. 'Life Itself: Global Nature and the Genetic Imaginary', in S. Franklin, C. Lurry and J. Stacey (eds), *Global Nature, Global Culture*. London: Sage, pp. 188–227.

_____. 2000b. 'Units of Genealogy', in S. Franklin, C. Lurry and J. Stacey (eds), *Global Nature, Global Culture*. London: Sage, pp. 68–96.

Greenwalt, D. and B. Creech. 2018. 'Nostalgic Environmentalities in the EPA's Documerica and State of the Environment Projects', *Visual Communication*, retrieved 28 January 2020, https://doi.org/10.1177/1470357218779119.

Hage, G. 2017a. *Is Racism an Environmental Threat?* Cambridge: Polity Press.

_____. 2017b. 'On the Relation Between Racial and Environmental "Othering"', in V. Prashad (ed.), *Will the Flower Slip through the Asphalt? Writers Respond to Capitalist Climate Change*. New Delhi: LeftWord Books, pp. 58–65.

Haraway, D. 2008. *When Species Meet*. Minneapolis: University of Minnesota Press.

Harlan, J.R. 1975. 'Our Vanishing Genetic Resources', *Science* 188: 618–21.

Ingold, T. 2000. *The Perception of the Environment: Essays on Livelihood, Dwelling and Skill*. London: Routledge.

Kirksey, E. and S. Helmreich. 2010. 'The Emergence of Multispecies Ethnography', *Cultural Anthropology* 25: 545–76.

Kirksey, E., N. Shapiro and M. Brodine. 2013. 'Hope in Blasted Landscape', *Social Science Information* 52(2): 228–56.

Klein, N. 2016. 'Let Them Drown: The Violence of Othering in a Warming World', in V. Prashad (ed.), *Will the Flower Slip through the Asphalt? Writers Respond to Capitalist Climate Change*. New Delhi: LeftWord Books, pp. 29–49.

Latour, B. 1991. *Nous n'avons jamais été modernes: Essai d'anthropologie symétrique*. Paris: La Découverte.

Louette, D., A. Charrier and J. Berthaud. 1997. 'In-Situ Conservation of Maize in Mexico, Genetic Diversity and Maize Seed Management in a Traditional Community', *Economic Botany* 51: 20–39.

Meskell, L. 2018. *A Future in Ruins: UNESCO, World Heritage, and the Dream of Peace*. Oxford: Oxford University Press.

Myers, N. 2017. 'From the Anthropocene to the Planthroposcene: Designing Gardens for Plant/People Involution', *History and Anthropology* 28(3): 297–301.

Nazarea, V. 2005. *Heirloom Seeds and their Keepers: Marginality and Memory in the Conservation of Biological Diversity*. Tucson, AZ: University of Arizona Press.

Neumann, R. 1996. 'Dukes, Earls, and Ersatz Edens: Aristocratic Nature Preservationists in Colonial Africa', *Environment and Planning D: Society and Space* 14: 79–98.

Ogden, L., B. Hall and K. Tanita. 2013. 'Animals, Plants, People, and Things: A Review of Multispecies Ethnography', *Environment and Society: Advances in Research* 4: 5–24.

Plucknett, D. and N. Smith. 1987. *Gene Banks and the World's Food*. Princeton, NJ: Princeton University Press.

Prashad, V. 2017. 'Introduction', in V. Prashad (ed.), *Will the Flower Slip through the Asphalt? Writers Respond to Capitalist Climate Change*. New Delhi: LeftWord Books, pp. 12–28.

Rosaldo, R. 1989. 'Imperialist Nostalgia', *Representations* 26: 107–22.

Seremetakis, C.N. 1994. 'The Memory of the Senses. Part I: Marks of the transitory', in C.N Seremetakis (ed.), *The Senses Still*. Boulder, CO: Westview Press, pp. 1–18.

Stengers, I. 2012. 'Reclaiming Animism', *e-flux journal* (36).

Stoler, A. 2013. *Imperial Debris: On Ruins and Ruination*. Durham, NC: Duke University Press.

Strathern, M. 1980. 'No Nature, No Culture: The Hagen Case', in C. MacCormarck and M. Strathern (eds), *Nature, Culture, and Gender*. Cambridge: Cambridge University Press, pp. 174–222.

Tsing, A. 2015. *The Mushroom at the End of the World: On the Possibility of Life in Capitalist Ruins*. Princeton, NJ: Princeton University Press.

Van Dooren, T. 2014. *Flight Ways: Life and Loss at the Edge of Extinction*. New York: Columbia University Press.

Van Dooren, T., E. Kirksey and U. Münster. 2016. 'Multispecies Studies: Cultivating Arts of Attentiveness', *Environmental Humanities* 8(1): 1–23.

von Uexkull, J. 2004. *Mondes animaux et mondes humains*. Paris: Pocket.

West, P., J. Igoe and D. Brockington. 2002. 'Parks and Peoples: The Social Impact of Protected Areas', *Annual Review of Anthropology* 35: 251–77.

Zeven, A.C. 1999. 'The Traditional Inexplicable Replacement of Seed Ware of Landraces and Cultivars: A Review', *Euphytica* 110: 181–99.

Zimmerer, K. 1996. *Changing Fortunes: Biodiversity and Peasant Livelihood in the Peruvian Andes*. Berkeley, CA: University of California Press.

CHAPTER 1

Thinking Through Nostalgia in Anthropologies of the Environment and Ethnographies of Landscape

Roy Ellen

> Here, in the vibrant, tactile scented gloom is the landscape of nostalgia and abandonment.
>
> —A. Gell, 'The Language of the Forest:
> Landscape and Phonological Iconism in Umeda'

Introduction

Memory is everywhere in current anthropological writing, whether as a subject of research or as a trope, such that some observers think it much overplayed, vacuous and semantically overextended (Berliner 2005; White 2006). I tend to agree. Memory is not just another word for culture, by which we usually mean everything transmitted from one generation to the next, while 'social remembering', in the sense of implying that societies have memories, entails a logical error in attributing an impossible capacity to an abstract second order category. In this chapter I treat memory as a cognitive property only of individual organisms, but also a property which organisms (especially human organisms) can instantiate through the 'extended phenotype' and re-organize through social distribution and the intelligent use of artefacts. I critically examine the treatment accorded to memory in the ways in which anthropologists have conceptualized cultural adaptation, especially in what we might conveniently call 'anthropologies of the environment'. In the first part, I argue that from being implicit in the explanatory apparatus of ecological and environmental anthropology since at least Julian Steward, the role of memory has not always been explicit. Indeed, as we move through successive and competing paradigms, so we transition from denial and ignorance to increasing acknowledgement of a place for memory. In this context ecological nostalgia might be seen as the selective use of memory by the subjects of our research to create potent and evocative valuations of particular scenarios which impact on how people store, represent and use environmental information; and the selective evocation of a romanticized past of the protagonists by those who study them. The consequences of all this vary depending on different socio-cultural configurations, and how these draw on emotional resources (White 2006) to reinforce particular kinds of memory.

In the second part of the chapter, I focus on two case studies that show how specific ecological nostalgias are dependent on the ways in which people make their environments, both physically and conceptually. In situations where states have come to re-define environmental relations, nostalgias can in various ways become 'false', through a process in which science, governments, stakeholder citizens, heritage specialists and traditional peoples may all in different ways be complicit. I illustrate this with reference to research conducted in and around the Batu Apoi forest reserve in Brunei during the mid-1990s, and among Nuaulu people on Seram, during the period 2000–2015 as they put together arguments in support of negotiations with the Indonesian government to establish an independent devolved administration. I show how what some people might describe as 'ecological nostalgia' has reinforced notions of ancient political autonomy that have transformed Nuaulu relations with the state, while at the same time the complexities of historical process prevent any easy definition of what, in this instance, this might actually constitute.

The Concepts of Memory and Nostalgia in Anthropologies of the Environment

The earliest theoretical formulations of the human-environment relationship accorded little ostensible role for memory (Ellen 1982). Where environments were seen to mechanistically determine cultural outcomes – as for example in the anthropogeography of some of the followers of Frederic Ratzel – there was no need for local cultural populations 'to remember' previous accommodations. However, as soon as the notion of 'cultural adaptation' becomes central to the modelling of human-environment relationships, as we find in the possibilism of Daryll Forde or in Julian Steward's cultural ecology, so memory becomes implicit, if not always explicit. People not only learn from their accumulated experience of a particular environment, but from the remembered experience of their predecessors. Cultural adaptation can be seen in the objective process through which certain practices allow one individual, group or population to survive better than another, but whether this is inadvertent or the consequence of premeditated action, the successful outcome depends on memory, either memories of past practices used to instantiate innovation into routine behaviour, or the transmission of instantiated practices and knowledge between individuals and populations over space and time. The role accorded to memory in post-Stewardian models is implicitly much expanded, but not always any more explicit, possibly because 'memory' as an analytical concept for a long time was assumed to be the preserve of psychologists rather than ecological anthropologists. But with the arrival of ethnoecology and the concept of 'indigenous knowledge', adaptation becomes an active rather than a passive process, its role reflected in the complex culturally transmitted classifications and protocols for organizing knowledge and using it to solve problems in material situations. The decision-making involved in environmental management is inevitably based on individual and collective memories. And in that other critical response to the mechanistic Stewardian theory of the separation of culture and environment systems, memory (as in the 'cognized models' of Rappaport 1979: 97–144) becomes a cybernetic loop supporting emic models of the world. Thus, successive re-workings of culture-environment theory have gradually recognized how initial responses to environmental problems faced by people in low energy small-scale subsistence systems, generally beginning as short-term problems for individuals, become institutionalized in the longer term through personal life-histories and sharing, such that the individual episodic response is transformed intergenerationally and collectively into a mimetic cultural memory.

We must, of course, distinguish the memories and nostalgias attributed to the subjects of anthropological research from the (oftentimes covert) nostalgia reflected in the assumptions and methodologies of anthropologists themselves. There can be little doubt that historically, anthropologists looking at traditional pre-capitalist and pre-industrial modes of subsistence, that were in decline and under threat at the moment when they were being studied, have often been tempted to see them as the remnants of systems that once functioned in ways that were fully adaptive and had been, until the present, perfectly evolved for their environmental circumstances. In such views we find a convenient convergence between in-harmony-with-nature and pristine ecology arguments (Ellen 1986). Thus, Lee (1966) argued for a model of 'affluent' and autonomous hunter-gatherer subsistence among !Kung San bushmen that required downplaying their precarity of existence, intermittent arduous work schedules and the role of exchange with outside agricultural societies. This interpretation has since been extensively critiqued, and later partially retracted (e.g. Konner and Shostak 1986). Similarly, Rappaport, who argued persuasively in the first edition (1968) of *Pigs for the Ancestors* for self-sustaining cybernetic loops involving ritual regulation amongst Tsembaga of New Guinea just as these systems were 'breaking down', had by the second edition in 1984 to back-track somewhat. Certainly, it is very clear to me that both Lee and Rappaport were influenced by covert nostalgia in their assumptions and reconstructions regarding the 'pristine' systems they were describing. Friedman (1974) disparagingly described the models on which such reconstructions were based as 'ecological functionalism', thus linking the new ecology to a more general anthropological functionalism which had by then been discredited. Although for Friedman the linkage was 'ideological', it was also in almost equal measure encouraged by the fairly standard liberal and romantic anthropological imagination of primitive arcadias linked to the emergent environmentalist concerns of the late twentieth-century West, including (agro-)biodiversity loss, landscape despoiliation and ecological transformation. Such analyses were hardly uncommon in anthropology during the second half of the twentieth century, and arguably continue in much work motivated by ethnoecology, indigenous knowledge studies, concerns for environmental justice and post-humanist (more-than-human) perspectives.

Yet, what is missing in all this is any understanding of the role of nostalgia in shaping the memories of the people we study. We might reasonably assume that the neglect of nostalgia as an explanatory force in anthropologies of the environment simply reflects a generic distaste for resorting to psychological mechanisms during a particular period in the shaping of modern socio-cultural anthropology (Angé and Berliner 2015: 6), but as we have just seen, the neo-functionalist ecology of Rappaport had no problem in drawing upon cognitive psychology. What it ignored, or seemingly resisted, was a role for emotion in underpinning cognition. It is not until the appearance of the initially controversial ideas of Kellert and Wilson's (1993) 'biophilia hypothesis', and its echoes in the work of anthropologists such as Milton (2002), that it becomes acceptable to assume that emoting about whatever 'nature' might be for particular cultural populations is a basic human propensity. We can see now how nostalgia might be conceptually embedded, if we define it as an emotionally charged valorization of the past based on selective memories. Indeed, we now understand how emotion plays a key role in cultural cognition by fixing knowledge in the long-term memory through the limbic system of the brain. In the same way as personal experience can shape long-term memory, be transmitted to others and morph from individual episodic experiences to shared cultural mimesis, so individual nostalgia, precisely because of its emotional charge, can fuel and shape collective cultural memory. However, in terms of histories of anthropologies of the environment it is not until the appearance of approaches that we now describe as historical ecology, political ecology and the humanistic ecologies (Biersack 1999; Kottack 1999) that we find an appropriate theoretical framing for understanding the role of nostalgia. But these theoretical contexts are less conducive to claims for its possible cognitive role in reinforcing adaptive memories.

The paradigm of historical ecology is of particular interest because of its foundational tenet that people make their environment, which they do both conceptually and physically. The Vietnamese Mnong Gar are famously described by George Condominas (1957) as having 'eaten the forest', and in his analysis the swidden cycle provides a framework which simultaneously measures time, structures activity and valorizes space as people pass through a landscape. Mnong Gar emotionally invest in landscape as they pass through it, changing it along the way, and using the physical markers so created to recall events and stories. Thus, our ecological nostalgias are to a considerable extent the consequence of how we have altered the environment and left our individual and shared marks upon it.

By comparison, the paradigms of political and humanistic ecology confound the line of explanation so far developed by reminding us that environments are not simply made and emoted in the process but contested, and that the value placed on one place, resource or landscape may be very different depending on the relationship between social groups who relate to it in alternative ways, often in ways that entrench hierarchical relationships and inequalities. Thus, because different groups with an interest in the same environment invest different memories in it, their comparative nostalgias will be different as well. Moreover, following the 'deconstruction of nature' debates and the subsequent 'ontological turn', these representations have become associated with Latourian 'naturecultures' (Haraway 2003, Tsing 2015), that is variable cultural constructions of what nature constitutes in particular places. One of the most discussed, contested and iconic landscapes in this context is tropical rainforest. The West has created rainforest in the imagination, based on its ur-naturalness as wilderness, paradoxically on the one hand as a feared, impenetrable, externalized nature associated with all manner of dangers summed up in the term 'jungle', and on the other as a basically benign landscape associated with many positive virtues (non-timber forest products, biodiversity, carbon sinks and indigenous peoples with their associated folk wisdom), the threats to all of which are rehearsed through narratives of destruction.

The Batu Apoi Nature Reserve: Brunei 1991–1995

In 1991 I was invited by the Earl of Cranbrook (otherwise known as Lord Medway, or Gathorne Gathorne-Hardy) to participate in the joint Universiti Brunei Darussalam/Royal Geographical Society Brunei Rainforest Project (BRP), which had been launched in 1990. The aim was to set up a Field Studies Centre at Kuala Belalong in 'undisturbed lowland tropical rainforest' (Cranbrook 1990: 2) on the edge of the Batu Apoi Forest Reserve, Temburong district (Map 1.1). The invitation was motivated by the observation that the proposed study of an extensive tract of rainforest would be incomplete without an anthropologist or ethnobotanist to monitor traditional extraction practices within the reserve used by local Dusun-speaking peoples and other linguistic minorities living on its periphery. The BRP as a whole had the highest level patronage possible in the persons of the Sultan of Brunei and HRH the Prince of Wales, and therefore a significant international profile as a scientific endeavour, while the Kuala Belalong centre was set up with funds provided by the Brunei government, Brunei-Shell Petroleum and many other corporate sponsors. My part in the project was funded by the British Economic and Social Research Council (ESRC), as part of its Global Environmental Change initiative.

Until we were well into the planning phase, including appointing staff, all seemed to be going well. Unfortunately, those agencies of the government of Brunei who were closely involved in supervising the project decided, rather late in the day, to take the view that since Batu Apoi was a protected area in which hunting and gathering by local peoples was prohibited then there would be nothing to study. In other words, 'what should be' was determining the interpretation of 'what was', or put differently, empirical reality became subservient to a legal reality. This was despite the existence of very good evidence that (a) the reserve area had been shaped by patterns of human settlement and extraction over some hundreds if not thousands of years; and (b) that local Dusunic-speaking people were continuing to traverse the reserve area. In addition, at a conference hosted by the Universiti Brunei Darusalam in Bandar Seri Begawan on 'Tropical rainforest research', held in April 1993 in connection with the Batu Apoi project (Edwards, Booth and Choy 1996), there was an attempt by overseas scientists present to vote on a motion opposing the Batu Apoi dam that was being proposed for the watershed by the Brunei government. Here then was a three-way clash between several visions of the Batu Apoi reserve: one by the scientific community which saw it as a classic case of virgin jungle in need of protection; a second by the BRP leadership who wished to pursue science but recognized that humans

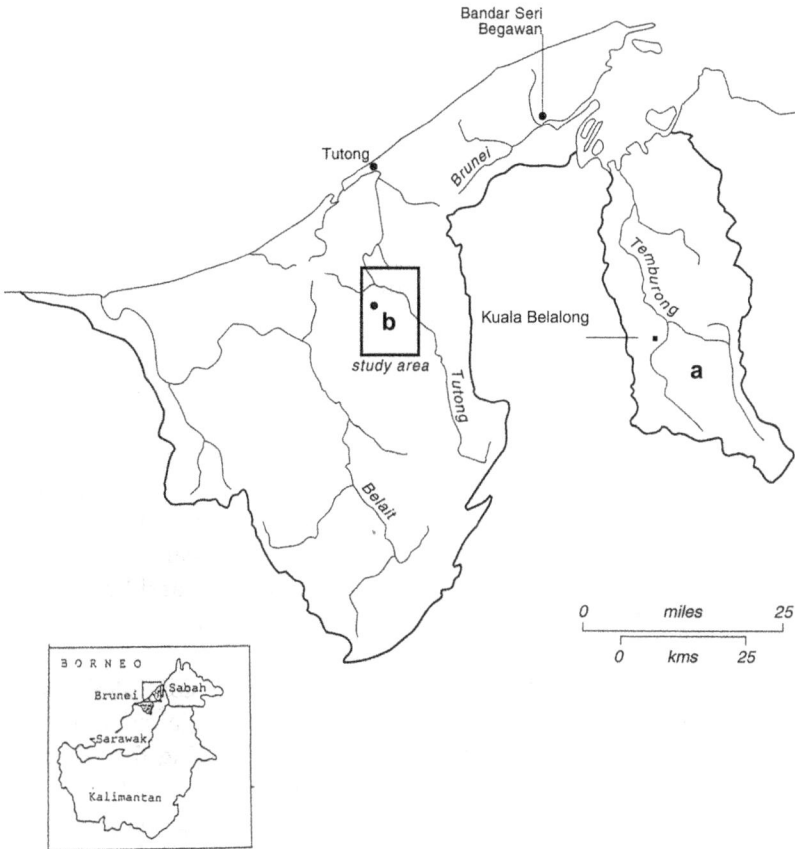

Map 1.1. The river systems and state boundaries of Brunei, showing the locations of the Batu Apoi reserve (a) on the Temburong, and Tasek Merimbun (b) in Tutong District. The inset indicates the position of Brunei on the island of Borneo. © Roy Ellen.

were part of a dynamic ecosystem; and a third by the government which for political reasons was happy to be seen establishing a nature reserve to protect the patrimony and heritage of the state. At the same time as denying the historicity of forest, the government wanted the freedom to dramatically alter the watershed in the interests of development. Both the scientists and the government, publicly at least, either contested or were ignorant of the historicity of the forest. On the part of the scientists this view was possibly informed by generic 'functionalist' modelling assumptions then still current concerning rainforest ecology, which were formed without the benefit of local memories and experience of the indigenous

Temburong communities, let alone the insights of the emerging discipline of historical ecology. On the other hand, the government view was formed by an institutional and political memory of forest as the natural 'other' of the historical Sultanate, the periphery over which it traditionally exerted authority and nowadays had controlling power. If the government claimed by fiat that the forest now had no inhabitants then that was the reality that had to be dealt with. In this model with all its contradictions, memory was suitably selective but informed by a nostalgia born out of recollections of the relations between centre and periphery under the Sultanate, in which ethnic affinity conveniently coincided with environmental zone and degree of subjugation (Brunei Malay on the coast, Dusun in upriver areas, and Penan and other groups in deep forest): a nostalgia more for a particular political dispensation than for a distinctive ecology (Brown 1970).

Meanwhile, unable to conduct work in the Batu Apoi reserve, Jay Bernstein and myself moved the project to Tasek Merimbun, another albeit less politically contentious Dusun area (Map 1.1). However, here too, as in much of Brunei, there was a difference between how local Dusun viewed and invested in forest through their cultural memories, and how the site was viewed by the politically dominant Brunei Malays and their government.

In order to understand the context in which these contested perceptions of forest occurred, it is necessary to note the special circumstances of Brunei with respect to deforestation. When comparing the otherwise compositionally similar dipterocarp rainforest of Brunei and other contiguous territories in northern Borneo, the neighbouring forests of Sarawak and Sabah have obviously been heavily logged for timber, while the forests of inland and upland Brunei are still largely intact. As Bernstein and I have shown in an earlier piece (Ellen and Bernstein 1994) this is largely a function of Brunei being a 'hydrocarbon society'. A small total state population and the overall revenue brought in by oil exports has meant that logging is unimportant to the overall economy, while people no longer rely on extensive upland farming in any significant way to survive. Indeed, income levels and standards of living for most Bruneians are such that they have no need to ever see, let alone interact with, forest. However, there is still a difference between how Brunei Malay, the government and local Dusun still living in upland areas conceptualize and emote about forest. For Brunei Malays the forest has become an empty space, its historicity denied, a place to be occasionally visited for recreational purposes, and which the Forestry Department has suitably domesticated in various places to enhance the visitor experience. Around the Forestry

Centre at Sungai Liang and at Sungai Lumut, walkways, signage and other facilities have been installed, similar picnic spots and associated furniture have been constructed near Sukang on the upper Belait, while Tasek Merimbun itself had been designated a National and ASEAN Heritage Site as early as 1984 to maintain it as a 'wilderness with recreational and tourism' values (Wong 1993), derived from it being a unique wetland habitat (Said 1991). On the basis of a consultancy report, the Ministry of Development produced a plan to turn Tasek Merimbun into Brunei's first national park, with recommendations for a boathouse, campsites, education centre, parking spaces, restaurants and accommodation. However, because of ecological deterioration unrelated to deforestation the plan had not been implemented by 1993, and the Brunei Museum had strongly advised against further development, instead recommending a programme of restoration and research. Our part in this proposal was to document the ethnobiology of Dusun people living around the lake.

Meanwhile, although local Dusun no longer relied on the forest for sustenance, it was still symbolically important in quite specific ways. Male Dusun engaged in recreational hunting, while women collected medicinal plants, and Dusun more generally (certainly during the 1990s) were still cutting at least one communal swidden a year to supply the glutinous rice needed for rice wine and feasting, for purposes such as traditional *temarok* and shamanic curing ceremonies still being practiced today (Pudarno 1989, n.d.; Antaran 1984; Kershaw 2000). Dusun farmers continued to engage in collective swidden practices (Figure 1.1), such as cutting, burning, planting, managing and harvesting by driving to fairly remote sites in 4x4 SUVs, and in one case that I observed having a fire tender on hand in case a swidden fire got out of hand (Ellen 2012: 27). Thus, on the one hand there was a generic empty and restructured memory of forest reinforced by generic nostalgia regarding the state's traditional political relations with upriver areas and peoples, while on the other hand there was for the Dusun a specific and very concrete nostalgia that led to the retention of residual cultural practices associated with forest.

Nuaulu Landscape and the Argument for Autonomy

The second case is rather different. The character and cultural significance of forest features prominently, as do memories of the past, but Nuaulu on the island of Seram in the Indonesian province of Maluku, unlike Dusun, still have a strong subsistence dependence on forest, and are certainly not alienated from it (Map 1.2). They continue to rely on a

Figure 1.1. Dusun part-time farmers sowing seed rice in a recently cleared swidden, Tutong District, Brunei, 1991. Photograph by the author.

multi-dimensional use of a complex rainforest environment, engaging in hunting, sago extraction, cutting timber for house construction, and gathering many different non-timber forest products (NTFPs), both for local use and for sale. Their memories of forest are instantiated through the temporal regularities and systematic movements of the swidden cycle, through other physical inputs associated with forest modification and patterns of extraction, and through visits to old village sites. However, their political relationship with forest has changed significantly over a 150-year period. Before 1880 Nuaulu clans were dispersed in hamlets throughout the central highlands of Seram. In the 1880s most clans submitted to the authority of the Dutch colonial government and the Muslim raja of Sepa and re-settled in villages along the south coast. Although Nuaulu clans continued to extract from their mountain territories where logistically possible, and there was much local acknowledgement of traditional Nuaulu territorial rights, they retained fewer of these rights after 1949, under the Agrarian and Forestry Laws of the new Indonesian state. The expansion of the extractive economy under the late New Order led to much logging activity and in-migration of transmigrants, particularly along the Ruatan valley (1970–1990). This in turn led to tensions between settlers and Nuaulu, and increasing resentment of the political hege-

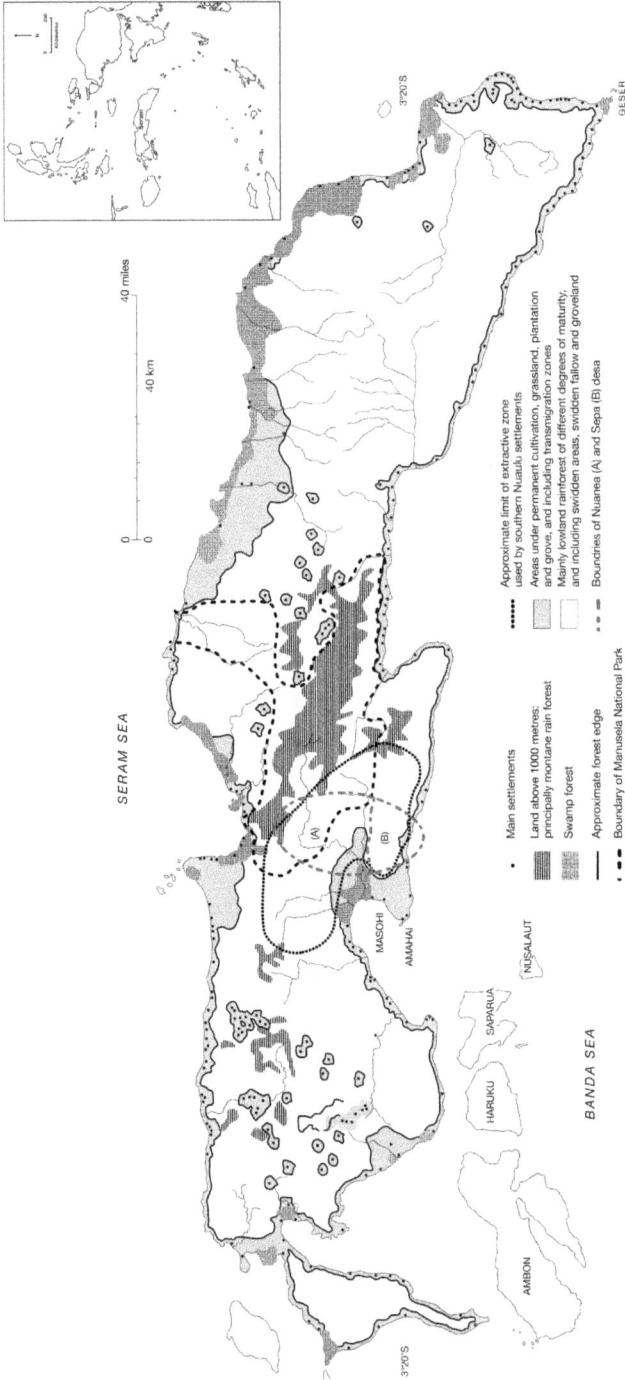

Map 1.2. Seram, showing boundaries of the recently established *desa* of Nuanea (a) and that of Sepa (b), in relation to the Nuaulu extractive environment as a whole, and the overlapping area of the Manusela National Park. © Roy Ellen.

mony of Sepa. Logging and transmigrant activity had adverse ecological consequences too for Nuaulu. Although some of the initial developments were in the short term beneficial, the long-term consequences were not. For Saite, speaking in 1995 about the consequences of logging during the 1980s:

> Before the lumber companies came we got around well. We found food well because the deer slept nearby, pigs lived nearby, and cassowaries lived nearby. But when they levelled and destroyed these animals' places and caves they ran away. So it is very hard for the Nuaulu people to find food because they chased away all the pigs and deer so that they are now far away. (see Ellen 1999: 151–52 for full text)

At the same time – and paradoxically – the opening up of the Ruatan valley on traditional Nuaulu land and construction of access roads allowed the movement of some Nuaulu to form new settlements at the confluence of the Nua and Ruatan valleys, on land originally constituting the territories of Nuaulu clans (Map 1.2). These developments accelerated after the overthrow of Suharto in 1998, and the arrival of an age of *reformasi* (reformation) and *otonomi daerah* (local autonomy), and even more so as a consequence of communal conflict between Christians and Muslims between 1998 and 2002 (in which the Nuaulu were technically neutral). This encouraged Nuaulu to seek (or as they saw it, regain) direct control over their traditional lands (Ellen 1993, 1999, 2014). In 2008 they succeeded, with recognition by the Indonesian government of a separate Nuaulu *desa* (Nuanea) comprising some 125,00 square kilometres with boundaries encompassing many old clan territories around the headwaters of the Nua river (Figure 1.2).

Thus, in this case, we can see continuing collective memories of a homeland supported in myth and history, combined with nostalgia (*rihu* [*anoi ererihu*], Ind. *rindu*) for both a lost ecological and political dispensation. Nuaulu nostalgia is not for a past that is irrevocably over, but for an environmental present that is continually under threat, combined with an attempt to regain a political past: autonomy from the hegemony of Sepa, and a move back to ancient territories. In the context of the post-1998 Indonesian government policy of *otonomi daerah* this has become realistic politics and not simply a yearning. It is true that in the Moluccan diaspora in the Netherlands some exilic nostalgia for *Ambon manise* (sweet Ambon) persists, but in most of Seram the passing of a traditional way of life (Ind. *tempo dulu*, in the sense of 'the olden days') is self-evident. It has gone forever, and there is no attempt at or possibility of regaining it (see e.g. Grzimek 1991; Hagen 2006). This is nostalgia of the 'wistful longing' variety, an acknowledgment that traditions and en-

Figure 1.2. Sonohue Matoke surveying his land: Sama (looking north) from head-waters of Sune Ukune near Rouhua, South Seram, February 1996. Photograph by the author.

vironments are irrevocably lost, with no hope of return, which have left people with no other option than to focus on a golden future rather than a golden past, one promised through the politics of *pembangunan* (development) and a commitment to all things *moderen* (modern) and *ramai* (in this sense, busy, bustling and enlivened) (Schreer 2016). In regaining a large part of their territory, in achieving a fair degree of autonomy, in appearing to control their forest resources and in a commitment to their customary religious practices, Nuaulu have – paradoxically – replaced a sentiment of loss and displacement with pursuit of a 'traditional path to modernity' (Ellen 2014).

Discussion

The two case studies presented here both deal with memories of the recent ecological past, a past in which what we call tropical rainforest is the predominant material and experiential reality. Both cases evince and evoke strong evidence for what White (2006: 333) calls 'the materiality of memory', although White does not address natural landscapes but rather the built environment, and only then addresses decontextualized representations of the past. It is well understood now (e.g. Quak, London and Talsma 2015) that memory processing is multisensorial and synaesthetic, one sense informing and cross-referencing another, and we should hardly be surprised that the triggering of a nostalgic reverie often occurs in senses we associate with lower, more primitive, parts of the brain. One need only mention that super cliché the Proustian madeleine to make this point effectively. But rainforest too is encoded multisensorially by those who live on its borders and who interact with it on a daily basis (e.g. Feld 1996), registered through memories of a variety of familiar odiferous, gustatory, visual, tactile and acoustical stimuli. This is what makes it truly ambient or environmental rather than simply spatio-temporal. If 'ecological nostalgia' is to be a meaningful concept it must entail reminiscence of things that are deeply physical and material as well as relational. This is certainly as true for Nuaulu, as it is for Feld's (1996) New Guinean Kaluli, but unless there are occasions to acquire cognitive or emotional distance from the trigger experiences, as when travelling in radically different environments and deprived of its sensations, or temporally (for example, after it has been removed and replaced with a fundamentally different vegetative landscape), it is difficult to conceive of a conceptually distinctive experience.

But rainforest as a lived reality for the Nuaulu is rather different from how it is experienced by the rest of the emotional stakeholders I have described in the first case study from Brunei, where the sensorial density and extensiveness is much diminished. Even with Dusun, who continue to intermittently enter and make use of forest, their physical displacement and current economic and cultural orientation makes their appreciation of rainforest no less semantically dense, but paradoxically because of the conceptual distancing 'rainforest' has become more of an entified thing or phenomenon, contrasting with other more routine day-to-day environments with which they interact, such as the built townscape of Bandar Seri Begawan, or the secondary brush around Tasek Merimbun, or the cultivated coastal strip and manicured edges of the main highways. By comparison, the nostalgias of rainforest associated with the other groups discussed, such as the official versions of government, the versions of urban Bruneians and of international rainforest biologists, and Western environmentalists who may never have visited rainforest but who might be committed to 'rainforest crunch' type views (Dove 1993), are even more semantically depleted. While rainforest biologists know a great deal about the biology of the forest and no doubt feel that affinity that comes with fieldwork, their appreciation cannot be the same as those for whom it is the dominant lived reality from cradle to grave. While their sensory faculties are potentially no less acute than those who live the forest, their nostalgic relationship to it inevitably has less multi-dimensionality, and is informed by their own cultural background and process of socialization, in which tropical rainforest for the most part only makes a rare appearance, and then often as 'jungle'.

When it comes to the attribution of notions of nostalgia, the two cases indicate the juxtaposition of different versions, each in contention with the other. In the Brunei case we can separate out the scientific nostalgia associated with the objectives and sentiments of the Brunei Rainforest Project, the international group of scientists working at Kuala Belalong and participating in the rainforest conference. For many tropical forest biologists (and the subset of these who might be described as conservationists) the dominant narrative is one of an 'evolutionary Eden' of global utility, and their public projection is of rainforest destruction and how they will save it (Richards 1992: 138). Although we think of destruction of the rainforest as a theme and concern of the modern environmentalist era, it was anticipated by the earliest European travellers and naturalists in the tropics, such as Alexander von Humboldt (Nicolson 1990). European representations from Humboldt onwards have varied in their emotional and romantic burden, by turns Hobbesian 'jungle' or Conradian 'heart of darkness', and by turns idyllic Rousseauesque fantasy. Either way, they are seen as 'natural' in the old-fashioned sense of this word. Until the rise of historical ecology, scientists no less than other people who did not live in them assumed that rainforests were dynamic natural systems that worked as functioning wholes, as well-illustrated in the ruling scientific consensus of the twentieth century exemplified by the influential work of Paul Westmacott Richards (1952). Since Richards, our scientific understanding of rainforest ecology has been revolutionized by increasing recognition of the variability of its habitats, its 'patchiness', and the discovery that rainforests have histories, and that moreover these are cultural and social histories. There are several dramatic empirical demonstrations of this. One is Michael Dove's (1992) critical study of the transformation of Sanskrit *jangala* (meaning 'arid savanna pasture') to Urdu *jangal* (English 'wild forest', and from which we derive 'jungle'), showing how a change in the meaning of words reflects an altered historical relationship between people and the natural world, and how they construct 'their' nature. A second is the important work of James Fairhead and Melissa Leach (1996) on the colonial 'misreading' of the West African forest landscape to suggest that local people were wilfully destroying it when in fact the present forest turns out to be a consequence of deliberate and systematic human interventions. A third is the archaeological discovery of 'black earths', and complex mounded and ditched settlement patterns underlying the remote rainforest of southwest Amazonia, first reported by Anna Roosevelt (1994). Nowadays, in sophisticated intellectual circles we take it for granted that vast tracts of lowland rainforest owe much to the impact of human patterns of extraction, forest-fallow cultivation and movement. Thus, both Nuaulu and Dusun not only lived in historically anthropic forests, but their own understanding of them and their nostalgia is informed by the knowledge that they, in a very physical sense, have made them.

The official memories and the quasi-nostalgia associated with Brunei state institutions who seek to manage rainforest in a period when its subsistence role has much diminished is a different matter. This is, in part, informed and legitimized by a scientific consensus on how rainforest works, by internationally articulated assumptions as to its necessary function in the biosphere, and in part encompasses the history of the Sultanate itself, with the sultan and Brunei Malays at the centre seeking to control an unruly inland periphery (the *ulu*) through exchanges with other ethnic groups, including Dusun, who only share their political culture up to a point. This model also reinforces the ignorance of most contemporary urbanized and post-subsistence Bruneians who see rainforest as a void occasionally punctuated with recreational facilities. In so far as ordinary Bruneians feel nostalgic about it, it is of the curious wistful longing *tempo dulu* variety, reinforced through (material) culture enactments of the kind displayed in the galleries of the Brunei Museum, full of objects of impenetrable meaning for the younger generation but evoking reminiscences for their grandparents. The representations and memories of Dusun who retain a semi-subsistence way of life living in upriver locations such as Tasek Merimbun is different again, articulated through a depleted knowledge of the rainforest kept alive through limited hunting and collecting activity and attenuated swidden practices. Attenuated or not, the connection is important for Dusun, whose very identity is under threat as they have progressively become de-culturated, and defined mainly negatively by 'not being Muslim' (Bernstein 1997, Ellen and Bernstein 1994). These connections become, therefore, vital nostalgic threads linking them to a past way of life through which they find their *raison d'être*.

In the Nuaulu case, scientifically driven rainforest nostalgia is irrelevant, except where Nuaulu are able to harness the rhetoric of rainforest conservation to pursue their own interests, and where the few politically weak conservation groups and NGOs reflect it (Ellen 1999). Likewise, there is yet no official nostalgia in a part of Indonesia where the dominant state discourse is almost entirely driven by development and reconciliation agendas following communal violence. Nuaulu themselves evince paradoxical notions. Like many other Indonesians living in remote areas they are attached to the state goals of development, which promise a life that is *ramai*. In the past this was strongly associated with conversion to either Christianity or Islam. However, in the light of the failure of the religious model of development that they see in the civil war between 1998 and 2001 they have sought a third way: a traditionalist path to modernity. They see themselves as having moved some way to achieving this nativistic ideal. In so far as this is fuelled by nostalgia, it is nostalgia for both the traditional autonomy that they enjoyed before 1880 and nostalgia for a forest environment that has been progressively eroded since 1970. When Nuaulu sing their *ahinae* during the great circle dances (*kahuae*) that accompany major rituals, through the words and stanzas that recall mythologized historic events, they are performing nostalgia. When Nuaulu talk about their longing for the kind of fecund and negotiable forest that existed before the depredations of loggers and transmigrants they are performing nostalgia. But since they have, for the time being at least, convinced themselves that they have gone some way to recouping such losses in establishing their Nuanea, theirs is a 'restorative nostalgia' rather than simply the reflective nostalgia (Boym 2001: xviii) that we find in every contested version of the Brunei idea of rainforest: a basis for action in the present.

Conclusion: Does the Concept of Ecological Nostalgia Serve Any Purpose?

In the literature on the concept of adaptation, both biological and anthropological, there is wide agreement that it is an essentially conservative process. Populations in small-scale traditional societies, while mostly seeking the accoutrements of modern life, also tend to want to maintain things as they are in the face of challenges to some existing system, and consequently engineer paradoxical changes that seek to maintain current conditions. It is likely that how our memories work evolved to support this strategy.

It is this same cognitive impulse that underlies the sense in which nostalgia seems to assume change and decline from some golden age (Turner 1987: 150). While on the one hand it conjures up fantasies of the past determined by the needs of the present, and serves to mnemonically 'fix' (Bloch 1998) positive memories that are potentially adaptive, by being selective and simplifying memory, it also becomes a symptom and cause of memory distortion (Lowenthal 1989). Such a 'disease of the afflicted imagination', as Angé and Berliner (2015: 4) put it, is comparable to the way that some have seen fetishism as the pathological extension of an otherwise cognitively normal process, one reifying anthropically representations that in themselves are evolved forms of mental processing utilizing cultural inputs (Ellen 1988). Nostalgia can seem like a flakey concept for anthropologists of a certain persuasion, but although it is not without its conceptual difficulties, when harnessed to the practical (political) needs of the present it must be seen as part of a group of processes in which emotion and cultural cognition combine with powerful effect to achieve what Roy Rappaport (1971) called 'sanctity'.

Acknowledgements

Research in Brunei was funded through ESRC Grant R 000 23 3088, 'The ecology and ethnobiology of human rainforest interaction in East Brunei', organized jointly by the University of Kent at Canterbury and the Brunei Museum (1991–1994), with additional support from the British Academy (BA-AN561-APN582, 'Dusun Forest Use in Brunei and Social Change: Final Phase', 1994) and the British Council. In connection with the work in Brunei I would like to thank the following: the Brunei Forestry Centre, the Royal Botanic Gardens at Kew (particularly Professor John Dransfield), the Tutong District Office and the people of Kampong Merimbun for their cooperation, Bantong Antaran, Pundarno Binchin, Dr Marina Wong, Lord Cranbrook, Chair of the UK Planning Committee, Dr J.C. Nuttman, then Dean of the Faculty of Management and Administrative Studies at UBD, and Dr David Edwards of the Biology Department, Dr Morni bin Othman, Director of Forestry, the British High Commisioner Roger Westbrook, and Professor Haji Sharom Ahmat, Permanent Academic Adviser to UBD, Dr Peter Eaton and Mr Lim Chung Tat. The work at Tasek Merimbun was undertaken by Jay Bernstein.

Research in Seram has been conducted periodically between 1970 and 2015 and its full funding and support reported elsewhere. The work since 1996 most relevant to the matters discussed here was supported as follows: ESRC, 1995–1998, 'Deforestation and forest knowledge in south central Seram, eastern Indonesia' (R000-236082); ESRC, 2001–2004, 'Frequency and periodicity in Nuaulu ritual reproduction' (R000-239310); British Academy, 2014–2017, 'Demography, kinship and ritual reproduction: Nuaulu cultural resilience in the "New Indonesia"' (SG131590); and a Leverhulme Emeritus Fellowship, 2018–2020, 'Nuaulu ethnobotanical cognition and knowledge (Seram, eastern Indonesia)' (EM-2018-057-6). All recent fieldwork in Maluku has been conducted under the auspices of Pattimura University in Ambon within the terms of a Memorandum of Understanding with the University of Kent.

Roy Ellen is Professor Emeritus of Anthropology and Human Ecology at the University of Kent, where he initiated the programmes in environmental anthropology and ethnobotany, and founded the Centre for Biocultural Diversity. He has undertaken field research in island Southeast Asia, mainly in the Moluccas, and has published widely. His recent books include *On the Edge of the Banda Zone* (2003), *Nuaulu Religious Practices* (2012), and *Kinship, Population and Social Reproduction in the 'New Indonesia'* (2018). An earlier collection of his essays has appeared as *The Categorical Impulse*. He was elected to the British Academy in 2003 and was President of the Royal Anthropological Institute from 2007 to 2011.

References

Angé, O. and D. Berliner. 2015. 'Introduction: Anthropology of Nostalgia – Anthropology as Nostalgia', in O. Angé and D. Berliner (eds), *Anthropology and Nostalgia*. Oxford: Berghahn, pp. 1–16.

Antaran, B. 1984. 'Kepercayaan Temarok: Sebuah Pengenalan Ringkas', *Berita Muzium* 6(1): 24–29.

Berliner, D. 2005. 'The Abuses of Memory: Reflections on the Memory Boom in Anthropology', *Anthropological Quarterly* 78(1): 197–211.

Bernstein, J.H. 1997. 'The Deculturation of the Brunei Dusun', in R.L. Winzeler (ed.), *Indigenous Peoples and the State: Politics, Land, and Ethnicity in the Malayan Peninsula and Borneo*. New Haven, CT: Yale University Southeast Asia Studies, Monograph 46, pp. 159–79.

Bernstein, J.H., R.F. Ellen and B. Antaran. 1997. 'The Use of Plot Surveys for the Study of Ethnobotanical Knowledge: A Brunei Dusun Example', *Journal of Ethnobiology* 17(1): 69–96.

Biersack, A. 1999. 'Introduction: From the "New Ecology" to the New Ecologies', *American Anthropologist* 101(1): 5–18.

Bloch, M. 1998. *How We Think They Think: Anthropological Approaches to Cognition, Memory and Literacy*. Boulder, CO: Westview Press.

Boym, S. 2001. *The Future of Nostalgia*. New York: Basic Books.

Brown, D.E. 1970. *Brunei: The Structure and History of a Bornean Malay Sultanate*. Brunei: Brunei Museum.

Condominas, G. 1957. *Nous Avons Mangé la Forêt de la Pierre-génie Gôo*. Paris: Mercure de France.

Cranbrook, Earl of. 1990. 'Brunei Rainforest Project 1991-2'. Universiti Brunei Darussalam – Royal Geographical Society.

Dove, M.R. 1992. 'The Dialectical History of "Jungle" in Pakistan: An Examination of the Relationship Between Nature and Culture', *Journal of Anthropological Research* 48(3): 231–53.

_____. 1993. 'A Revisionist View of Tropical Deforestation and Development', *Environmental Conservation* 20(1): 17–24.

Edwards, D.S., W.E. Booth and S.C. Choy (eds). 1996. *Tropical Rainforest Research: Current Issues*. Monographieae Biologicae 74. Dordrecht and Boston: Kluwer Academic Publishers.

Ellen, R.F. 1982. *Environment, Subsistence and System: The Ecology Small-scale Social Formations*. Cambridge: Cambridge University Press.

_____. 1986. 'What Black Elk Left Unsaid: On the Illusory Images of Green Primitivism', *Anthropology Today* 216: 8–12.

_____. 1988. 'Fetishism', *Man* 23(1): 1–23.

_____. 1993. 'Rhetoric, Practice and Incentive in the Face of the Changing Times: A Case Study in Nuaulu Attitudes to Conservation and Deforestation', in K. Milton (ed.), *Environmentalism: The View from Anthropology*. London: Routledge, pp. 126–43.

_____. 1999. 'Forest Knowledge, Forest Transformation: Political Contingency, Historical Ecology and the Renegotiation of Nature in Central Seram', in T. Li (ed.), *Transforming the Indonesian Uplands: Marginality, Power and Production*. Amsterdam: Harwood, pp. 131–57.

_____. 2012. 'Studies of Swidden Agriculture in Southeast Asia Since 1960: An Overview and Commentary on Recent Research and Syntheses', *Asia Pacific World* 3(1): 18–38.

_____. 2014. 'Pragmatism, Identity and the State: How the Nuaulu of Seram have Re-invented their Beliefs and Practices as "Religion"', *Wacana: Jurnal Ilmu Pengetahuan Budaya* 15(2): 254–85.

Ellen, R.F. and J.H. Bernstein. 1994. 'Urbs in Rure: Cultural Transformations of the Rainforest in Modern Brunei', *Anthropology Today* 10(4): 16–19.

Fairhead, J. and M. Leach 1996. *Misreading the African Landscape: Society and Ecology in a Forest-savanna Mosaic*. Cambridge: Cambridge University Press.

Feld, S. 1996. 'A Poetics of Place: Ecological and Aesthetics Co-evolution in a Papua New Guinea Rainforest Community', in R. Ellen and K. Fukui (eds), *Redefining Nature: Ecology, Culture and Domestication*. Oxford: Berg, pp. 61–88.

Friedman, J. 1974. 'Marxism, Structuralism and Vulgar Materialism', *Man (N.S.)* 9(1): 44–69.

Gell, A. 1995. 'The Language of the Forest: Landscape and Phonological Iconism in Umeda', in E. Hirsch and M. O'Hanlon (eds), *The Anthropology of Landscape*. Oxford: Clarendon Press, pp. 232–54.

Grzimek, B.R.O. 1991. 'Social Change on Seram: A Study of Ideologies of Development in Eastern Indonesia', PhD thesis. London School of Economics and Political Science, University of London.

Hagen, J.M. 2006. *Community in the Balance: Morality and Social Change in an Indonesian Society*. Boulder, CO and London: Paradigm.

Haraway, D. 2003. *The Companion Species Manifesto: Dogs, People, and Significant Otherness*. Vol. 1. Chicago: Prickly Paradigm Press.

Kellert, S.R. and E.O. Wilson. 1993. *The Biophilia Hypothesis*. Washington DC: Island Press.

Kershaw, E.M. 2000. *A Study of Brunei Dusun Religion: Ethnic Priesthood on a Frontier of Islam*. [Borneo Research Council Monograph 4] Phillips, ME: Borneo Research Council.

Konner, M. and M. Shostak. 1986. 'Ethnographic Romanticism and the Idea of Human Nature: Parallels Between Samoa and !Kung San', in M. Biesele (ed.), *The Past and Future of !Kung Ethnography: Critical Reflections and Symbolic Perspectives. Essays in Honour of Lorna Marshall*. Amsterdam: John Benjamins Publishing Company, pp. 69–76.

Kottack, C. 1999. 'The New Ecological Anthropology', *American Anthropologist* 101(1): 23–35.

Lee, R. 1966. 'What Hunters Do for a Living, or, How to Make Out on Scarce Resources', in R. Lee and I. Devore (eds), *Man the Hunter*. Chicago: Aldine Publishing, pp. 30–48.

Lowenthal, D. 1989. 'Nostalgia Tells it Like it Wasn't', in C. Shaw and M. Chase (eds), *The Imagined Past: History and Nostalgia*. New York: Manchester University Press, pp. 18–32.

Milton, K. 2002. *Loving Nature: Towards an Ecology of Nature*. London: Routledge.

Nicolson, M. 1990. 'Alexander von Humboldt and the Geography of Vegetation', in A. Cunningham and N. Jardine (eds), *Romanticism and the Sciences*. Cambridge: Cambridge University Press, pp. 169–88.

Pudarno, Binchin. N.d. 'Fungsi Upacara Temarok Sebagai Saluran Pengukuhan dan Penyatuan Pengalaman dalam Kontek Keluargaan Masyarakat Kampung Ukong.' Unpublished.

_____. 1989. 'Temarok: Fungsi Upacara dan Pembentukan Struktur Sosial Masyarakat Dusun.' Unpublished.

Quak, M., R.E. London and D. Talsma. 2015. 'A Multisensory Perspective of Working Memory', *Frontiers of Human Neuroscience* 9: 197. Retrieved 26 September 2019, doi: 10.3389/fnhum.2015.00197.

Rappaport, R.A. [1968] 1984. *Pigs for the Ancestors: Ritual in the Ecology of a New Guinea People*. New Haven, CT and London: Yale University Press.

_____. 1971. 'The Sacred in Human Evolution', *Annual Review of Ecology and Systematics* 2: 23–44.

_____. 1979. *Ecology, Meaning and Religion*. Richmond, CA: North Atlantic Books.

Richards, P. 1992. 'Saving the Rain Forest? Contested Futures in Conservation', in S. Wallman (ed.), *Contemporary Futures: Perspectives from Social Anthropology*. London: Routledge, pp. 138–53.

Richards, P.W. 1952. *The Tropical Rain Forest*. Cambridge: Cambridge University Press.

Roosevelt, A. (ed.). 1994. *Amazonian Indians from Prehistory to the Present: Anthropological Perspectives*. Tucson, AZ and London: University of Arizona Press.

Said, I.M. 1991. 'Tasek Bera Under Threat', *Asian Wetlands News* 4(2): 5–6.

Schreer, V. 2016. 'Longing for Prosperity in Indonesian Borneo'. PhD thesis. University of Kent, Canterbury.

Soumori, S. and R.H. Bolton. 1999. 'Nuaulu People of Indonesia: Voices of the Earth', in D.A. Posey (ed.), *Cultural and Spiritual Values of Biodiversity*. London: Intermediate Technology Publications, pp. 146–47.

Tsing, A.L. 2015. *The Mushroom at the End of the World: On the Possibility of Life in Capitalist Ruins*. Princeton, NJ: Princeton University Press.

Turner, B. 1987. 'A Note on Nostalgia', *Theory, Culture and Society* 4(1): 147–56.

White, G. 2006. 'Epilogue: Memory Moments', *Ethos* 34(2): 325–41.

Wong, M. 1993. 'Proposed Development of Research Facility at Tasek Merimbun'. Bandar Seri Begawan: Brunei Museum. Reference: 3/JMB/490/76/2, 06 pp., unpublished.

CHAPTER 2

High Arctic Nostalgia
Thule and the Ecology of Mind

Kirsten Hastrup

The lands of the far North were imagined well before they were penetrated by Europeans. Since Pytheas' classical writings around 300 BC, an image of *Ultima Thule* had circulated and the rumour of a land surrounded by a frozen sea, where winter and darkness reigned for the better part of the year, had spread (Hastrup 2007). The European mind began to imagine the Arctic as a distinct geographical matter; this intensified from the seventeenth century onwards, when exploration and commercial interests deepened. Many Europeans perished in the attempt to conquer the icy world, all while the locals continued their marginal lives as before.

Exploration was followed by colonization. In High Arctic Greenland it took shape in the establishment of the Thule Station in 1910, a trade station in the northernmost inhabited region, definitively locating the dreamt-up Thule of the ancients, or so it seemed. In early 2019, Ultima Thule became the name of an icy celestial body in outer space, recently photographed by the NASA spacecraft *New Horizons*, which succeeded in making 'the most distant flyby' ever. Meanwhile, the earthly Thule apparently remains in place, if somewhat shattered and evoking many different sentiments.

The Thule Station gave its name to a larger geographical region in Northwest Greenland, and to a prehistoric Inuit population, the Thule Inuit, whose traces were first identified close to the Station, having wandered along the American Arctic coast from Alaska and entered into Greenland c.1250 (McGhee 1997). By this move a new ecology materialized, in the sense proposed by Gregory Bateson as an 'ecology of mind' (1972: xv), implying that 'the unit of survival is the flexible organism-in-its-environment' (ibid.: 451). Bateson reminds us that it is never the territory that gets onto the map, but '*difference*, be it a difference in altitude, a difference in vegetation, a difference in population structure, difference in surface, or whatever.

Figure 2.1. Meeting on the sea ice – still the most important infrastructure. The anthropologist to the left. Photograph by the author.

Differences are the things that get onto a map' (ibid.; original emphasis). The difference between the European and the High Arctic landscapes, not least the omnipresence of ice, the absence of trees, and the annual cycle of extensive periods of either darkness or light, impinged deeply upon the European perception both of the place and of the community, and it still does. Now, the ice is melting and minds are changing; in the process, the region and its inhabitants increasingly feature as a disappearing world.

This change precipitates a new nostalgia, adhering both to the High Arctic landscape, and to people who are seen as the 'last hunters', and even as the 'last Eskimos', even if they are always resilient – meaning flexible and ready to contemplate new opportunities (Hastrup 2009). Changes and movements have been ingrained elements in their lives, and a measure of strategic opportunism along with fine-tuned technologies has made their community viable. Despite these obviously contemporary skills and the necessary attention to the future, people have been portrayed in a nostalgic mode, also by anthropologists, for whom this has been a disciplinary habit (Ange and Berliner 2015; Berliner 2015). For the Inughuit, as they call themselves today, counting some 750 people, the sense of loss and longing for the past is not obvious; they never lived in the past tense and are, as always, ready to embrace new possibilities. Living in the Thule Region means living within a particular geo-sociality – a concept we shall explore in combination with ecological nostalgia.

Invincible Worlds: Exploring the Last Wilderness

The Arctic was explored and mapped rather late in the European history of exploration because of its forbidding nature. Although some Arctic seas and coasts had at least been partly known by whalers since the seventeenth century, the mapping of the Thule Region, situated between 76° and 79° North, was a nineteenth-century charge that would continue into the first part of the twentieth century. The practice of mapping is never simply a representational exercise, as we know from Sarah Whatmore's discussion of the limitations of the grid, given that bodily practices, travels and writing itself are inscribed on the map (Whatmore 2002) – always so much more than a territory. Edward Said suggested that geography is always in some sense imaginative; in drawing upon received images and categories, in geography there is always 'something *more* than what appears to be merely positive knowledge' (Said 1979: 55; original emphasis). The mind is always operative, and our ideas of place are predicated upon particular images and social conventions; Orientalism, as discussed by Said, is a key example of how 'regions' are implicated in imaginaries. With less impact, the notion of Arcticality was later suggested as a Northern version of Orientalism (Pálsson 2002). As outsiders' notions, both carry an implicit colonial nostalgia to which anthropology has also contributed (Bissell 2005).

Arctic nostalgia took off well before the Arctic was mapped, however. It began on the seas, where one expedition after the other sought to identify unknown coasts and penetrate ice-packed passages. Fridtjof Nansen (1861–1930), a major explorer of the Arctic around 1900, describes the driving force of exploration:

> It is our perpetual yearning to overcome difficulties and dangers, to see hidden things, to penetrate into the regions outside our beaten track – it is *the call of the unknown* – the longing for the Land of Beyond, the divine force deeply rooted in the soul of man which drove the first hunters out into new regions – the mainspring perhaps of our greatest actions – of winged human thought knowing no bounds to its freedom. (Nansen 1927: 20; original emphasis)

This perpetual longing propelled exploration along in Europe from the Enlightenment until the twentieth century. The multitude of expeditions patronized by kings and emperors in the eighteenth and nineteenth centuries were explicitly aimed at mapping the world, not only in terms of resources and trade routes but also in terms of 'the natural order' (Pratt 1992: 15ff). This order was based on perceived differences between places and peoples that tended to merge in the process of classifying species of plants, animals and humans. Once mapped, the territories were always more than geography.

The people living in the (not yet named) Thule Region became known to the outer world only in the nineteenth century and remained on the edge of vision until far more recently. The first to report on their existence was Captain John Ross, who had been sent out by the British admiralty to find the North West Passage in 1818, and who wrote that they exist in a corner of the world 'by far the most secluded which has yet been discovered', having no knowledge of how they had come there, and believing themselves alone in the universe (Ross 1819: 123–24). The discovery went both ways, and while Ross made it back to report what he found, thus attracting other sailors and whalers, the locals began assembling at Cape York, the southernmost promontory in the region, each summer, hoping for more ships and more foreign goods for barter. For them, too, a new world had opened up. During the cool period of the Little Ice Age (c.1350–1800), they had been cut off from their more southerly relatives in Greenland, but were now reminded of the world beyond their confines – a world that could supply them with new materials that made their lives easier, while also exposing them to new epidemics that threatened the survival of the small group, down to just a hundred people around 1860 (Hastrup 2018a, 2018b).

Other expeditions followed, often to be stopped by the ice, or to go down. The fevers and delusions that had accompanied penetration into central Africa (Fabian 2002: 3) were replaced with different perils of exposure in the Arctic. Quite apart from the cold, the pack ice and the blizzards, there were strange visual effects that – when reported – made the public wonder about facts and fantasies, all while confirming the sublime nature of the frozen experiences at a safe distance. The recurrent whitening out of all distinction between land, sea ice and sky remains an unsettling experience. In the late nineteenth century, the most powerful image-maker of unknown lands had become the press, where 'explorers, confirming as they did the heroism, romance and adventure of empire, were a particularly celebrated genre' (Riffenburgh 1993: 2). The resulting maps are inscribed with bodily practices and fearful travels, and as the reading public took them in, a particular ecology of mind took root.

One of the early mapmakers in the Thule District was Robert Peary (1856–1920), who spent the greater part of the years between 1891 and 1909 there; his quest was personal and ultimately concerned the North Pole. It took a long time to identify the best way to get there, possible only with the help of local hunters. While exploring and mapping the options, Peary got himself a second family among the Inuit and came to master both worlds, bodily and technologically. When seeking funding in America, the symmetry was broken, however. On a campaign in Washington he said:

> I have often been asked: Of what use are the Eskimos to the world? They are too far removed to be of value in commercial enterprises, and furthermore they lack ambition. They have no literature, nor, properly speaking, any art. They value life only as does a fox, or a bear, purely by instinct.
>
> But, let us not forget that these people, trustworthy and hardy, will yet prove their value to mankind. With *their* help, the world shall discover the Pole. (Peary 1907: 390; original emphasis)

Reducing the locals here to instruments for the American hero, Peary did credit his helpers with a lot of insight and skills in other works (Peary 1898). They knew how to live where others would perish. Not least, they knew how to navigate the sea ice, ever a comprehensive memento of one's own insignificance. This still impresses itself forcefully on the fieldworker, travelling along on a hunter's dog sledge, and results in a powerful emotional topography (Hastrup 2010).

By its nature, the icy region is a volatile space, and therefore unscalable in the convention of mapping. Anna Tsing has discussed scalability and non-scalability and called for a theory of the latter, which 'recalls attention to the wild diversity of life on the earth'; this offers an alternative to the conceptual bias of exploration and colonialism as bound up with an idea of scalability, that is, 'the ability to expand – and expand, and expand – without rethinking basic elements' (Tsing 2012: 505). Her model case is the plantation designed for colonial extraction, possibly the archetypal view of colonial enterprise, illustrating how 'scalable projects are those that can expand without changing' (ibid: 507). In the world of science, the ability to scale up (or down) is a virtue, while the 'art of noticing' – as known in ethnography and natural history – is considered archaic, because it does not 'add up' to a unified scheme (Tsing 2015: 37–38).

Yet, the art of noticing is what made Inuit survival in the High Arctic possible, and which makes ethnography. If outsiders came with definitive, grid-based mapping in mind, also of resources, the hunters always modelled their environment through a 'diagrammatic reasoning', operating through networks, images and sounds rather than concepts and numbers, allowing them to locate resources where others see none (Hastrup 2013a). In actual practice, ecology comprises both mind and matter; resources are not outside of human thought. As Bateson said, 'the unit of survival is the flexible organism-in-its-environment' (1972: 451).

Figure 2.2. Drying strips of narwhal meat on the island of Qeqertat; a composition of non-scalable elements. Photograph by the author.

Living in the Thule Region is predicated by the North Water, a High Arctic oasis of perpetually open sea water surrounded by ice and containing a remarkable diversity of life (Hastrup 2016; Hastrup et al. 2018a). This diversity is now under threat, and it has been suggested that the North Water be classified as a UNESCO Biosphere Reserve, to protect its specific physical and biological conditions (Speer et al. 2017). How such protection might work in the face of climate change is a major question among hunters in the region, who are always curious to know how scientists perceive their environment and are ready to single out certain elements for naming, for counting, or for protection, while the hunters know it as a totality of fluid boundaries and moving prey, whose trajectories may be storied but never predicted. Treaties and declarations rarely stall developments that are geo-social in nature, fusing geological, biological and social processes, each with their temporality yet always commingling (cf. Pálsson and Swanson 2016). Even so, they remind us of potential loss.

Recognizing geo-sociality, notably in the melting Arctic, poses a challenge to well-meaning attempts at protecting what is left of the (ancient) visions of the region. A case in point is found in a relatively recent attempt made by the United Nation's Environment Programme (UNEP 2006) to merge the Universal Declaration on Cultural Diversity (UNESCO 2001) with the Convention on Biological Diversity. The preamble of the 2006 declaration states (inter alia):

> *Aiming* to ensure full respect for the cultural and intellectual heritage of indigenous and local communities relevant for the conservation and sustainable use of biological diversity…

> *Recognizing* that respect and support for cultural diversity and the treatment of traditional knowledge, as co-equal and complementary to western scientific knowledge, are fundamental in order to ensure full respect for the cultural and intellectual heritage of indigenous and local communities.

These preambular exultations exhibit a disturbing classification of people, operating on a principle of distinction between indigenous (or local) communities and the rest of the world, and between traditional and Western, scientific, knowledge – as if the latter were not spatially, culturally and temporally contextualized. My point is that, while the international community takes the indigenous affect for animal species for granted, it also locates its own nostalgia with indigenous communities, implicitly portraying indigenous people as 'ecologically noble savages' (Redford 1991).

The local stakeholders in the North Water seem to have embraced this, through their own attempt at curbing the threats to the North Water at a more immediate human scale, gaining momentum from the international attention. In 2017 the Inuit Circumpolar Council (ICC) launched the idea of a North Water Commission on behalf of the Canadian and Greenlandic neighbours of oasis. In the process they agreed on a (West Greenlandic) name for the polynya: the Pikialasorsuaq (The Great Upwelling). Naming is a precondition for claiming, and in this the Pikialasorsuaq emulates the 'invention' of the name of the Inughuit – emerging in the 1970s when issues of indigenous populations entered the post-colonial global agenda. The aim of the North Water Commission is to curb the degradation of the habitat for both humans and animals, and to leave the management of the North Water to the locals on both sides of Smith Sound, whose life depends upon it. It is a political gesture that will have little impact on the actual development in the High Arctic, a region in deep trouble of global origin, which may be addressed but cannot be solved by declarations about the natural integrity of the North Water. It is defined by being enclosed in ice, for the better part of the year, but as it opens up and becomes an unmarked part of the open sea, it will soon become part of the ecological nostalgia attached to the region. The Commission serves to keep focus on the region as distinct.

The present inhabitants of the Thule Region do not ask for isolation; they eagerly engage with passing scientists, who may have come to estimate the stock of narwhal, to measure the thickness of the ice, to monitor the amount of soot on the glaciers, or are possibly on their way to even more northerly coasts in search of rare metals – of which one normally gets only scant information. Even secrecy fosters a hope of new possible sources of income, as the presence of marine mammals becomes more unpredictable. Conversely, scientists (including anthropologists) are totally dependent on the hunters' skill at navigation, at reading the ice, and at finding their way to the living resources for being able to scale their own attention properly (Hastrup 2013b). The hunters also assist in practical matters, such as tagging the animals with a view to mapping their foraging routes (Andersen et al. 2018). Yet, locally, biodiversity is not an abstract system of aligned species. It is a hard-won relationship to other species that are now (possibly) disappearing or at least moving elsewhere under the weight of new global realities of climate, sea ice and oceanic currents. The hunters are keen to share their views on the local ecology, just as before they awaited new arrivals; they are definitely part of a larger world. There is no nostalgic longing for isolation.

This brief tour to the High Arctic landscape, of which so much more may be said, brings us to what has been discussed in terms of environmental futures, ranging from the apocalyptic to the utopian, brought out by a range of very real concerns (Mathews and Barnes 2016). In contributing to the imaginations of new (resource) futures, anthropologists would be well advised to allow for the 'unruliness of our human and nonhuman interlocutors' (ibid.: 23), or, with the concept introduced above, the non-scalability of lives and landscapes. This may be a kind of intellectual nostalgia for social flexibility, defined by Bateson as an 'uncommitted potential for change' (Bateson 1972: 497), allowing for a diversity of action – badly needed.

Contaminated Landscapes: Measures of Modern Imperialism

Since the early twentieth century, the Thule region has been a site for varied and often intense research enterprises – including folklore, archaeology, biology, geology, oceanography and anthropology – if at different points in time. On top of the early explorations and mapping enterprises, itinerant scholars have contributed not only to knowledge published in foreign places, but also to the gradually shifting sense of place within the region. Involving themselves with the dwellers and their environment, scholars inadvertently contribute to a local experience of a shifting ground. While seeking out the true story of immigration, of walrus hunting, or of polar bears, they also unintentionally contribute to the design of the landscape (cf. Tsing 2015: 152). Minds and maps are inextricably linked, as claimed above.

Peary's long-lasting sojourns in the Thule region (1891–1909) signalled a qualitative shift in the ways in which strangers appropriated the newly 'discovered' place and its people, and, conversely, how the latter eagerly appropriated whatever they might use in their own interest. Epidemics still came and went, but the recurrent famines abated, due to regular influx of guns, etc. by which Peary paid for their services and which made hunting easier. When Peary withdrew after having attained his ulterior goal of reaching the North Pole in 1909, the Thule Trading Station was established in 1910 on the initiative of Ludvig Mylius-Erichsen and Knud Rasmussen, who had spent a year and a half in the region in 1903–1904 with the Danish Literary Expedition to Greenland, designed to collect tales and traditions of the 'New People', as the group who met them at Cape York was called (Rasmussen 1905, 1908). This was the first time their stories were written down in authoritative renderings of what was portrayed as a timeless world, becoming the baseline of future nostalgias.

With the Thule Station, a new monetary economy gradually emerged. For many years, the trade of fur, mainly from polar fox, was quite profitable and allowed the people to get guns and ammunition, utensils and cooking pots, new food items, and not least a steady supply of timber, so important for the dog sledges. The social situation had changed. When the expedition turned into a station, the relations between the newcomers and the local community changed (Fabian 2002: 47–48). In many ways the Thule Station also turned into a scientific field station at the instigation of Knud Rasmussen, the owner of Thule – still outside Danish state interests due to its inaccessibility. The surplus from the trade contributed to the funding of his many Thule Expeditions, whence their name, and over the years the Station as well as the inhabitants in the area serviced many archaeological, biological and geological expeditions, relying on the locals for transport and hunting.

The Thule Station was placed on a small headland beneath a huge moraine plain; the headland had been inhabited by Thule Inuit since their arrival in the region and there was still a small settlement, Uummannaq, referring to the 'heart-shaped' mountain on the tip of the headland. On the south side there was something like a natural deep-sea harbour, where the annual provision ship could anchor, and where the Station was built. It was well placed in the middle of the region with access to rich hunting grounds. With a permanent trade station, a mission, a school and eventu-

Figure 2.3. Remnants of the Thule-Station, with the emblematic 'heart-shaped' mountain at back. Photograph by the author.

ally a small hospital, the New People were definitively embraced by the Old World. This also extended to Old World scholarship, descending upon the region in its many forms and leaving its mark in local self-perceptions. Compared to earlier times, people were thriving; they had regular access to essential amenities and eventually to vaccination schemes. My own conversations with elderly friends in the region, who were children in the 1930s and 1940s, confirm that they saw it as a 'good time'.

Before the Thule Station, people had always been left to their own devices, and had lived in small, dispersed communities, where individual accidents might have great repercussions on the family's ability to hunt and to travel. Occupational hazards were numerous and often tolled hard among the hunters and their families. While neither sickness nor hunger abated totally with the trading station, fox skin could always be traded for food and rifles, and the safety net became ever more solid. With vaccination, the epidemics became manageable and the population, that had stabilized around 250 with Peary's introduction of rifles in exchange for services, continued growing (Gilberg 1976; Hastrup 2018b).

Renato Rosaldo has taken such views of improvement from the outside to task as a version of 'imperialist nostalgia' (Rosaldo 1989). This notion captures both the mourning of a lost traditional life and the guilt of foreigners, however well meaning they may have been. Anthropologists and other scholars arriving in the wake of 'discovery' to study the not-yet-vanished culture inadvertently contributed to its further demise, it could be claimed. Rosaldo also points to himself, stressing how 'The conditions that enabled us to stay among the Ilongots already made us complicit in imperialism' (Rosaldo 1989: 120). This is an important observation, yet some processes cannot be kept at bay by relinquishing documentation, and anthropologists have soldiered on, as have the local populations. Whose nostalgia is it anyway?

In Thule, imperialism reached a new scale, when in 1953 the settlement by the Thule Station was forcefully relocated from its vital centre at Uummannaq. The reason was the American establishment of the Thule Airbase, one of many tokens of the Cold War and of the build-up of the early warning system across the Arctic – the so-called DEW-line (Doel et al. 2014a, 2014b). The construction began surreptitiously – at least in relation to both the national and the international political community. Locally, it was not easy to overlook. Massive military gear and some 6000 soldiers (against some 400 local inhabitants) were deployed during the first couple of years. Imperialism was no longer an abstract process; it became part of the landscape.

A new story began; due to the Cold War militarization, with noisy airplanes, vast military ships during summer, the set-up of long-range missiles, the closing-off of the hunting grounds and so forth, the hunting landscape was de facto destroyed, and people were told to move from the headland. They had always been more or less itinerant, orienting themselves towards hunting possibilities along the entire coastline of the region stretching some 1000 kilometres, and of which they knew every bit in terms of resources. Yet, Uummannaq and the Thule Station were at the heart of their land – the gravitational centre in a decentred hunting world. Their sense of ecological integrity was deeply upset when they were forced to move.

Even though new houses were eventually built for them in other places, and the central functions of the Thule Station were recuperated in Qaanaaq further north, the heart had been broken. Their old landscape is visibly ruined; most of the turf houses at Uummannaq, where people had lived, ended up being destroyed to prevent people from using them on their way between the northern and southern regions of their land, stopping over on a hunting trip. The next step was to construct an under-ice city, Camp Century, in the late 1950s that would provide a safe haven for US personnel fighting against Soviet interests in the Cold War (Petersen

2008). It was argued that the observed retreat of glaciers and the 'polar warming' that had been predicted by scientists in the 1930s were a threat to US national security interests (Martin-Nielsen 2013: 52).

Camp Century was carved out in the deep of the ice cap some hundred kilometres from the Thule Airbase, widely seen as proof of American power at conquering the arctic environment (Nielsen et al. 2014: 455–56). A nuclear reactor had been installed in 1960, yet it had to be deactivated in 1963, because the moving ice made the entire construction bulge, leading to a near fatal contact between the reactor and the ice. The reactor was removed in 1964 and the entire experiment was abandoned. The personnel at the Thule Airbase decreased; by 1968, it was down to 3000 men, having peaked at 10,000 in 1962, and the airbase was transformed from an offensive to a defensive space (Martin-Nielsen 2013: 65). This made little difference to the people who had been ousted from their hunting grounds in 1953; they still depended on the broken landscape in its entirety, and having to circumvent the middle was a major problem.

The story reminds us how deeply the heated geopolitical situation had impinged on the global mind, barely noticing the consequences for people whose lands had been destroyed. For these people, the integrity of their hunting grounds was destroyed, and while times have changed and new possibilities have arisen, the past lingers as a sore point right under the surface of a new life. Some inhabitants voice a fear of there being nuclear waste still around in the now inaccessible Camp Century corridors that may eventually break off with a glacier, now nearing the sea. The local ecology has been irreparably shattered and the sense of loss has been reinforced by later incidents of contamination. When geo-sociality becomes part of a larger geopolitical scheme, a new sense of vulnerability and exposure takes root.

The ecological crisis lingers in people's minds; the ruined landscape cannot be obliterated – by however many clinical tests and political assurances. This has nothing to do with their being nostalgic; it has to do with a well-grounded fear of pollution that affects their future and subverts the hard-won sense of food security (Hastrup et al. 2016). Adding to this, the general contamination of the sea by heavy metals and persistent organic pollutants is an ominous presence in the Arctic region, where the hunting families are warned against eating too much meat and skin from the marine mammals (AMAP 2016; Dietz et al. 2018). Small wonder that people sometimes long for pre-anthropogenic waters.

The sense of the landscape having been ruined is not only a matter of contamination, but is also related to the political treachery by surreptitiously imperializing the land, and the long-term damages to the ecological integrity of the region. Place and politics are two sides of the same coin. Although in principle no one could own land or monopolize the resources, people were out-manoeuvred and the illegibility of the new neighbours left them with a deep sense of vulnerability (cf. Das 2004). The current climate scenarios feed into this. Like other people elsewhere, the Inughuit live in a landscape showing how 'empire's ruins contour and carve through the psychic and material space in which people live and what compounded layers of imperial debris do to them' (Stoler 2013: 2).

Living with imperial debris, including global ocean contamination, affects the local sense of a viable ecology, which again explains how the time 'before' the establishment of the Airbase is recalled in a nostalgic mode, even if the Thule Station was also some kind of foreign invasion and a game-changer. In numbers, the invasion was sparse, counting some three to five Danes, including the station manager and the doctor. Scale seems to make a difference to ecological nostalgia, rooted in matter as well as mind. This does not necessarily reflect an essentialist view of the past but reflects a memory of a viable community. While nostalgia may be about evoking a world that is distant in space and time (Bissel 2015: 222), the Thule people would not want to go back there. They certainly live in the present.

Disappearing Peoples: The Fusing of Past and Present

'Presentism' hinges on the past, of course, and we shall briefly revisit the earliest times of European exploration in the region. Norwegian Otto Sverdrup, on expedition in the High Arctic (1898–1902), found no living people. He was actually deeply affected by the fact that he only found ruins, from the 'time of the Eskimos', suggesting that they belonged to a prehistoric past. For him, the discovery of their traces underscored the unimaginable exposure to a hostile nature that would have been their plight. He noted:

> A few steps from our camp we encountered remnants of one construction after the other, from tents, meat caches and traps, clearly indicating that once upon a time these tracts were also inhabited.

> It is curious with these people. How vast the stretches they have claimed in these inhospitable lands with several months of night and under climatic conditions that would have led one to believe that all life would have come to a stop! What has happened to them? Have they moved south to milder regions? Or have they continued their hopeless fight against the oppressive darkness and frost of the winter night, until they all succumbed to the mighty enemy, who knows no mercy.

> One is gripped by a strange feeling of abandonment and waste when seeing these ruins, telling us that even here humans have lived with their sorrows and pleasures like us. (Sverdrup 1903, II: 275–76; personal translation)

Figure 2.4. Narwhal hunter in his kayak, silently waiting for his prey. Photograph by the author.

The chapter in which Sverdrup relates his finds, including a mummified human body in a stone grave, is called 'A dying people' and it underscores the sense of doom that clung to the region, and still does, if now in a new version – related to climate change and possible species depletion (AMAP 2017). The threat is linked both to the receding ice and to the contamination dealt with above, challenging the inter-species relations by which people live.

Zooming in on the life of hunters and their families in the Thule Region today, the heterogeneity of life forms formats their social life. This could be said of all humans, by their hosting multiple microbial creatures, and by their consuming animal and/or vegetable food (Bennett 2010: 38ff). Yet in the Thule region it is so very obvious. The most cherished foodstuff consists of meat from narwhal, seal, walrus, muskox, reindeer and sea-birds – notably little auks and guillemots. Food is 'one of the many agencies operative in the moods, cognitive dispositions, and moral sensibilities that we bring to bear as we engage the questions of what to eat, how to get it, and when to stop' (Bennett 2010: 51). The notion of biodiversity again falls flat, once we abandon the classificatory ambition and give in to the actualities of lived life in real-time landscapes where agents are always mixed up with each other.

When the hunters claim to need narwhal skin (*mattak*) to get through the long polar night where the sun is not seen for four months – 'otherwise we get depressed' – they voice a sense of self that incorporates their food. Medical studies point to the rich depositories of vitamin (A, C and D) in the whale-skin, but effectively they make the same case. The downside of the need for marine edibles is the growing anxiety about the heavy metals that pollute the sea and become ever more concentrated the higher up the food chain one gets – entirely by unintentional design (AMAP 2015, 2016). The demarcation of a bio-reserve makes no difference here; nature does not follow abstract ideologies, even if such may raise human awareness of its vulnerability.

Generally, people living in the High Artic landscape are all too aware of climate change, experienced directly in the sea ice breaking up earlier than before and compromising access to hunting grounds that have served people well for a long time, and of course eagerly followed on the Internet. The game also seems to seek out new territories and haul-out places, contributing to a definite sense that the liveable space is shrinking – all while globalization becomes increasingly obvious. Ancient sledge routes that connected settlements to each other, and to the distant haunts of walrus, polar bear or narwhal, to mention but the most emblematic species, are disappearing, and it is fair to say that their resource space is undergoing rapid change (Flora et al. 2018). Seal, seabirds, muskox and reindeer make a difference in the natural economy, but they are not essential in their social life as are the others, and often equally inaccessible. Fish – polar cod, arctic char, and halibut – also add to the diet, the latter increasingly so, because it has become an object of trade – and one that does not necessarily demand long-distance travelling. As the fox did before, the halibut has emerged as a new cash crop – improving the economy for many, but at a cost for people (not least the elderly) who used to get a share of the hunt, when it was marine mammals; however, one does not share money (Hastrup et al 2018b).

While the environment is changing, the materials and technologies by which people have lived for ages gradually become obsolete, including their spectacular skin clothes. Small wonder that international film-crews, journalists and researchers flock to the main town of Qaanaaq to document 'the last Eskimos' – as popular film titles often have it, be they in English, German, Japanese, Korean or Danish. The inhabitants of the region are already figuring as lost and gradually turning into heritage, becoming objects for conservation and 'mummified' in films, as it were, if not in the factual sense that so affected Sverdrup. In fact, their lives are still unfolding in response to both local and global trajectories, including the varying perceptions of outsiders. The formidable dog sledges are still the predominant technology of travel and an instrument of hunting and of community making – allowing people to move about and visit each other and to ferry film-crews and a few wildlife tourists around. The reporters swarming to the Arctic today have a parallel power to the nineteenth-century press; yet what was then a reporting on discovery and an expansion of the world has now become a kind of commemoration (cf. Bissel 2015: 222).

Locally, the influx of reporters of all kinds places the hunters who still have enough dogs for extensive trips in a dilemma; should they go for real, if uncertain narwhal hunts at the ice edge in spring, or should they collect a payment in cash for taking out tourists or film-makers, 'performing' as hunters? This is a delicate balance, not least because they often find tourists unprepared for the hardships of travel by sledge, and for the fact that one cannot 'book' an animal to show itself at a particular time, when it fits into the outsider's brief visit. Another, local dilemma has arisen between going for the new cash crop in the region, the halibut, or going for bigger game further away, if you still have your strength and your dogs. The halibut, too, can still only be caught from the ice on long lines, the same ice that may carry the hunters further afield. Even though destabilized, the ice remains the all-important infrastructure, with nothing as yet to replace it, and practical choices must be made.

My contention is that outsiders, including scholars, rushing to the place to experience 'the last hunters' or 'the last Eskimos' with their bearskin trousers, sealskin kamiks, dog sledges, kayaks and harpoons, contribute to an image of their life as if already just an exhibit. Through the circulating images, the 'Eskimos' become relegated to a past, in response to outsiders' perceptions, such as Sverdrup's in earlier times. However, when back from the hunt they change into different clothes, use their mobile phones, and consult the Internet for information about larger political issues, be it decisions made 'down south' about hunting quotas and health care issues, or the latest scientific predictions about the dwindling of the ice cap and the sea ice. Through the constant sharing of information between the homes in the village and with relatives elsewhere in Greenland and Denmark, the apparently isolated community is deeply integrated in a larger knowledge space, and people begin to resent being presented and addressed as if living in the past tense. They are attached to their place, but not in a particularly nostalgic mode; anthropological fieldwork makes this absolutely clear.

The High Arctic landscape was always marked out as inherently different and unknowable, because it seemed to defy mapping and knowing in established schemes and grids. This still seems to foster a particular perception of people actually living there as a kind of heritage, all while locally new imaginative horizons are opening up, sustaining new hopes (Crapanzano 2004). 'Hope is never far from nostalgia' (Berliner 2014: 384), yet hope for the Inughuit is not to bring back the past but to be able to remain in their region, however much it may change. Their life is there.

Ecological Nostalgias: Thinking through Friction

The High Arctic hunters, with whose history we have dealt above in various stories and accounts, were always inscribed in a truly global development – through climatic trends, exchange networks, animal migrations, human travels and encounters – even when most isolated. It is more conspicuous now than ever before, but it has been a fact forever. What is relatively recent is the intense outside interest, spurred by new knowledge about global warming and ocean contamination that contributes to an image of their life as doomed. What we should note is that the lives of hunters – like other lives – are part of and contribute to a particular geo-sociality. The geological processes fuel into and become part of biological and social developments.

The global processes are neither new nor predictable, because they are subject to frictions, in the sense suggested by Tsing, as such differences and vicissitudes that always get in the way of a smooth process (Tsing 2005: 4–6). The long-term climatic developments, the medium-term exploration interests, as well as the short-term political onslaughts, are all of them marked by (and creating) frictions that defy any linear vision of history and global development. These frictions are owed to the multiplicity of forces and agencies that surround social life, which is never stable because it is subject to both abrupt and gradual changes that challenge received wisdom and habits. Where nostalgia enters the picture, it glosses over the immanent frictions in the world, but it cannot really hide the motley processes that made it, whether of imperialist origin or fostered in a stone-and-turf hut, equally embedded in multi-scalar geo-social processes.

As anthropologists we are studying assemblages of all kinds, emerging or disappearing depending on the direction of the gaze and the analytical inclination within the geo-social framework. Ecological futures are always in the making, and we generally seek out a baseline for comparison. But even this is made up for the purpose and cannot be claimed to be the real thing, primordial or otherwise. Ecological nostalgias may have powerful emotional repercussions, as abstractions from the present they cannot guide the future. In times of Anthropocene thinking, the vision of nested ecological scales is untenable, and while we still have to write, we also have to explicitly acknowledge the nature of analysis – itself a scaling device.

This chapter took off from Bateson's concept of the ecology of mind, and it is worth remembering that for him, the mind represented ideas that extended, web-like, from individual brains out into nature; this implicitly connects humans with their environment. When mapping landscapes or regions, what gets on the map is perceived difference, according to Bateson. Differences – whether of landscapes, histories, economies, military dreams or life-styles – are sources of potential friction. These may be clad in different spatial vernaculars, a notion suggested by Whatmore, upsetting the geometric habits of conventional cartography by being 'fluid, not flat, upsetting coordinates of distance and proximity; local and global; inside and outside' (Whatmore 2002: 6). Such spatial vernaculars grow out of a particular engagement with an ecology of both matter and mind.

The Arctic has most often been portrayed as a unity, whether dreamt of or lived. Yet it is very much a differential space, also in the theoretical sense suggested by Henri Lefebvre, acknowledging the legitimacy of diverse knowledge interests (Lefebvre 1991: 399). Working on nature's edge as anthropologists (Hastrup 2014), we know that ecologies are double-edged in the sense that they point 'inwards' to people's perceptions, and possibly longings, and 'outwards' towards a landscape in permanent making.

Acknowledgements

Extensive fieldwork in Avanersuaq (the Thule region) was possible due to the project Waterworlds (2009–2014) funded by the European Research Council, Adv. Grant 229459. Later, the interdisciplinary North-Water Project (2014–2017) has allowed me to continue in the field and to embrace new perspectives. I am grateful to the Carlsberg Foundation and the Velux Foundations for generous financial support.

Warm thanks also to Olivia Ange and David Berliner for inviting me to participate in the conference in Brussels in early summer 2017, leading to this chapter. Thanks also to the anonymous reviewer for important notes.

Kirsten Hastrup is Professor Emeritus of Anthropology at the University of Copenhagen. She has worked in Northwest Greenland since 2007, and before that in Iceland. She has published numerous books and articles on both of these fields, with a sustained focus on the interface between nature and society. She was PI of *Waterworlds* (ERC Advanced grant) focussing on life with global climate change (2009–2014), and of the *North Water Project* on living resources and human societies in the Thule area, Greenland (2014–2018).

References

Andersen, A., O.J. Flora and M.P. Heide-Jørgensen. 2018. 'Is Sustainable Resource Utilization a Relevant Concept in Avanersuaq? The Walrus Case', *Ambio: A Journal of the Human Environment* 47(2): 265–80.

Ange, O. and D. Berliner 2015. 'Introduction: Anthropology of Nostalgia – Anthropology as Nostalgia', in O. Angé and D. Berliner (eds), *Anthropology and Nostalgia*. Oxford: Berghahn, pp. 1–15.

Arctic Monitoring and Assessment Programme (AMAP). 2015. 'AMAP Assessment 2015: Human Health in the Arctic'. Oslo.

_____. 2016. 'AMAP Assessment 2016: Chemicals of Emerging Arctic Concern'. Oslo.

_____. 2017. 'Snow, Water, Ice and Permafrost in the Arctic (SWIPA) 2017'. Oslo.

Bateson, G. 1972. *Steps to an Ecology of Mind*. New York: Ballantine Books.

Bennett, J. 2010. *Vibrant Matter: A Political Ecology of Things*. Durham, NC and London: Duke University Press.

Berliner, D. 2014. 'On Exonostalgia', *Anthropological Theory* 14(4): 373–86.

_____. 2015. 'Are Anthropologists Nostalgist?', in O. Angé and D. Berliner (eds), *Anthropology and Nostalgia*. Oxford: Berghahn, pp. 17–34.

Bissel, W.C. 2005. 'Engaging Colonial Nostalgia', *Cultural Anthropology* 20(2): 215–48.

_____. 2015. 'Afterword: On Anthropology's Nostalgia – Looking Back/Seeing Ahead', in O. Angé and D. Berliner (eds), *Anthropology and Nostalgia*. Oxford: Berghahn, pp. 213–23.

Crapanzano, V. 2004. *Imaginative Horizons: An Essay in Literary-Philosophical Anthropology*. Chicago: University of Chicago Press.

Das, V. 2004. 'The Signature of the State: The Paradox of Illegibility', in V. Das and D. Poole (eds), *Anthropology on the Margins of the State*. Santa Fe, NM: School of American Research, pp. 225–52.

Dietz, Rune, A. Mosbech, J. Flora, and I. Eulaers. 2018. 'Interactions of Climate, Socio-Economics, and Global Mercury Pollution in the North Water'. *Ambio. Journal of the Human Environment* 47, suppl. 2: 281–295.

Doel, R.E., U. Wråkberg and S. Zeller. 2014a. 'Science, Environment, and the New Arctic', *Journal of Historical Geography* 44: 2–14.

_____. 2014b. 'Strategic Arctic Science: National Interests in Building Natural Knowledge – Interwar Era through the Cold War', *Journal of Historical Geography* 44: 60–80.

Fabian, J. 2002. *Out of Our Minds: Reason and Madness in the Exploration of Central Africa*. Berkeley, CA: University of California Press.

Flora, J.K., K.L. Johansen, B. Grønnow, A.O. Andersen and A. Mosbech. 2018. 'Present and Past Dynamics of Inughuit Resource Spaces', *Ambio: Journal of the Human Environment* 47(2): 244–64.

Gilberg, R. 1976. *The Polar Eskimo Population, Thule District, North Greenland*. Copenhagen: Nyt Nordisk Forlag Arnold Busck.

Hastrup, K. 2007. 'Ultima Thule: Anthropology and the Call of the Unknown', *Journal of the Royal Anthropological Institute* 13: 789–804.

_____. 2009. 'Arctic Hunters: Climate Variability and Social Flexibility', in K. Hastrup (ed.), *The Question of Resilience: Social Responses to Climate Change*. Copenhagen: The Royal Danish Academy of Sciences and Letters, pp. 245–70.

_____. 2010. 'Emotional Topographies: The Sense of Place in the Far North', in J. Davies and D. Spencer (eds), *Emotions in the Field: The Psychology and Anthropology of Fieldwork Experience*. Stanford, CA: Stanford University Press, pp. 191–211.

_____. 2013a. 'Anticipation on Thin Ice: Diagrammatic Reasoning Among Arctic Hunters', in K. Hastrup and M. Skrydstrup (eds), *Anticipating Nature: The Social Life of Climate Models*. London: Routledge, pp. 77–99.

_____. 2013b. 'Scales of Attention in Fieldwork: Global Connections and Local Concerns in the Arctic', *Ethnography* 14(2): 145–64.

_____. 2014. 'Nature: Anthropology on the Edge', in K. Hastrup (ed.), *Anthropology and Nature*. London: Routledge, pp. 1–26.

_____. 2016. 'The North Water: Life on the Ice Edge in the High Arctic', in K. Hastrup and F. Hastrup (eds), *Waterworlds: Anthropology in Fluid Environments*. Oxford: Berghahn, pp. 279–99.

_____. 2018a. 'The Viability of a High Arctic Hunting Community: A Historical Perspective', in M. Brightman and J. Lewis (eds), *The Anthropology of Sustainability: Beyond Development and Progress*. New York: Palgrave Macmillan, pp. 145–63.

_____. 2018b. 'The Historicity of Health: Environmental Hazards and Epidemics in Northwest Greenland', *Journal of Cross-Cultural Research* 53(3): 291–311.

Hastrup, K., A.O. Andersen, B. Grønnow and M.P. Heide-Jørgensen. 2018. 'Life Around the North Water Ecosystem: Natural and Social Drivers of Change over a Millennium', *Ambio: A Journal of the Human Environment* 47(2): 213–25.

Hastrup, K., B. Grønnow and A. Mosbech. 2018. 'Introducing the North Water: Histories of Exploration, Ice Dynamics, Living Resources, and Human Settlement in the Thule Region', *Ambio: A Journal of the Human Environment* 47(2): 162–74.

Hastrup, K., A.M. Rieffestahl and A. Olsen. 2016. 'Food Security: Changing Health Concerns in the Global North', in M. Singer (ed.), *Wiley's Companion to the Anthropology of Environmental Health*. Hoboken, NJ: Wiley and Son, pp. 257–80.

Hayes, I.I. 1866. *The Open Polar Sea: A Narrative of a Voyage of Discovery towards the North Pole, in the Schooner United States*. London: Sampson Low, Son and Marston.

Lefebvre, H. 1991. *The Production of Space*, trans D. Nicholson-Smith. Oxford: Blackwell.

Martin-Nielsen, J. 2013. '"The Deepest and Most Rewarding Hole Ever Drilled": Ice Cores and the Cold War in Greenland', *Annals of Science* 70(1): 47–70.

Mathews, A.S. and J. Barnes. 2016. 'Prognosis: Visions of Environmental Futures', *Journal of The Royal Anthropological Institute*, Special Issue: 9–26.

McGhee, Robert. 1997. *Ancient People of the Arctic*. Vancouver: University of British Columbia Press.

Nansen, F. 1927. 'Adventure', in *Adventure and Other Papers*. London: Leonard and Virginia Woolf.

Nielsen, K.H., H. Nielsen and J. Martin-Nielsen. 2014. 'City under the Ice: The Closed World of Camp Century in Cold War Culture', *Science as Culture* 23(4): 443–64.

Pálsson, G. 2002. 'Arcticality: Gender, Race, and Geography in the Writings of Vilhjalmur Stefansson', in M. Bravo and S. Sörlin (eds), *Narrating the Arctic: A*

Cultural History of Nordic Scientific Practices. Cambridge: Cambridge University Press, pp. 275–309.

Pálsson, Gísli and Heather Swanson. 2016. 'Down to Earth: Geosocialities and Geopolitics'. *Environmental Humanities* 8(2). doi:10.1215/22011919-3664202.

Peary, R.E. 1898. *Northward over the 'Great Ice': A Narrative of Life and Work along the Shores and upon the Interior Ice-Cap of Northern Greenland in the Years 1886 and 1891-1897*, vol. I & II. London: Methuen & Co.

_____. 1907. *Nearest the Pole: A Narrative of the Polar Expedition of the Peary Arctic Club in the S.S. Roosevelt*. London: Hutchinson & Co.

Petersen, N. 2008. 'The Iceman that Never Came', *Scandinavian Journal of History* 33(1): 75–98.

Pratt, M.L. 1992. *Imperial Eyes: Travel Writing and Transculturation*. London and New York: Routledge.

Rasmussen, K. 1905. *Nye Mennesker*. Copenhagen: Gyldendal.

_____. 1908. *The People of the Polar North*, trans. G. Herring (ed). London: Kegan Paul, Trench, Trübner & Co.

Redford, K. 1991. 'The Ecologically Noble Savage', *Cultural Survival Quarterly* 15(1): 46–48.

Riffenburgh, B. 1993. *The Myth of the Polar Explorer: The Press, Sensationalism, and Geographical Discovery*. London and New York: Belhaven Press and Scott Polar Research Institute, University of Cambridge.

Rosaldo, R. 1989. 'Imperialist Nostalgia', *Representations* 26: 107–21.

Ross, J. 1819. *Voyage of Discovery, Made under the Orders of Admiralty, in his Majesty's Ships Isabelle and Alexander, for the Purpose of Exploring Baffin's Bay, and Inquiring into the Probability of a North-West Passage*. London: John Murray, Albemarle-Street.

Said, E. 1979. *Orientalism*. New York: Vintage Books.

Speer, L., R. Nelson, R. Casier, M. Gavrilo, C. von Quillfeldt, J. Cleary, P. Halpin and P. Hooper. 2017. *Natural Marine World Heritage in the Arctic Ocean: Report of an Expert Workshop and Review Process*. Gland, Switzerland: IUCN.

Stoler, A.L. (ed.). 2013. *Imperial Debris: On Ruins and Ruination*. Durham, NC and London: Duke University Press.

Sverdrup, O. 1903. *Nyt Land: Fire Aar i Arktiske Egne*. Bd. I & II: Kristiania: Forlaget Aschehoug & Co. (W. Nygaard).

Tsing, Anna L. 2005. *Friction: An Ethnography of Global Connection*. Princeton, NJ: Princeton University Press.

_____. 2012. 'On Nonscalability: The Living World Is Not Amenable to Precision-Nested Scales', *Common Knowledge* 18(3): 505–24.

_____. 2015. *The Mushroom at the End of the World: On the Possibility of Life in Capitalist Ruins*. Princeton, NJ and Oxford: Princeton University Press.

UNEP 2006. *Marine and Coastal Ecosystems and Human Well-Being: A Synthesis Report Based on the Findings of the Millenium Ecosystem Assessment*. United Nations Environment Programme.

UNESCO 2001. *Universal Declaration of Cultural Diversity*. Paris: Unesco.

Whatmore, S. 2002. *Hybrid Geographies: Natures, Cultures, Spaces*. London: Sage.

Chapter 3

Nostalgic Confessions in the French Cévennes

Politics of Longings in the Neo-Peasants Initiatives

Madeleine Sallustio

Introduction

Today is a beautiful autumn day. I'm staying at the farm of Chambalou:[1] a community of eight people who maintain a *maraîchage* (market gardening) system with animal-drawn vehicles and a small herd of goats, who also sell their homemade cheeses and wood-oven bread in the nearby markets. Among them is Pierre, who left Paris a few years ago to settle in the Cévennes where he built a small wooden hut on the farm's site, and became very passionate about organic gardening. Although he is busy with the work that this activity requires, he offers to show me around the hills nearby. The land we are crossing, covering several tens of hectares, very little of it maintained, belongs to various owners in the region. It is an idyllic expedition for me, whose knowledge of nature is limited to such places as parks in Brussels. For Pierre, it is an abandoned landscape: the ruins of a world that no longer exists.

The access paths are covered by the brambles and holm oaks that grow all over the place, destroying the dry-stone terracing walls. The passage of game and herds of adventurous goats contributes to the collapse of these walls and creates a network of passages through bushes and shrubs that are sometimes more convenient to follow than the original paths. In addition to these dry-stone walls, there are ruins: small buildings whose former status as a habitat, shepherd's hut or sheepfold has been forgotten; stone staircases embedded in the walls that provide access from one terrace to another; remains of gutters that once enabled the irrigation of these terraces; and the development of basins downstream from the river and other remains of peasant agriculture that were still active at the beginning of the twentieth century. During the climb, Pierre explains what he knows (or guesses) about the use of these remains. He seems particularly affected by his lack of knowledge of landscape archaeology. Several times during the walk, we find ourselves in front of cavities carved into the walls of the terraces. He comments: 'Here is a big mystery. No one knows what it could be made for. Shelter maybe? To keep out the rain when they were herding the animals? It drives me crazy that we've lost all this knowledge, that we've forgotten what it was meant for, what these terraces used to look like'. Further up the mountain, basalt flows contribute to an atmosphere of neglect and desolation. We sit at a place where we enjoy a clear view down over the valley. I particularly enjoy this contemplative break between serenity and physical exhaustion. Pierre shares what he then presents as a confession:

> Well, I'm telling you because I know you're interested. But here, when I see this, I get really nostalgic, it gets me here [he touches his chest, hesitates]. I realize that it's not possible to recreate these, though. I mean, there's all kinds of things you don't have to produce anymore, you can just buy them. But all of that made an entire world disappear.

> *Are you sorry this world is over?*

> [He hesitates…] It's not that I regret it, I definitely don't want to go back to that. … You know, we are always called utopians, hippies, dreamers. But no, on the contrary, the dreamers are those who believe that we can continue to exploit the land as we do! We have become so specialized that we have completely lost our grip on basic knowledge and know-how such as producing our food, maintaining our environment, building our house… It's not that I want to go back, but it would be a shame to lose everything.[2]

This conversation, in which my interlocutor shows a certain nostalgia which he then immediately nuances and justifies with political discourse, is no exception. It is a recurrent rhetorical strategy on the part of the people I have met in the field. In this chapter, I will explore this confessional modality of neo-peasants' nostalgia for traditional peasantry. I will examine the different temporalities that surround the daily lives of people who have chosen to leave the city to live in farms, and documents eco-nostalgic practices that are symptomatic of Western society in the face of climate change and ecological upheavals. Analysing the nostalgia for traditional peasantry experienced by these actors highlights the salient aspects of the social and ecological critique they carry.

To understand the roots of this confessional dimension, I will examine the mobilization of rural nostalgia over the long term. This historical approach is inspired by the concept of 'structural nostalgia' introduced by Michael Herzfeld (2007: 173–213). Through his study of the nostalgic rhetoric of Cretan shepherds, he showed how the same nostalgic representation is passed through history while being re-appropriated in very different ideological discourses. I will seek to understand how the archetype of the traditional peasant, invoked as the basis of stability and human wisdom, has been used in the course of history for differing fascist, reactionary, anarchist or ecological projects. Although they are in the historical continuity of the mobilization of this rural nostalgia, neo-peasants are nevertheless reluctant to assume the nostalgic emotion within a political discourse for fear of being accused of lacking rational discernment. Their attachment to past agricultural traditions thus takes the form of a 'nostalgic confession'.

Furthermore, I will draw on Svetlana Boym's thought about the 'Future of Nostalgia' to demonstrate that the nostalgic temporality of the neo-peasants is neither strictly oriented towards the past nor strictly towards the future. It involves the interweaving of different temporalities with the past, present and future horizons that constitute them, in accordance with her assertion that nostalgia seems 'stifled within the conventional confines of time and space' (2001: xiv). The neo-peasant collective projects are inspired by past knowledge and know-how with the aim of proposing an alternative way of life that is more respectful of the environment. This chapter intends to account for the composition of this complex temporality.

French Rural Nostalgia throughout History

The nostalgic reference to traditional peasantry or vernacular countryside is not new. In France, the social transformations that took place in the countryside between the end of the eighteenth and the beginning of the twentieth century provided fertile ground for the emergence of a collective nostalgia that allows for a 'sense of historical continuity' in times of uncertainty (Davis 1979: 49). In the course of history, the peasant archetype has often asserted itself as 'the only witness to pre-industrial civilization and … the bearer of valuable experience that can provide a remedy against the evils of so-called technical progress' (Jollivet 1978: 25, personal translation). The same applies to the countryside, invoking the idea of a salvific balance and harmony in the face of the 'ravages of modernity' (Chamboredon 1980: 114; Chevalier et al. 2000: 54–55; Eizner 1978; Jollivet 1978; Léger and Hervieu 1979). Such a melancholic idealization of traditional forms of popular sociability and rural family economic organization in opposition to the growth of cities thus already existed in the eighteenth century with thinkers such as Jean-Jacques Rousseau (Rauchs 1999: 286; Dobré 2002: 141–42).

However, at about the same time in France, a completely different temporality dominated the discourse towards the rural world: that which was associated with progress. This temporality is characterized by the conviction that we are witnessing a unidirectional historical process, a 'single evolutionary line' (Simmel 1984: 219–20, personal translation) oriented towards an ever-increasing improvement in the human living condition. By the end of the nineteenth century, the countryside became the site of unprecedented national integration policies: literacy became a priority; the modalities of collective organization and management of the peasantry were institutionalized; the first phase of mechanization had as a consequence more individualization of peasant work, these in turn freeing up labour (Bleton-Ruget 2002; Fel 1985; Weber 1983; Lejeune 1991). People within this temporality started migrating to the cities.

In reaction to these social transformations and the advent of modern capitalist industry, some intellectuals of the time questioned the humanism of the Scientifics and denounced the inequalities in the distribution of the benefits from the industrial revolution (Noble 2016). Thus, authors such as Charles Fourier and Elisée Reclus (1899: 3) opposed the progress of industry and urban development in favour of communalized agricultural life. For these authors, the countryside and 'corporate agriculture' (Fourier 1833: 292) became the primary place for the creation of a liberated society and for the well-being of the people. In the nineteenth century, the French countryside was indeed the site of the installation of the first anarchist communities: the *Milieux libres* (Steiner 2016). These precursors of neo-peasantry wanted to distance themselves from the industrial world and reconstitute in the countryside a communitarian society, free from the proletariat, the Church and the State. The anarchists of the time thus put the work of the land in the spotlight. The first criticisms of capitalist industrialization were thus built in parallel with a re-evaluation of the peasantry.

However, the idealization of traditional peasantry within political discourses was not exclusive to progressive libertarian thinking. At the end of the nineteenth century, for example, agrarianism was born. This conservative and anti-Semitic European ideological trend emerged as a result of the political organization of an elite composed of landowners and families in power directly descended from the fallen Christian aristocracy: the *Notables*. Faced with the endangerment of the foundations of a hierarchy directly inherited from the *Ancien Régime*, the massive rural exodus emptying the countryside of its craftsmen and peasants and, above all, the rise of revolutionary workers' forces in the cities, this elite then in-

Figure 3.1. 'The land doesn't lie', Limoges, 1942. Propaganda Épinal image under the Régime de Vichy showing the *Maréchal* Pétain saluting the hard work of the French peasants. Used with permission.

tended to rely on a sense of rural identity to establish its legitimacy (Barral 1968). Strongly supported by the Catholic Church, the rural world was then invoked as the 'privileged place of Christian life' (Hervieu and Léger 1980: 17, personal translation). The peasant family and village life were presented as moral emblems and systematically placed the city and industrialization at odds with each other. Peasant pride and working the land then became one of the stabilizing symbols of the French nation (idem). Agrarianism and its hatred of cities, elites and the 'decadence' linked to progressive social values resurfaced with the rise of fascism as witnessed by its apogee under the Vichy regime.

In the post-war years, the imperative was to modernize agriculture. This time, the isolation of the countryside from the cities' cultural entertainment environments was emphasized, the permanent social control of the villages was criticized, and the austere peasant lifestyle was poorly perceived (Jollivet 1978: 22–23). The modernist ideology of the time and the green revolution it was preparing seemed to have overcome the collective nostalgia for a myth of nobility and peasant wisdom (Guérin 2002: 233–35; Mendras 1976: 297–300; Weber 1983: 687–88). The doors opened up to the agri-food industry as we know it today. This agricultural system is understood to be the intensification of productivity, the generalization of monocultures, the widespread use of chemical pesticides and fertilizers, and the development of hybrid plants, but also the large-scale competition between farms throughout the world thanks to the deployment of competitive imports and exports (Haubert 1991: 726; Deléage 2011; Dupont 2005; van der Ploeg 2014). Facing this, small-scale agriculture struggled to maintain itself. Peasantry shifted from a 'way of life' to a professional status, as it was entering a process of specialization.[3] The rural exodus of those who could not bear the new commercial constraints increased as well.

Although the rural world had already witnessed the disappearance, creation and transformation of traditions over the course of history (Chevalier et al. 2000: 22; Weber 1983: 567), this time the elites and intellectuals sounded the alarm in favour of the past against 'the death of tradition' (Weber 1983: 669, personal translation), and set out in search of 'authenticity' (Bendix 1997). Using a Marxist perspective, these intellectuals constructed an ideal-typical description of the peasantry as a social category fundamentally opposed to industrial capitalism (Alphandéry and Sencébé 2009; Bernstein and Byres 2001: 7). The traditional peasant was indeed presented as a victim disappearing under the injunction to modernize and make agricultural work more productive (Weber 2015; Mendras 1976; Kayser 1990; van der Ploeg 2014: 47; Fel 1985; Jollivet 1968; Deléage 2013).

This critical perspective, which stood for the social and ecological merits of the traditional peasantry, was appropriated by the early neo-peasants. When they arrived in the deserted countryside after the events of May 1968, these activists carried with them a nostalgia articulated as a project of 'return to the land'. This notion of 'return', commonly used by the actors themselves, is quite revealing of the nostalgia at stake. Most of them had indeed not lived in rural areas before. The 'return' should be understood here as nostalgia for a world they did not directly experience, an 'exo-nostalgic' (Berliner 2014) characteristic of neo-peasant initiatives. This longing for traditional peasantry nourishes the will of a 'return to the roots', to a pre-industrial stage where a long-term sustainable ecological balance would prevail. The figure of the traditional peasant was then erected as a symbol of resistance and an icon of a pre-industrial and collectivist way of life. This is illustrated, for example, by the birth of the trade union La Confédération Paysanne in 1987 or the organization of the international movement Via Campesina. The peasant archetype underpins a sustainable, small-scale, environmentally friendly agricultural project, but also advocates decent working conditions and village solidarity (Demeuleunaere and Bonneuil 2011). In addition, the reference to peasantry carries with it the search for the transmission of vernacular wisdom and skills and a taste for local products, which are presented as being directly opposed to contemporary 'junk food' (Jollivet 1978).

The popularization of the romantic and idealized portrait of the French peasantry and countryside was thus directly linked to its political construction, sometimes humanist and anarchist, sometimes regionalist and reactionary. As has already been studied by other anthropologists in different fields (Herzfeld 2007: 173–213; Berliner 2012), the mobilization of the same nostalgic reference in political discourse has thus served very different, sometimes even opposite, ideological projects and this ideological ambivalence has percolated throughout history. This sheds light on the ideological tensions and misunderstandings that are embedded in the nostalgic stories I collected during my stay in the Cévennes.

Neo-Peasants' Life Projects in the Cévennes: An Ethnographic Outline

Since the end of the 1960s, the Cévennes has been the scene of a 'rural renaissance' (Kayser 1990, personal translation) following the arrival of city people. Among the actors that sociologists generally identify as 'neo-rural', I chose to meet those who decided to settle in the countryside and whose goal was to establish a field of experiments for the creation of new libertarian and self-managed micro-societies. They had wanted to boycott the political scene, which is considered disappointing and corrupt, and wished to escape the control of institutions and the State. They intended to live on the margins of the 'system', understood as the organization of work based on the wage relationship, the pyramidal institutionalization of power relations, as well as inegalitarian and anti-ecological modes of production. In order to respect their identification with the peasantry, I have chosen to call them 'neo-peasants'.

During the year and a half of participant observation in the field, I lived and worked in about ten collectives, composed of between five and twenty-five inhabitants. These collectives bring together people aged between twenty-five and forty years old (in addition to children, up to eleven years old), generally from middle-class backgrounds (two thirds of the people) or from more precarious backgrounds (one third). A very large majority of them also come from the cities.

These actors organize themselves according to self-management principles, in particular by ensuring horizontality in decision-making concerning daily life and the organization of work. In addition to building spaces for social experimentation (collective life, mutualism, rejection of private property, self-management, multi-family life), most of the activities that the neo-peasants set up revolve around the desire to learn how to 'do by themselves' and to become autonomous regarding the consumption of their most basic needs. This ambition focuses primarily on their food self-sufficiency through the implementation of small-scale organic farming, the raising of goats or sheep, and knowledge about the cooking of agricultural products (sourdough bread, jams, cheeses, lacto-fermentation, wine-making, beer brewing, cold meats, etc.). The desire to improve their autonomy also concerns the ability to build their own homes or to understand the functioning of the tools they use (mechanics, ironwork, electricity, craftsmanship, carpentry, low-tech engineering).

These daily activities are seen as a way to self-empower and to have more control over the environment. These tasks occupy a large part of the time of neo-peasants. They are valued as emancipatory as opposed to the repetitive, compartmentalized and decontextualized tasks of line work or office work, which are taken as examples of typically urban occupations and seen as numbing and alienating. However, these activities are rarely sufficient to generate individual income, and neo-peasants usually receive social assistance in parallel with their activities.

The neo-peasants' search for independence is also associated with an anxious approach to the future. While continuing the rural nostalgia whose history was presented above, the contemporary regret of the traditional peasantry is accentuated by the temporality of the 'emergency' (Dubar 2011). This vision of the future has been conceptualized, according to the authors, as a 'crisis of the future' (Dubar 2011: 2; Leccardi 2011, personal translation), 'loss of the future' (Anderson 2017: 4), 'death of the future' (Lowenthal 1992), 'eclipse of the future' (Taguieff 2002: 83–123, personal translation), 'dystopian times' (Levitas 1982), 'apocalyptic times' (Godard 2002; Foessel 2012, personal translation) or even as 'catastrophism' (Dupuy 2002, personal translation). All these works refer to the relatively pessimistic approach to the future and the erasure of long-term future temporalities in progressive political discourse: utopia seems to have lost its place in political thinking.

Since the 1990s, the Intergovernmental Panel on Climate Change (IPCC) has produced unqualified assessment reports on the responsibility of human activity in the process of global warming (Pachauri and Meyer 2014). Increasingly, research shows that the related systemic consequences include the degradation of biodiversity, the increasing scarcity of drinking water sources and dramatic consequences for health and food. The work that has been carried out on concrete cases of cascading extinctions and abrupt transfigurations of ecosystems has produced a specific relationship to time: that of the apprehension of an irreversible environmental disaster.

What is then called the 'ecological crisis' thus carries with it the idea of a 'breaking point' (Servigne and Stevens 2015: 89, personal translation), of a 'catastrophic shift' (Scheffer et al. 2001) by which the ecosystem would suddenly collapse, accompanied by an unprecedented global humanitarian crisis. On this basis, neo-peasants maintain the idea of a world in which environmental pressures on human life, such as the difficulty of feeding one's self or accessing water, would plunge people into barbarism. Faced with this approach to the future, it is tempting to conclude that 'living in the present', according to a formula very frequently used by neo-peasants, is an emotional 'withdrawal' strategy (Hartog 2015; Leccardi 2011: 4), allowing them to avoid having to justify their actions in a long-term, carefully planned political project:

> I'm a bit too pessimistic to have a real ambition for social change… I relieve myself by doing littles things, going to dig potatoes and thinking about how beautiful my potato field is. I say to myself, 'well, I'm doing something good, right now, it's concrete, I'm indirectly exploiting almost no one, I have a minimal ecological footprint, and it's nice, I have good potatoes, it's in my interest …' And if it can inspire people to do the same thing, who knows, maybe we can build an alternative. But [sighs], it's hard to believe.

The cynical attitude towards the future that can be observed in this interview with Mathieu helps us to understand how neo-peasants associate 'living in the present' with 'giving meaning' to their lives and seeking personal fulfilment. It is precisely this search for meaning that motivates neo-peasants to settle in collective farms, which allow a way of life in line with the imperative of ecological sustainability. The opening of the future in less catastrophic terms then seems possible only on the condition of working 'here and now' to implement concrete alternatives, without submitting to the bureaucratic lengths or actions deemed too indirect of classical political processes. Faced with the temporal nature of the urgency conveyed by the ecological crisis, neo-peasants are impatient to see the 'return' to sustainable agriculture, without depending on equipment whose modes of production are based on the excessive exploitation of natural resources (including fossil fuels) and on the enslavement of part of humanity.

The fact that people seek above all the instantaneous pleasure of living and think of their project in terms of a local scale does not imply an individualistic and indifferent approach to the wider social world. What brings pleasure is in fact evaluated in terms of a 'post-capitalist ethic of existence', to quote Christian Arnsperger (2009, personal translation), on the basis of which a whole regime of values is constructed, such as respect for animal and plant life, the valorization of self-production and poly-activity, the rejection of neo-colonial exploitation, and others. This ethic also presupposes a self-realization that is re-situated in a universal perspective of social transformation ('if everyone did like me it would change things', 'I want to show that it is possible'). By setting up agricultural collectives and developing self-sufficiency practices, neo-peasants intend both to refuse to participate in a production system deemed harmful, and to weaken it, as the practice of boycotts implies. This is the whole logic of the 'interstitial strategy' (Wright 2017: 513), common to anarchist initiatives, which supposes a weakening of the capitalist system 'from the margins'.

The Past as a Source of Inspiration: The Cases of Ancestral Seeds and Animal Traction

Rather than freezing in anxiety, neo-peasants are therefore working to refocus scale, both spatially (relocated economy, local production, communal policies, etc.) and temporally (future envisaged in the short term). This change of scale implies the re-appropriation of agricultural practices that prevailed before industrial expansion, awakening an interest in rural history. However, it is not by idealization of the past that neo-peasants are re-appropriating past craft and agricultural know-how (Chevalier et al. 2000: 23). Rather, it is because the updating of this heritage is linked to their personal emancipation projects and their ecological and social concerns. The study of the rehabilitation of tools and techniques rendered obsolete by the progressive industrialization of the countryside thus offers a prime field for analysing how past and future time horizons interact.

Among the different activities that crystallize this 'sustainable nostalgia' (Davies 2010), we can count first the use and reproduction of ancestral seeds and the latter's self-production. With the advent of the controversy over GMOs and hybrid seeds from the late 1970s onwards, various activist, association and union networks defended the use and reproduction of so-called 'peasant' seed varieties (Demeulenaere and Bonneuil 2011: 204). Like the debates in which rural nostalgia has historically been inscribed, this issue is divided between defenders of progress (genetics this time) and those who oppose it in the ancestral peasant tradition (Bonneuil et al. 2006: 29). The choice of neo-peasants to turn to the use of local seed varieties and, based on these, to produce their own, is part of this debate.

This choice is not exclusively justified by a nostalgic desire to conserve and save ancestral plant varieties from oblivion. First of all, it is about contemporary environmental issues. Given that the seeds sold by the industry are selected to meet the standards of conventional agriculture (Bonneuil and Hochereau 2008: 1333; Demeulenaere and Goldringer 2017: 56), market gardeners who wish to implement organic agriculture without pesticides, herbicides, heated greenhouses or fertilizers turn to the varieties best suited to the region's terroirs and climate: heirloom and traditional varieties. These different seed varieties, resulting from successive selection by farmers up until the seed industry developed with the advent of the green revolution, make it possible, for example, to save water (in the case of regions where summers are particularly drought-prone) and do not require inputs to reach maturity (Bonneuil and Thomas 2009; Demeulenaere and Bonneuil 2011: 205). Second, the reintroduction of traditional varieties into the agricultural production of neo-peasants aims to increase biodiversity. This biodiversity makes it possible to choose the seeds best adapted to the cultivated area, to diversify the diet, but also to protect market gardeners from a bad harvest. If one variety of wheat does not tolerate the drought of one year, another, earlier or more resistant variety may be able to cope more easily. For example, it is quite common to use a mixture of seeds in the culture of wheat plots, without necessarily knowing exactly which varieties are used. In addition to the savings in annual expenses from buying back seeds, self-production of seeds also gives neo-peasants control over the entire production and work chain and, therefore, autonomy from the monopolies of large seed groups. Managing the entire production process is part of the search for autonomy and independence that is dear to them and corresponds to their vision of peasantry as a holistic way of life (Mercier and Simona 1983: 258).

A second convincing example of the re-appropriation of practices rendered obsolete by the green revolution and rehabilitated in a perspective of ecological alternative is the use of animal traction. In many valleys of the Massif Central, it is common to find remains of dry-stone terracing on which the different cultures were organized. This system made it possible to make use of sloping land, protecting crops from erosion, drought and damage caused by the autumn rains known as the *épisodes cévenols*. As a result, the agricultural land was fragmented and the use of motorized tools such as tractors was practically impossible. Although the local inhabitants have finally abandoned agriculture due to the drudgery of manual labour, the need for constant maintenance of these areas and the impossibility of improving agricultural productivity, the neo-peasants have decided to reinvest in these types of crops. The willingness of neo-peasants to acquire an intellectual and practical mastery of the tools they use and to look for alternatives to fossil fuels in agriculture has led them to re-appropriate the know-how of yesteryear. For these individuals, it is therefore a question of recognizing (and valuing) what the pressure of a pre-industrialized rustic environment has made human beings do, without them being aware of the long-term ecological value of their activities. It is therefore not peasant morality that is idealized here, but rather the prospects offered, in the cur-

Figure 3.2. Practice of animal traction in the case of mound crops. The trained horse walks between the mounds and works following the neo-peasant's commands and movements. Photograph by the author.

rent context, by functional uses dating from before the advent of motorized farm work. Neo-peasants thus often refer to pragmatic efficiency and virtuous austerity to explain choices of crops or tools, which are therefore not simply the result of nostalgic attachments.

In addition to being presented as more sustainable, the re-appropriation of devolved agricultural practices is also defended through indirect criticism of hygienism, over-consumption, waste, and the static and compartmentalized work of city dwellers. The agricultural work that neo-peasants are putting in place is erected in opposition to these practices as ultimately healthier, more sustainable and empowering. The 'hardness of life', the material sobriety or the physical and manual work are valued. For the desire to re-appropriate the production chain of daily-use goods also stems from the idea of learning to appreciate their value. The aim here is mass consumption: there is no longer any question of systematically wasting or throwing away worn-out everyday objects.

The pleasure of the task and the attachment to romanticized practices of their project nevertheless play a driving role in the neo-peasants' initiatives. That said, these affects are very rarely verbalized as such by the actors encountered. As the excerpt from an interview with Pierre shows in the introduction, nostalgic attachment is generally not displayed in the discourse of neo-peasant initiatives. In addition to the historical overview outlined above, sociological analyses of the nostalgic rhetoric on the political scene help us to understand the nostalgic shame shown by these actors. As Paum Zawadski argues, 'to describe someone as nostalgic in a political discussion is generally not laudatory' (2002: 36, personal translation). In the French media scene, protagonists from both the Marxist left and right-wing politicians have publicly accused neo-peasants of being reactionaries. The first ones, like journalists Jean-Baptiste Malet[4] and Yann Kindo,[5] accuse the neo-peasants of conservatism because they consider that the glorification of the traditional peasantry generates a disassociation from workers' struggles. They thus draw a dangerous kinship with extreme right-wing discourse and an anti-scientific attitude (see above). The second ones, like former French President Nicolas Sarkozy, accuse his detractors of being anti-progressive and paranoid towards new technologies and the market opportunities they open up.[6] In the media or in the mouths of political figures, this accusation is frequently used to caricature radical environmentalist positions by categorizing them as anti-progressive. This rhetoric reveals the difficulty of devising a social critique of industrialization and capitalism that is not necessarily backward-looking (Dobré 2002: 145). It corroborates the fact that nostalgia is 'always suspect' (Atia and Davies 2010: 181), in line with the medical perspectives that introduced it in the seventeenth century as an indicator of a pathological state (Dames 2010: 271; Davis 1979: 1; Illbruck 2012: 29–42; Jovicic 2016: 49–50; Sedikides et al. 2008: 304; Boyer 2006: 364–68).

This strategy of de-rationalizing an idea through the denunciation of a nostalgic attitude and the systematic devaluation of the past in relation to the present on the part of the detractors of environmental projects is not an isolated case. As authors such as Daphne Berdahl (2010: 195), Dominic Boyer (2006: 374), Mitja Veikonja (2009) and Ayse Parla (2009) demonstrate in their respective fields, the same applies to the positive evocation of the communist era in anti-capitalist political arguments. These arguments are systematically linked to a nostalgic attitude considered as an error of judgement, betraying the 'objective' and darker historical facts. Thus, when reference is made to the past in the discourses regarding the aspiration of a return to communism, two types of argumentation face each other: on the one hand, those that evoke stability, prosperity, solidarity, equality among citizens; and, on the other hand, those that depict a dictatorial, libertarian, threatening, violent and corrupt context. On another level, the reference to traditional rural life suffers the same fate when it is evoked in environmentalist discourse. On the one hand, it is praised for its state of stability, autonomy, independence and respect for ecosystems.

On the other hand, it is contrasted with inequalities between men and women, superstition, omnipresent social control, isolation and the harshness of life and work.

Confronted with this reaction from a section of public opinion, those who support questioning scientific progress made for the capitalist market have constructed a defensive line of argument. During my walk with Pierre in the terraces, it was clear how he quickly retracted his sensitive, introspective and notoriously fleeting impulse just right after evoking these. The latter then directly integrates his nostalgic feeling into a rhetorical figure mobilizing a variety of emotions that veil the evanescent nostalgic spark. This furtive 'nostalgic confession' does not indeed fit into the same temporal register as rationalized eco-nostalgia integrated into a social critique. In the same way, Pierre also tries to avoid the accusation of 'idealism', which would invite some to categorize him as utopian, in its chimerical connotation. The intellectualization of his nostalgia, as well as part of his utopia, is carried out in the name of the objective efficiency of traditional peasant practices. In this vein, neo-peasants insist on their desire to re-appropriate the advances made in the field of science and technology in the name of 'real' progress, with the goal of improving the lives of as many people as possible without devastating the environment (Zimmer 2011: 165). Rather than rejecting the very notion of progress, actors are re-appropriating its definition and objectives and reconciling it with an a priori antinomic time horizon: the past. In doing so, it is a matter of seeking in the traces of a past life 'the basis of future prospects for the evolution of society-nature relations at the local level' (Giusepelli, 2006: 139, personal translation).

Multiple Nostalgias

Analysing the nostalgia manifested by neo-peasant projects certainly helps to better understand the meaning that neo-peasants give to their daily activities. It also allows us to take an original perspective on the relationships that neo-peasants entertain with other inhabitants who appreciate the natural environment of the Cévennes with different values: tourists and holiday-home owners on the one hand and locals on the other. The tensions between neo-peasants and holiday-home owners is epitomised by the discrepancy between their two different idealizations of the traditional rural world. Several disagreements between the inhabitants of second homes and neo-peasants have indeed been reported to me. They concern, for example, the installation of electrified fences,[7] the use of certain plots of land for grazing herds or the burning and felling of trees.

On the one hand, the owners of holiday homes (often renovated old Cévennes houses, possibly inherited family homes) project a romantic vision of country life on the territory. Urbanite lovers of bucolic walks, they are looking for a change of scenery. During their holidays, they aspire to be immersed in a supposed time from the past, idealized and unchanged, reminiscent of the romantic images of the French countryside. In this critical imaginary of air pollution and concrete pavements in the city, electric fences take away the aesthetic value of the landscape and it is the trees that need to be protected. Their discourses display a willingness to preserve the 'natural environment'. Yet, summer residents demonstrate a kind of longing similar to the 'imperialist nostalgia' conceptualized by Renato Rosaldo (1993). This concept enlightens how people innocently mourn the loss of a traditional world that they actually contribute to through their colonial domination. Indeed, the popularity of rural and heritage tourism has led to real estate inflation and an explosion in the second home market. Through the favourable balance of power implied by their economic capital, the owners of holiday homes freeze the possibilities of settlement and reduce the prospects for economic development in the valleys. This process is known as 'rural gentrification' (Cognard 2012: 64; Perrenoud 2008; Richard et al. 2014; Martin et al. 2012). They block rural development opportunities, other than through tourism, for being considered to be detrimental to heritage 'authenticity' (Berliner 2010). The neo-peasants' desire, not without nostalgic foundations, to participate in local cultural life and their desire to revitalize interpersonal and economic ties in the area is thus frustrated.

Secondly, a balance of power is at stake between holiday-home owners and neo-peasants in the relationship that these two types of actors maintain with regard to the landscape. For example, the forests idealized by tourists are the object of a reverse appreciation by neo-peasants who read in them the mark of the abandonment of the countryside. Described as *déprise agricole* (agricultural decline), these forests have effectively invaded the terraces after the abandonment of agriculture following the massive rural exodus, leaving the land lying fallow for sometimes a hundred years. The terraced landscapes in ruins, invaded by brambles, holm oaks and chestnut trees, awaken nostalgia among neo-peasants, just as much as a willingness to act on this landscape. This is particularly true when the traces of history are still present enough to reinvent themselves. So they cut down the trees and uproot the brambles so that the grass can grow back under the chestnut trees. This allows better use of the potential pastures or simply easier access to harvest the chestnuts, which are then processed and sold at markets.

The neo-peasants claim superior territorial legitimacy vis-à-vis the inhabitants of second homes. This legitimacy is directly linked to their identification with the Cévennes peasantry and is in line with the idea of continuity of use rather than family heritage. As illustrated by the following excerpt from an angry neo-peasant after the owner of the land on which he used to graze his herd told him that he was now forbidding him access: 'He dared to say to me, "you are not Cévenol"! He comes three times a year and thinks he's a Cévenol because his father lived here, but I'm more Cévenol than he is! Who works here all year round? Who is keeping the paths clean? I know the territory way better than he does!' Conducting agricultural activities thus influences the way in which the landscape is conceived. Indeed, it appears that as their agricultural, pastoral or artisanal practices become more professional, the neo-peasants themselves re-evaluate their nostalgic impulses for their project. For many of them, the notion of ecological coherence is relativized and food autonomy ceases to be an end in itself. As for the use of motorized tools, it is not uncommon for their necessity to resurface as the issue of comfort, ergonomics and efficiency at work becomes important.

Both the nostalgia of the neo-peasants and the nostalgia of the summer residents is for a past they have not experienced personally. Their 'exo-nostalgic' quarrels (Berliner 2014) do, however, raise questions of legitimacy. Faced with the same landscape, the owners of holiday homes and neo-peasants do not see the same thing. The former see a wild natural green space that must be preserved and the latter see it as a sign of a world that has long since been lost and whose loss is deplored. For the neo-peasants, it is not a question of preservation from imminent destruction, but rather of rehabilitating and transforming a landscape so that it corresponds to an image that evokes a peasant way of life, based on pre-industrial and family use of the land. Yet, the neo-peasants consider that their nostalgia is more legitimate than that of tourists since it is supposed to be more similar to that of the so-called 'local' Cévenols. The neo-peasants like Pierre often refer to the sadness of the old Cévenols to see the 'work of the ancestors' falling into ruin:

> The death of the Cévennes, it's these lands that close under the brush. And for the old people, that's what's painful… When people who live in second homes see us cutting down trees and they say, 'oh my God, you're destroying the forest!' It's because they don't understand the pain of picking chestnuts from the brambles. If you want biodiversity, you have to prune the trees to allow others to grow.

If these exo-nostalgic disagreements here take on the appearance of neighbours' anecdotes, they nonetheless take on more significant economic and political stakes in the negotiation relations of neo-peasants with public actors such as the Cévennes National Park. Indeed, the Cévennes National Park has made the preservation of fauna and flora a priority, to the point that agriculture is prohibited and construction projects on territories that were once cultivated and inhabited are drastically limited. This situation of tension is due to the desire to preserve a different kind of nature (wild nature on the one hand and peasant life on the other). Without denying the need to protect natural spaces against capitalist extractivism, this observation nevertheless raises the whole question of heritage fixation on the part of 'preservation agents' (Berliner 2012: 770, personal translation) who freeze a given ecosystem, endemic or not, in a given time, signalling the existence of 'multiple nostalgias' (Bissel 2005; Berliner 2012) depending on the cultural frameworks of the actors and their daily practices.

The trend towards French rural heritage does not only play to the disadvantage of neo-peasants (Bossuet and Torre 2009: 147). The maintenance of the regional specificities that neo-peasants demonstrate can indeed open up economic and tourist potentialities of what are, for example, local products. The nostalgia of tourists for the oblivion of local traditions, the loss of regional culture, the standardization of vernacular specificities, the transformation of the rural landscape and so on are also used in a utilitarian way (Valceschini and Torre 2002: 273–90). As Olivia Angé has studied (2012, 2015), nostalgia can thus be instrumentalized for commercial strategy purposes. Playing on the rusticity of products such as local salads bearing the name of the region, homemade flower syrups, 'granny style' jam, sourdough spelt bread baked over a wood fire or other homemade products adds significant added value once in the markets.

Invoking the preservation of the heritage of natural areas or rustic products such as chestnut cream or sourdough bread baked over a wood fire can also be linked to 'awareness-raising devices' (Clavairolle 2013: 314, personal translation) to defend biodiversity, fight against the food industry or oppose extractivism. However, the anti-capitalist nature of their political positioning is not always evident. In the collective of Chambalou, where Pierre lives, the practice of animal traction, for example, has several times crystallized ideological misunderstandings between the inhabitants of the collective and extreme right-wing protagonists. The latter saw in the rehabilitation of animal traction the enhancement of the image of the traditional French peasant, and with it a racist regionalist identity opposed to multiculturalism and the supposed Islamization of France. These ideological misunderstandings raise questions among neo-peasants, most of whom are progressive and anti-racist.

Conclusion: Nostalgia, a Utopia in the Past Tense?

The neo-peasants' nostalgia is a continuation of a rural nostalgia documented throughout history. Today, it is a reaction to a context of 'crisis of the future', which is particularly based on an anti-capitalist critique and an anxiety about the degradation of the environment on a global scale. Faced with the impossibility of envisaging a stable and serene future, the neo-peasants I met implement an alternative way of living and working that reveals a singular interaction between past, present and future. By re-appropriating old-fashioned craft and agricultural skills such as animal traction, the reproduction of ancestral seeds or the re-appropriation of rustic recipes and food processing, the neo-peasants mobilize a traditional heritage in order to achieve their utopian projects of personal emancipation, the quest for well-being and the construction of a way of life that would be radically ecological and based on egalitarian social relations. I argue that the eco-nostalgia of the individuals I have observed is both an affective state and an allegorical technique, as researcher Jeremy Davies (2010: 265) has already formulated. The evocation of the past among neo-peasants is the result of a constant negotiation between an emotional yearning for nostalgia and the desire to inscribe their political proposals for organic agriculture in a historical continuity.

Following Olivia Angé and David Berliner, I have mobilized nostalgia here as a 'power/resistance paradigm' (2015: 5). I have studied its 'critical potential' (Atia and Davies 2010: 181) to grasp its role in the construction of contemporary contesting claims (Boym 2001; Bissel 2005). This study makes it possible to distinguish between imperialist eco-nostalgia and political eco-nostalgia. The first one, which I have observed among owners of second homes in the Cévennes, enjoys a balance of power in their favour because of their purchasing power and the protection of their private property. By seeking to preserve a presumed natural state of wilderness, they are blocking the ability of the inhabitants to act in their environment and hampering the possibility of economic development that would not be geared towards tourism in this region. The second, demonstrated by the neo-peasants, relates to the desire to 'revitalize' the Cévennes countryside by seeking to maximize autonomy and localized food self-sufficiency. In this perspective, the recognition of certain positive aspects of the past is taken as the basis for a critical analysis of progress and capitalist modernity (Pickering and Keightley 2006: 921; Bissel 2005: 216). If the mismatch between the agricultural practices of neo-peasants and the land grabbing by summer visitors can lead to neighbourhood quarrels, neo-peasants do not hesitate to mobilize the heritage nostalgia of tourists when selling their products in markets, which also becomes a communication strategy about their activities and political ideas.

This study provides a better understanding of the concrete interweaving of nostalgia and utopia within contemporary ecological practices. Neo-peasants' eco-nostalgia unfolds an ambivalent temporality. It is at once a reaction to a catastrophic future, a positive value placed on traditional peasantry, but also the potential breeding ground for 'utopian impulses' aspiring to change society (Pickering and Keightley 2006: 936). This idea that nostalgia is ultimately equivalent to utopia combined with the past has already been defended by the anthropologist Mitja Velikonja. He presents nostalgia as a 'retrospective utopia' (2009: 13–14) that consists more of the implementation of a sustainable agricultural project and the hope for a better future than an irrational interest in the past.

In this context, the idealized past becomes a source of inspiration for the development of sustainable agriculture projects. Nostalgia as studied here makes it possible to understand how temporalities that are regarded as antinomic in our Western culture in fact interact with each other. Dystopian, utopian, nostalgic and presentist temporalities interact with each other and reciprocally shape their essence. This re-establishes the interactional perspective of our relationship to time and offers a contribution to the consideration of the coexistence of multiple temporalities in anthropology.

Madeleine Sallustio studied Sociology and Anthropology at the Université libre de Bruxelles and Visual Sociology at the Université d'Évry-Val d'Essonne. In 2019, she got her PhD in Political and Social Sciences in the Laboratoire d'Anthropologie des Mondes Contemporains (LAMC). She is interested in topics such as temporalities, contemporary anarchy, labour value and the social dynamics surrounding ecological crisis. She is also committed to the research of alternative forms to scientific narratives notably through the co-presidency of the association Atelier d'Hybridations Anthropologiques (AHA).

Notes

1. All the names of places and people have been changed for the sake of anonymity.
2. All these words were transcribed just after the walk but were not recorded.
3. This is notably evidenced by the increasing number of professional categories within the French agricultural status (grain farmer, dairy farm manager, market gardener, seed producer, etc.).

4. Journalist for the Marxist-oriented newspaper *Le Monde Diplomatique*. See https://www.monde-diplomatique.fr/2018/08/MALET/58981 or https://www.monde-diplomatique.fr/2019/08/MALET/60145 (both last accessed 24 June 2020).
5. Marxist journalist for the online and far-left newspaper *Médiapart*. See https://blogs.mediapart.fr/yann-kindo/blog (last accessed 24 June 2020).
6. In a speech to defend nuclear energy production in France in 2011, Nicolas Sarkozy, for example, accused his ecological critics of wanting to 'go back to the Middle Ages' and 'go back to the candle'. See https://blogs.mediapart.fr/edition/les-invites-de-mediapart/article/011211/la-centrale-ou-la-bougie (last accessed 24 June 2020).
7. They are used to protect the pastures from wild boars which, in their search for worms and roots, turn the earth upside down and destroy the rare and precious meadows of the Cévennes mountains.

References

Alphandéry, P. and Y. Sencébé. 2009. 'L'émergence de la sociologie rurale en France (1945–1967)', *Etudes Rurales* 183: 23–40.

Anderson, B. 2017. 'Emergency Futures: Exceptions, Urgency, Interval, Hope', *Sociological Review* 32: 1–17.

Angé, O. 2012. 'Instrumentaliser la nostalgie: les foires de troc andines (Argentine)', *Terrain* 59: 152–67.

_____. 2015. 'Le goût d'autrefois: Pain au levain et attachements nostalgiques dans la société contemporaine', *Terrain* 65: 34–51.

Angé, O. and D. Berliner (eds). 2015. 'Introduction: Anthropology of Nostalgia – Anthropology as Nostalgia', in O. Angé and D. Berliner (eds), *Anthropology and Nostalgia*. Oxford: Berghahn, pp. 1–15.

Arnsperger, C. 2009. *Éthique de l'existence post-capitaliste: Pour un militantisme existentiel*. Paris: Editions du Cerf.

Atia, N. and J. Davies. 2010. 'Nostalgia and the Shapes of History', *Memory Studies* 3(3): 181–86.

Barral, P. 1968. *Les agrariens français de Méline à Pisani*. Paris: Armand Colin.

Bendix, R. 1997. *In Search of Authenticity: The Formation of Folklore Studies*. Madison, WI: University of Wisconsin Press.

Bensa, A. 2006. *La fin de l'exotisme: Essai d'anthropologie critique*. Toulouse: Anarchasis.

Berdahl, D. 2010. '"(N)Ostalgie" for the Present: Memory, Longing, and East German Things', *Ethnos* 64(2): 192–211.

Berliner, D. 2010. 'Perdre l'esprit du lieu: Les politiques de l'Unesco à Luang Prabang (RDP Lao)', *Terrain* 55: 90–105.

_____. 2012. 'Multiple Nostalgias: The Fabric of Heritage in Luang Prabang (Lao PDR)', *Journal of the Royal Anthropological Institute* 18: 769–86.

_____. 2014. 'On Exonostalgia', *Anthropological Theory* 14(4): 373–86.

Bernstein, H. and T.J. Byres. 2001. 'From Peasant Studies to Agrarian Change', *Journal of Agrarian Change* 1(1): 1–56.

Bissel, W.C. 2005. 'Engaging Colonial Nostalgia', *Cultural Anthropology* 20(2): 215–48.

Bleton-Ruget, A. 2002. 'La France et ses paysans: 130 ans d'histoire nationale', in M. Sylvestre (ed.), *Agriculteurs, ruraux et citadins: les mutations des campagnes françaises*. Dijon: Educagri, pp. 19–34.

Bonneuil, C., E. Demeulenaere, F. Thomas et al. 2006. 'Innover autrement? La recherche face à l'avènement d'un nouveau régime de production et de régulation des savoirs en génétique végétale', in *Dossiers de l'environnement de l'INRA*. Paris: Institut national de la recherche agronomique, pp. 29–51.

Bonneuil, C. and F. Hochereau. 2008. 'Gouverner le "progrès génétique": Biopolitique et métrologie de la construction d'un standard variétal dans la France agricole d'après-guerre', *Annales, Histoires, Sciences Sociales* 6: 1305–40.

Bonneuil, C. and F. Thomas. 2009. *Gènes, pouvoirs et profits: Recherche publique et régimes de production des savoirs, de Mendel aux OGM*. Versailles: Éditions Quae.

Bossuet, L. and A. Torre. 2009. 'Le devenir des ruralités: Entre conflits et nouvelles alliances autour des patrimoines locaux', *Économie rurale* 313–314: 146–62.

Boyer, D. 2006. 'Ostalgie and the Politics of the Future in Eastern Germany', *Public Culture* 18(2): 361–81.

Boym, S. 2001. *The Future of Nostalgia*. New York: Basic Books.

Chamboredon, J.-C. 1980. 'Les usages urbains de l'espace rural: du moyen de production au lieu de récréation', *Revue française de sociologie* 21(1): 97–119.

Chevalier D., I. Chiva and F. Dubost. 2000. 'L'invention du patrimoine rural', in D. Chevalier (ed.), *Vive campagnes: le patrimoine rural, projet de société*. Paris: Autrement, pp. 11–57.

Clavairolle, F. 2013. 'Le retour des camisards: Émotions et mobilisations en faveur d'une vallée menacée', in D. Fabre (ed.), *Émotions patrimoniales*. Clamecy: Edition de la Maison des sciences de l'homme, pp. 313–34.

Cognard, F. 2012. 'L'application du concept de «migration d'agrément» aux moyennes montagnes françaises', in N. Martin, P. Bourdeau and J.-F. Daller (eds), *Les migrations d'agrément: Du tourisme à l'habiter*. Paris: L'Harmattan, pp. 57–67.

Dames, N. 2010. 'Nostalgia and its Disciplines: A Response', *Memory Studies* 3(3): 270–76.

Davies, J. 2010. 'Sustainable Nostalgia', *Memory Studies* 3(3): 262–68.

Davis, F. 1979. *Yearning for Yesterday: A Sociology of Nostalgia*. New York: Free Press.

Deléage, E. 2011. 'Les mouvements agricoles alternatifs', *Informations sociales* 2(164): 44–50.

———. 2013. *Ravages productivistes, résistances paysannes*. Lormont: Éditions Le Bord de l'Eau.

Demeulenaere, E. and C. Bonneuil. 2011. 'Des semences en partage: Construction sociale et identitaire d'un collectif paysan autour de pratiques semencières alternatives', *Techniques et Culture* 57: 202–21.

Demeulenaere, E. and I. Goldringer. 2017. 'Semences et transition agroécologique: Initiatives paysannes et sélection participative comme innovations de rupture', *Natures Sciences Sociétés* 4: 55–59.

Dobré, M. 2002. *L'écologie au quotidien: Éléments pour une théorie sociologique de la résistance ordinaire*. Paris: L'Harmattan.

Dubar, C. 2011. 'Temps de crises et crise des temps', *Temporalités* 13: 1–10.

Dupont, Y. 2005. 'Pourquoi faut-il pleurer les paysans?', *Écologie & politique* 5(31): 25–40.

Dupuy, J.-P. 2002. *Pour un catastrophisme éclairé: Quand l'impossible est certain*. Paris: Seuil.

Eizner, N. 1978. 'Le rétro: un certain goût de lenteur', *Autrement* 14: 13–21.

Fel, A. 1985. 'Les révolutions vertes de la campagne française (1955-1985)', *Vingtième Siècle. Revue d'histoire* 8: 3–17.

Foessel, M. 2012. *Après la fin du monde: Critique de la raison apocalyptique*. Paris: Seuil.

Fourier, C. 1833. 'Le progrès, le progrès masque des faux amis du peuple', *La Réforme industrielle ou le Phalanstère* 2(25): 292–95.

Giuseppelli, E. 2006. 'Place et fonctions de l'agriculture en zones périurbaines de montagne: modes d'habiter et représentations du rural', *L'Espace géographique* 35: 133–47.

Godard, O. 2002. 'L'impasse de l'approche apocalyptique de la précaution: De Hans Jonas à la vache folle', *Éthique Publique* 4(2): 1–22.

Guérin, M. 2002. 'Entre secteur et territoire: l'évolution des politiques rurales en France. Quelques enseignements d'une approche de longue période', in M. Sylvestre (ed.), *Agriculteurs, ruraux et citadins: les mutations des campagnes françaises*. Dijon: Educagri, pp. 225–50.

Hartog, F. 2015. *Régimes d'historicité: Présentisme et expériences du temps*, 3rd edn. Paris: Seuil.

Haubert, M. 1991. 'Introduction: Le retour des paysans: mythes et réalités', *Tiers-Monde* 32(128): 725–40.

Hervieu, B. and D. Léger. 1980. 'Recours à la ruralité et crise', *Économie rurale* 140: 16–20.

Herzfeld, M. (ed.). 2007. 'Nostalgie structurelle: Le temps et le serment dans les villages de montagnes de Crète', in *L'intimité culturelle: Poétique sociale de l'État-Nation*. Québec: Presses de l'Université de Laval, pp. 173–213.

Illbruck, H. (ed.). 2012. 'Nostalgia's Early Modern Origins: Cultural Backgrounds', in *Nostalgia: Origins and Ends of an Unenlightened Disease*. Evanston, IL: Northwestern University Press, pp. 29–42.

Jollivet, M. 1968. 'Structures agraires et changement économique en agriculture', *Revue française de sociologie* 9(3) : 339–54.

———. 1978. 'Les pièges de la Mère Denis', *Autrement* 14: 22–30.

Jovicic, J. 2016. 'La Nostalgie, de la maladie au sentiment national', *French Politics, Culture & Society* 34(1): 48–65.

Kayser, B. 1990. *Renaissance rurale: Sociologie des campagnes du monde occidental*. Paris: Armand Colin.

Leccardi, C. 2011. 'Accélération du temps, crise du futur, crise de la politique', *Temporalités* 13: 1–16.

Léger, D. and B. Hervieu. 1979. *Le retour à la nature: 'Au fond de la forêt, l'État'*. Paris: Seuil.

Lejeune, D. 1991. *La France de la Belle Epoque: 1886-1914*. Paris: Armand Colin.

Levitas, R. 1982. 'Dystopian Times? The Impact of the Death of Progress on Utopian Thinking', *Theory Culture and Society* 1: 53–64.

Lowenthal, D. 1992. 'The Death of the Future', in S. Wallman (ed.), *Contemporary Futures: Perspectives from Social Anthropology*. London: Routledge, pp. 23–36.

Martin, N., P. Bourdeau and J.-F. Daller (eds). 2012. *Les migrations d'agrément: Du tourisme à l'habiter*. Paris: L'Harmattan.

Mendras, H. 1976. *Société paysannes*. Paris: Armand Colin.

Mercier, C. and G. Simona. 1983. 'Le néo-ruralisme: Nouvelles approches pour un phénomène nouveau', *Revue de géographie alpine* 71(3): 253–65.

Noble, D. 2016. *Le progrès sans le peuple*. Marseille: Agone.

Pachauri, R.K. and L.A. Meyer. 2014. *Climate Change 2014: Synthesis Report. Contribution of Working Groups I, II, and III to Intergovernmental Panel on Climate Change*. Geneva: Intergovernmental Panel on Climate Change (IPCC)."

Parla, A. 2009. 'Remembering across the Border: Post-Socialist Nostalgia among Turkish Immigrants from Bulgaria', *American Ethnologist* 36(4): 750–67.

Perrenoud, M. 2008. 'Les artisans de la "gentrification rurale": Trois manières d'être maçon dans les Hautes-Corbières', *Sociétés contemporaines* 3(71): 95–115.

Pickering, M. and E. Keightley. 2006. 'The Modalities of Nostalgia', *Current Sociology* 54(6): 919–41.

Rauchs, P. 1999. 'La nostalgie ou le malentendu du retour', *Évolution psychiatrique* 64: 281–88.

Reclus, E. 1899. *À mon frère le Paysan*. Paris: Bureaux des Temps Nouveaux.

Richard, F., J. Dellier and G. Tommasi. 2014. 'Migration, environnement et gentrification rurale en Montagne limousine', *Revue de géographie alpine* 102(3): 1–16.

Rosaldo, R. 1993. *Culture & Truth: The Remaking of Social Analysis*. Boston: Beacon Press.

Scheffer, M., S. Carpenter, J.A. Foley et al. 2001. 'Catastrophic shifts in ecosystems', *Nature* 413: 591–96.

Sedikides, C., T. Wildschut, J. Arndt and C. Routledge. 2008. 'Nostalgia: Past, Present and Future', *Association for Psychological Science* 17(5): 304–307.

Sencébé, Y. 2004. 'Être ici, être d'ici: Formes d'appartenance dans le Diois (Drôme)', *Ethnologie française* 34(1): 23–29.

Servigne, P. and R. Stevens. 2015. *Comment tout peut s'effondrer: Petit manuel de collapsologie à l'usage des générations présentes*. Paris: Seuil.

Simmel, G. 1984. *Les problèmes de la philosophie de l'histoire: Une étude d'*épistémologie, 2nd edn. Paris: Presses Universitaires de France.

Steiner, A. 2016. 'Vivre l'anarchie ici et maintenant: Milieux libres et colonies libertaires à la Belle Époque', *Cahiers d'histoire. Revue d'histoire critique* 133: 43–58.

Taguieff, P.A. 2002. 'Faillite du progrès, éclipse de l'avenir', in P. Zawadzki (ed.), *Malaise dans la temporalité*. Paris: Presses de la Sorbonne, pp. 83–123.

Valceschini, E. and A. Torre. 2002. 'Politique de la qualité et valorisation des terroirs', in J.P. Sylvestre (ed.), *Agriculteurs, ruraux et citadins: Les mutations des campagnes françaises*. Dijon: Educagri, pp. 273–90.

van der Ploeg, J.D. 2014. *Les paysans du XXIe siècle: Mouvements de repaysannisation dans l'Europe d'Aujourd'hui*. Paris: Editions Charles Léopold Mayer.

Velikonja, M. 2009. 'Lost in Transition: Nostalgia for Socialism in Post-socialist Countries', *East European Politics and Societies* 23(4): 535–51.

Weber, E. 1983. *La fin des terroirs: La modernisation de la France rurale 1870- 1914*. Paris: Fayard.

Weber, M. 2015. 'Capitalisme et société rurale', *Tracés* 2(29) : 133–58.

Wright, E.O. 2017. *Utopie Réelles*. Paris: La Découverte.

Zawadzki, P. (ed.). 2002. *Malaise dans la temporalité*. Paris: Presses de la Sorbonne.

Zimmer, M. 2011. 'Les AMAP en France: Entre consommation de produits fermiers locaux et un nouvel ordre de vie', in G. Pleyers (ed.), *La consommation critique, Mouvements pour une alimentation responsable et solidaire*. Paris: Desclée de Bouwer, pp. 47–69.

Chapter 4

The Nature of Loss

Ecological Nostalgia and Cultural Politics in Amazonia

Casey High

Introduction

Recent academic writing, anthropological and otherwise, has made clear that nostalgia can take many different forms and express diverse sentiments of loss. Like any practice or form of personal reflection, longings for past times and places are historically constituted in changing social and political contexts. The editors of this volume describe a semantic shift from nostalgia's original etymology as the pain and grief of homesickness to the temporal dimensions of 'nostalgic trauma' in modernist notions of progress and rupture, despite an emphasis on the spatial disjuncture that came with capitalism and agricultural enclosures in nineteenth-century Europe (Ange and Berliner, this volume). Increasingly, Western nostalgic sentiments have presented a form of social memory concerned with the irreversibility of time and longings for a past irrevocably lost. As Berliner (2012: 770) observes, contemporary nostalgias for lost or 'disappearing worlds', whether spatial or temporal, in some cases glorify the past in the absence of first-hand nostalgic memories.

Like other forms of memory, the multiple expressions of longing and loss anthropologists encounter in contemporary social life should be understood in terms of the changing historical contexts that frame them. The diversity of nostalgic sentiments is as evident within particular societies as it is across them. As Bissell (2005) suggests in his study of colonial nostalgia, such expressions of disjuncture not only co-exist, combine and come into conflict, but are also part of the very process of intergenerational transformation. In this chapter I describe how, in Amazonian Ecuador, Waorani people of different generations lament ecological loss in ways that confound some of the key categories of conventional modernist nostalgia rooted in distinctions between tradition and modernity and nature and culture. Although Waorani ecological nostalgias appear to reject the temporal and spatial concerns of conventional nostalgia, my young adult interlocutors live in a world where discourses of history, nature and culture are becoming integral to indigenous political action.

A certain nostalgia, whether expressed as a lost time or disappearing world, has been a recurrent theme in Western imaginings of Amazonia (Hutchins and Wilson 2010; Slater 2002; Whitehead 2002). After the devastating impacts of colonialism and state development on indigenous communities and their environments, the Amazon is often conceptualized in terms of loss. This is perhaps best illustrated by popular media coverage of the last remaining 'uncontacted' groups, whose assumed isolation from modernity is often valued as representing a time lost to history (High 2013). The Amazon is today routinely seen as a place of unique natural and cultural attributes under immanent threat from the forces of modernity. Conventional views of Amazonian 'nature' and 'culture' seem to be equally nostalgic and tragic. Whether seen as the 'lungs of the earth' under threat from extractive economies and industrial agricultural or a vanishing world of ancient cultural knowledge of medicinal plants, this is a part of the world often associated with – and valued as – a place of ongoing and irrevocable loss.

These perspectives point to legitimate and pressing concerns about the fate of Amazonia in the contemporary world. They also reflect an enduring tendency to situate Lowland South America and its indigenous peoples as, in Susan Silver's description, 'a fertile site for personal nostalgic discourse' (Silver 2011: 117). As Silver and Whitehead (2002) note, nostalgia has often mediated between the old and new worlds not only in early European travel writing in South America,[1] but also anthropology. This is evident in Lévi-Strauss's famously melancholic view of Brazil in *Tristes Tropiques* (1976 [1955]), where he described the sense of loss inherent in the Americas and what this implies for the limits and possibilities of studying Amerindian peoples:

> The problems are so vast, the guidelines at our disposal so tenuous and uncertain, the past, over huge tracts of time, has been so irrevocably wiped out, and the basis of our speculations is so precarious, that even the most insignificant reconnoitering of the terrain puts the researcher into a state of uncertainty in which he oscillates between the most humble kind of resignation and the wildest ambition: he knows that the essential evidence has been lost and that all his efforts will amount to no more than a scratching of the surface; yet may he not stumble on some miraculously preserved clue that

> will shed light? Nothing is possible, so all is possible. The darkness through
> which we are groping is too thick for us to make any pronouncements about
> it; we cannot even say that it is doomed to last. (Lévi-Strauss 1976: 338)

Though in some ways distinct from the interests of travel writers and anthropologists, in the second half of the twentieth century the environmental movement and increasing global recognition of indigenous rights in
Amazonia were also inflected by a certain nostalgia. The 1970s and 1980s
saw increasing international concerns about the speed of deforestation
and the acculturation or disappearance of Amazonian people as a result
of large-scale national development projects – especially in Brazil (Davis
1977; Schmink and Wood 1984; Slater 2002). These concerns have recently
returned to the global spotlight in response to the increasing rate of deforestation and the alarming suppression of indigenous rights in the Brazilian
Amazon since President Jair Bolsonaro took office in January 2019.

Such concerns about past or imminent loss – whether cultural or ecological – can also inspire political action. I grew up in the 1980s, seeing pop
stars like Sting on TV visiting Brazil to raise awareness of indigenous land
rights and global campaigns to save the rainforest by paying to conserve
tracts of forest or buying sustainable rainforest products.[2] When I began
fieldwork in Ecuador in the 1990s, a professor commented that it was a
good thing that I was studying Amazonian people now since they would
surely soon be completely gone. The professor was not an anthropologist,
and like most people, was not aware that despite the mass population decline of Amazonian peoples in the initial centuries of the colonial period,
indigenous populations have steadily grown in recent decades (Viveiros
de Castro 1996). Some groups have also made substantial gains in terms
of land claims and political power as they become more aware of their
positioning in national and regional socio-political dynamics (Fisher 1994;
Turner 1991, 2002; Zanotti 2016).

And yet, nostalgic sentiments continue to have a strong presence in
the anthropology of Amazonia – much as they have elsewhere (Berliner
2015). Whether describing the impending acculturation of indigenous
peoples, attempting to identify resonances of a pre-Columbian cosmology
in present societies, or insisting on the value of indigenous knowledge,
Amazonianist anthropology exemplifies what Berliner (2015) describes as
'exo-nostalgia' for other peoples and places in its critical stance against modernity.[3] Berliner contrasts encompassing exo-nostalgic discourses of loss
that tend to be more detached from personal experience to endo-nostalgia,
which he describes as 'nostalgia for the past that one has lived personally'
(2015: 21). My intention is not to criticize exo-nostalgic representations
of Amazonia, nor do I deny their influence on my own formation as an

anthropologist. There are good reasons to be concerned about the ongoing pressures on ecology and indigenous peoples in Amazonia – and the real prospect of loss in this part of the world. Important projects of cultural and linguistic revitalization – whether initiated by indigenous communities, external researchers or both – often draw on nostalgic sentiments for past times and practices perceived to be under threat.[4] However, as ethnographers we should be careful not to allow our own nostalgias prevent us considering ideas about change and possibility we encounter in fieldwork that do not share the same sense of irrevocable loss – whether cultural, ecological or otherwise. Such nostalgia, whether in searching for Lévi-Strauss's 'miraculously preserved clues' to lost worlds or describing the imminent disappearance of indigenous knowledge, risks temporally distancing Amazonia and thus, in Fabian's (1983) terms, denying the 'coevalness' of Amazonian people in the contemporary world.

In this chapter, I contrast anthropology's traditional disciplinary exo-nostalgia to the ways that Waorani people with whom I work lament threats to their own socio-natural world in Amazonian Ecuador. In a context where familiar categories of 'nature' and 'culture' are not easily mapped onto a Waorani lived world, I explore memories of and longings for the productive relations that oil development, colonization and changing settlement patterns have altered within their territory. I draw on Waorani memories of what has been lost in this process to explore the ontological status of what my interlocutors call *wao öme* (Waorani land/territory) or *monito öme* (our land). In contrast to modernist concepts of nature, culture and history, their memories of the past and the future possibilities they evoke contradict conventional Western nostalgias for what is often seen as irrevocably lost.

And yet, the premise of modernist nostalgia is increasingly co-implicated with Waorani ideas of land and the socio-natural relations of which they are part. This process is complicated by their involvement with state and NGO agendas for ecological preservation and emerging discourses of 'culture'. By exploring what is transmitted across generations in memories of ecological change, and young adults' ideas about the future, I draw contrasts between Waorani ecological nostalgias and Western formulations of history, heritage and modernity. In the absence of a modernist ecological nostalgia rooted in ideas of irreversible loss, young people insist on their ability to recreate the socio-natural relations that constitute *wao öme* despite the social transformations and ecological degradation of recent decades.

Divergent experiences and increasing involvement with broader cultural and ecological politics point to multiple ideas of the past in Waorani expressions of change and loss. In this context I argue that we should not simply assimilate the memories and longings we encounter in fieldwork to our own ecological nostalgias, as attention to endo-nostalgia points to what is at stake for people as they situate themselves and engage in processes of transformation. What we might call Waorani endo-nostalgias, and the different temporalities they evoke, pose certain challenges to the conventional sentiments of many environmentalists and indigenous rights advocates, including anthropologists, who tend to reproduce modernist assumptions in our nostalgia for Amazonia. In this way, Waorani ideas of ecological loss, longing and future possibility might help us think beyond external understandings of Amazonian culture and environment. And yet, in the context of their ongoing battles with oil companies and the state, as well as alliances with international environmental activists, Waorani ideas about land, change and loss are increasingly intertwined with exo-nostalgic ideas about Amazonia as a site of history, culture and nature.

Oil and *Wao Öme* Beyond Nature

During much of the twentieth century, Waorani people were best known for their general isolation and resistance to contact with outsiders (Robarchek and Robarchek 1998; Rival 2002; Yost 1981). For many people of my parents' and grandparents' generations in the United States, they were associated with the killing of five North American evangelical missionaries in 1956, an event that was widely publicized in news media and Christian writing around the world (*Life* magazine 1956; Wallis 1960). The subsequent period of missionization, led in part by close relatives of the deceased missionaries, was carried out in alliance with extensive oil development and the colonization of what was once part of Waorani ancestral lands (Cabodevilla 1999; Kimerling 1991, 1996; Stoll 1982). Renewed oil exploration in the 1980s and 1990s culminated in high-profile confrontations between Waorani people and oil companies.[5]

In recent decades intensive oil production in and around what is today a legally recognized Waorani territorial reserve has made this industry a major part of life for many if not most Waorani villages. Oil well platforms, pools of industrial waste, immense residential compounds to house workers, and an extensive network of oil roads have left a highly visible mark on Waorani lands. As academics, political activists and Waorani themselves observe, the noise and pollution of oil production has had a major impact on game populations, as well as the Waorani's ability to plant gardens and fish in rivers in certain areas. Alongside the profound socio-ecological effects of oil in many Waorani communities, the expanding oil frontier has also created and exacerbated conflicts between communities, including those involving groups living in voluntary isolation (Cabodevilla 2013; Gilbert 2017; High 2013, 2015a; Lu et al. 2017).[6]

The social impact of oil is striking, not only in areas where wells are operated close to Waorani homes, but in villages located many miles from oil production. In addition to bringing Waorani into close contact with a range of non-Waorani oil workers and connecting some villages to frontier cities by road, the oil industry has employed a significant proportion of Waorani men as labourers. When Laura Rival began her fieldwork in the late 1980s, she estimated that around 90 per cent of Waorani men had worked for oil companies between 1985 and 1992 (2000: 248). Similarly, at the start of my fieldwork in the 1990s, I rarely met an adult man who had not at some point worked for *la compañía* (the oil company), even in areas distant from oil installations. As oil work became their primary source of cash income, Waorani incorporated the visible material wealth of oil companies into a highly egalitarian and non-reciprocal demand-sharing economy (Rival 2000). Rival described how Waorani treated them as a source of 'natural abundance' much like they see in the forest. She argued that Waorani 'naturalized' the oil industry as a host that would provide abundantly for them as guests on demand, much as they see givers of manioc feasts.

Rival's analysis of what Waorani came to see as the 'endlessly renewable wealth' of oil companies in terms of 'natural abundance' (2000: 257) is part of a wider body of scholarship that contrasts indigenous cosmologies and practical engagements with the environment to modernist understandings of 'nature' as a domain distinct from human activity (Blaser 2009, 2013; de la Cadena 2010; Descola 1994, 2013; Escobar 1999). Waorani people, for example, see the abundance of forests not as a natural phenomenon independent from human participation, but as the result of past human activity (Rival 1993, 2016). As with work highlighting socio-natural relations in Amazonia and animistic or perspectivist cosmologies (Århem 1996; Cormier 2003; Kelly 2011; Viveiros de Castro 1998), Waorani talk about the *omaëre* (forest) or their *öme/ögïpo* (land/territory) as a place peopled by a range of different social beings, many of which either share human perspectives or communicate with human beings (High 2012). Rather than a kind of 'natural' backdrop for human activity,[7] the seemingly inexhaustible abundance of *wao öme* is the product of relations between humans and other beings.

This formulation of *wao öme* as a nexus of socio-natural relations that includes human beings has an important bearing on what Waorani people see as being lost or under threat in the wake of decades of oil development. Some Waorani continue to talk about the vast scale of *wao öme* and the wealth of products that results from their interactions within it. This

Figure 4.1. A remote part of *wao öme* where gardens, fish and game remain plentiful for Waorani residents in the area. Photograph by the author.

abundance is closely connected to the idea, expressed by many of my Waorani interlocutors, that they are living in a period of remarkable (yet fragile) population expansion – in contrast to a history of violence, instability and losing kin. And yet, many now understand the productive potential of *wao öme* as finite and ultimately under threat by oil extraction, new settlement patterns and the colonization of their lands. In a context where 'nature' and 'culture' are not easily distinguished, what is at stake in their understandings of potential loss is most often not 'Waorani culture' or even environmental conservation, but the socio-natural relations within *wao öme* that make life possible for Waorani people (see also Hastrup, this volume).

Remembering Abundance

Narratives of loss have a conspicuous presence in Waorani oral histories, particularly in the stories elders tell of how their close kin died during an intense period of revenge killing prior to mission settlement (High 2015a). They remember the subsequent mission period, widespread conversion to

Christianity and the coming together of mutually hostile Waorani groups in larger sedentary villages, as the time of *civilización* (civilization). Even in a largely post-Christian context today, 'civilization' is a particular form of historical consciousness that conveys less a sense of irrevocable loss than a mode of sociality associated with relative peace and social expansion (High 2016). Deceased ancestors and non-human features of the land are seemingly inseparable in Waorani memories of loss and change. This becomes clear when accompanying Waorani people on long treks to distant areas of forest where people lived in the past, such as particular hills where ancestors lived, groves of trees where they gathered food, or streams where they were killed by enemies. As Rival (1993) pointed out twenty-five years ago, Waorani people appear to conceptualize their social relations in line with their perceptions of the forest, whether in terms of growth, destruction and decay, or the capacity to provide abundantly. This observation helps contextualize why Waorani narratives of loss are often as much about plants and animals – and their relationships with people – as they are about human beings themselves.

Even if the forest presents an ideally abundant arena of socio-natural relations, decades of oil development and colonization have made clear to many of my Waorani interlocutors that this productive capacity can be lost. For elders, this was demonstrated in the early years of the oil boom along what is now known as the Via Auca, an oil road that connects the frontier city of Coca to an area many elders today remember as the northern boundary of *wao öme*. During decades of oil production, colonists occupied and deforested much of the land along the road, which today is not included as part of the official Waorani territorial reserve. And yet, features of the land routinely appear in Waorani accounts of particular people who once lived there. Remembered as a site of abundant life, it is sometimes lamented by my Waorani informants as having been lost to *kowori*, a broad category to which they assign non-Waorani people. Although it is clear to them that the area has been heavily deforested and polluted, what they seem to lament most about the Via Auca and areas like it is the absence of a particular kind of productive potential of which Waorani people are part. While oil companies, colonists involved in agriculture, and loggers have seen a vast productive potential in these areas, for many Waorani these extractive economies appear more destructive than productive in terms of how they see *wao öme*. Despite what are obviously visible ecological discontinuities, my interlocutors also describe certain continuities in the (now untapped) potential of the land that appears to be the result of previous Waorani occupation.

What I want to highlight here is how, in contrast to ecological nostalgias premised on modernist ideas of history, the sense of loss these places evoke

Figure 4.2. Oil roads, pipelines and drilling installations have become part of everyday life in the northern and eastern areas of the Waorani ethnic reserve. Photograph by the author.

for my Waorani interlocutors is not one that is necessarily irrevocable. Without dismissing their recognition of the disastrous effects of oil, what appears to be at the centre of Waorani concerns is the kinds of beings who live and interact in *wao öme. Kowori* people, whether oil companies, loggers or Kichwa-speaking people accused of poaching animals, are understood to pose a threat to the kind of productivity that constitutes Waorani livelihood. This point of view should not be mistaken for a conservationist logic of protecting 'the environment' for its own sake, as if it had a distinct standing outside of human action. It is precisely the productive capacity in *wao öme* that my Waorani interlocutors understand themselves to be part of – rather than separate from. The term *kowori* itself, which was once associated with a semi-human state of cannibalism, appears to evoke a kind of antithesis to the growth and abundance that emerges as a product of socio-natural relations in *wao öme*, of which Waorani sociality is part. *Kowori* people, especially in the form of past missionaries and present oil companies, have been associated with a source of extraordinary abundance not through productive engagement in *wao öme*, but the provision of foreign manufactured goods without any obvious origin or method of production. This stands in stark contrast to the productivity that my interlocutors often describe as the result of the specifically Waorani qualities of *waponi kiwimonipa* (living well), which involves hunting, gardening, collecting forest fruits, and sharing this abundance with kin and visitors.

Kowori people, despite their apparent wealth of goods, whose origins and method of manufacture remain a key point of interest and speculation in rural Waorani villages, pose a threat to the productive abundance of *wao öme*. Adult informants describe the destructive tendencies of *kowori* as a threat not just to Waorani people, but also to non-human features of *wao öme*. In the context of oil extraction, they often express their concerns about ecological destruction from the point of view of game animals that flee noisy oil installations, are poisoned and die from pollution, or become the targets of mass slaughter by poachers along oil roads. They lament not the violation of a pristine state of 'nature' separate from themselves and in need of conservation, but something that threatens their own livelihood. Even as *wao öme* is ideally a place of abundance, most Waorani adults I know are keenly aware of how different plants and animals interact and depend on each other within it. Just as the ideal of plentiful animals and forest fruits is mirrored by a Waorani emphasis on the growth of their human communities (Rival 1993), the depletion of human and animal populations are closely intertwined in their discussions of how oil and *kowori* people can deplete such abundance.

Several years ago a young woman told me a story that illustrates the concerns many of my informants share about oil extraction as both a threat to Waorani livelihoods and an assault on specific animals within *wao öme*. She described how her kinsmen had recently encountered the scene of a mass slaughter of animals near one of the major rivers in the oil block. What surprised her and other Waorani was less the fact that poachers had shot and killed so many monkeys, birds and other game animals with rifles, but that the carcasses were then simply left to rot in and around abandoned camps. They were horrified by the idea that these animals, which they see their own quality of life depending on, were needlessly killed. In hearing this account I was in some ways as perplexed as my hosts, wondering why the poachers would not have at least taken the game meat to sell at a regional market.[8] What also struck me about this story was how its telling mirrored the oral histories Waorani elders tell me about spear-killing raids they and their kin suffered in the past. Although many of

Figure 4.3. *Waponi kiwimonipa*: 'living well' in everyday household life. Photograph by the author.

these attacks were, and to some extent continue to be, part of long-standing vendettas between families, they are most often described from the victim's point of view, emphasizing the excessive and needless killing of the narrator's kin (High 2009, 2015a; Rival 2002). The fate of the animals in the woman's account also evoked a broader sense of victimhood in the face of aggression from *kowori* outsiders that is central to indigenous expressions of what it means to be a Waorani person (High 2015a; Rival 2002).

Even if *kowori* are understood to be antithetical to the relationships that constitute *wao öme*, it has also become clear to many Waorani how their own actions are placing this productive ideal under threat. In particular, the increasing size and permanence of their villages, combined with more intensive gardening practices and access to hunting rifles, have led to the scarcity of game animals in some areas (Lu 2001). In the largest villages, which now rely heavily on fishing and gardening, hunting certain animals requires travel to distant areas. While the constraints this depletion imposes on subsistence stands in clear contrast to stories of past abundance, Waorani women and men do not tend to see such changes in terms of irrevocable loss. They instead identify themselves as able to manage questions of scarcity in ways that *kowori* cannot, describing how they allow certain game populations to replenish for certain periods or travel long distances to hunt large game. Alongside these strategies, income from oil work, inter-ethnic marriages, village schools and engagement with indigenous politics all figure in the complex relationships Waorani people have with both *wao öme* and the market economy.

Despite dramatic social, economic and demographic changes in recent decades,[9] most Waorani people I have met remain confident in their ability to engage productively and 'live well' in *wao öme*. Some describe their recent participation in extensive digital mapping of their territory (the result of collaboration with an international environmental NGO) as a technology for ensuring this possibility. One young man described to me how, though he saw the mapping as a *'kowori* technology', it would enable Waorani people to protect their territory from extractive industries and transmit knowledge of *wao öme* to young people. Waorani accounts of successful hunts and huge manioc beer drinking feasts in the past evoke less a sense of nostalgic loss than an ideal of present and future relations that continue to be enacted under the right conditions. Similarly, what they see as the productive capacity of Waorani people within *wao öme* (in contrast to *kowori*) bears little resemblance to popular ideas of indigeneity that assume deep historical links between land and people. Since the beginning of my fieldwork, older adult informants have described to me how certain parts of *wao öme* were in the past inhabited not by their own ancestors, but other indigenous groups. What is at stake for them in *wao öme* is not as much a historical link to the lands on which they live, but a particular mode of relations that generates livelihoods and, more specifically, the prospect of 'living well'.

Contrasting and Emergent Temporalities of Transformation

My argument that Waorani understandings of loss and change are fundamentally different from the notion of irrevocable loss in certain modernist nostalgias does not suggest that we should ignore major social changes and generational shifts that have occurred in recent decades. Even as my informants' engagements in *wao öme* and memories of 'civilization' appear to resist modernist thinking, these shifts and the intensifying relations with *kowori* that define them have transformed Waorani experiences in many ways. These changes can be seen as much in their engagements with the land and marriage practices as in the ways in which Waorani people imagine and define themselves in relation to outsiders. So even if their ideas of loss challenge modernist nostalgia, we should also recognize how generational changes have increasingly placed young adults in situations defined by conventional ideas of nature, culture and history. In these contexts, different forms of nostalgia, and the contrasting ideas of time, loss and social transformation they evoke, are at times closely intertwined in social and political practices.

One of the most clearly identifiable of these contexts in everyday life is in village schools where, instead of joining their elders in hunting, gardening or collecting forest products from a young age as their parents did, children learn a national curriculum primarily in Spanish. Whether teaching that Waorani are deficient because of their 'savage' or 'wild' ways (Rival 1992), or that they are part of a distinct cultural heritage to be preserved and publicly displayed (High 2015a), schooling has simultaneously removed Waorani children from their everyday productive practices in *wao öme* and defined them in culturalist terms (High 2015c). Since colonial times, popular imagination has often located Amazonian people within the domain of nature, whether as innocent noble savages, representatives of a supposedly violent human nature, or as a source of rich ethnobiological knowledge. The primarily *mestizo* and Kichwa-speaking teachers who worked in Waorani villages during my primary fieldwork in the early 2000s presented an interesting twist on this tradition, seeing their onerous educational mission as to ideally 'civilize' the wildness of their students and to recognize their cultural uniqueness as Amazonian people. The emphasis in schooling on removing children from forest activities and celebrating their cultural difference takes us a long way from Waorani ideas of *wao öme* as a nexus of productive relations of which Waorani people are part.

As has occurred elsewhere in Amazonia (Graham 2005; Oakdale 2004; Turner 2002), some Waorani youths with whom I work, as well as some older adults, have readily adopted discourses of *cultura* (culture) in talking about specific practices and their relations with non-indigenous people (High 2015a). Ideas of culture that are often implicit in school have become central to indigenous politics and Waorani engagements with the state, academics and international environmental activists as part of a wider politics of recognition (Coulthard 2014; Povinelli 2002; Taylor and Gutmann 1992). In these contexts, as elsewhere in Latin America, Waorani are popular symbols and active participants in a socio-political arena often defined in terms of 'interculturality' (Walsh 2009; Whitten and Whitten 2011).

Alongside a growing awareness of themselves as cultural citizens of a 'plurinational' Ecuadorian state (Jameson 2011; Sawyer 2004; Whitten and Whitten 2011), they are also part of national and global ecological agendas that define their territory in terms of environmental conservation

(Conklin and Graham 1995; High and Oakley 2020). Even as conventional conservationist approaches to nature and environment do not map easily onto Waorani understandings of *wao öme*, they do seem to share a notion of Waorani people being intrinsically connected to the land. What appears to be changing in this context is how Waorani are coming to understand *wao öme* in terms of scarcity, as a bounded entity to be demarcated with physical boundaries and ultimately to be defended in the face of external pressures (High 2020). In their work with NGOs to map and delineate *wao öme* in order to deter further colonization, some young adult Waorani have adopted the language of *naturaleza* (nature) and *medio ambiente* (environment), though the extent to which they are translating a concept like *wao öme* or coming to understand their territory in new ways is not always clear in their use of these terms in Spanish.

Waorani alliances with Ecuadorian and international environmental activists and indigenous rights advocates are an increasingly important part of this context. These relationships, part of an ever-more globally oriented environmental politics in Amazonian Ecuador (Erazo 2013), tend to portray 'nature' and Waorani 'culture' as under threat from extractive economies. This became particularly clear in recent Waorani protests against the Ecuadorian government's plans to expand oil extraction on their lands in the province of Pastaza.[10] In February 2019, hundreds of Waorani marched through the regional capital city, Puyo, delivering to the local judiciary office a formal lawsuit against the government's decision to sell oil concessions without adequately consulting Waorani communities. Attending the protest, I observed Waorani of multiple generations marching alongside other Ecuadorians and international activists. Some Waorani protestors carried large banners denouncing oil and calling for the defense of *monito öme* ('our land'). And yet, this protest, and the wider Waorani resistance movement of which it was part, was strengthened by young adult Waorani leaders calling for the defence of 'nature' and the conservation of Waorani 'culture' in the face of oil.

It appears that such expressions, even if distinct from everyday understandings of *wao öme*, were successful in engaging national and global audiences concerned about the potential destruction of pristine nature and the loss of traditional culture in Amazonia. In what has been seen by many as a landmark victory for indigenous rights against corporate and state agendas, the provincial court subsequently ruled in favour of the lawsuit, resulting in the suspension of oil concessions on Waorani lands in Pastaza. There is little to be gained in criticizing the deployment of nature and culture as key categories of environmental activism and international solidarity, especially given the importance of this result for Waorani communities and others in Ecuador. This example instead highlights how Waorani ideas

Figure 4.4. In February 2019, Waorani and other indigenous peoples of the Ecuadorian Amazon march through the city of Puyo to protest against the government's selling of oil concessions on indigenous lands without adequate community consultation or informed consent. Photograph by the author.

of territorial loss and change are intertwined, at times productively, with dominant discourses of modernist nostalgia they encounter beyond their own communities. Their alliances with international activists and challenges to national development agendas require translating between *wao öme*, nature and culture, as well as Waorani people learning new ways of communicating their concerns about threats to *wao öme*.

And yet, the expressions of nostalgic longing I hear from many of my Waorani informants in everyday life appear to still insist on a distinct temporality of change. In the context of key generational shifts, of which schooling, oil work and inter-ethnic marriages are part, young adults talk more about the productive potential they see in *wao öme* than immanent or irreversible loss. When school-educated adults contrast their life in large villages to that of their elders and ancestors prior to 'civilization', they often express a longing for the abundance and ability to *vivir libre* ('live freely') that they associate with the past. These comments often emerge in conversations about the desirability and prospect of living *durani bai* ('like the ancient ones'). And yet, this apparent nostalgia is tempered by memories of a time of mutual fear between groups, instability and ultimately the loss of kin to violence. As I have suggested, if we approach Waorani ideas of change and loss in terms of nostalgia, this is not nostalgia for a way of life or an ecology understood as entirely lost in historical terms. Whether in their everyday conversation or in Facebook postings, young adults often describe their future plans to inhabit *wao öme* much in the same way as their elders and ancestors once did (High 2010). Young men in particular have proudly explained to me how they will someday leave their villages to found new households and live 'free' in remote areas of *wao öme*. The lives of elders, ancestors or indigenous groups who continue to live nearby in voluntary isolation all figure as points of reference in these statements, in which the idea of being 'like the ancient ones' indexes future possibilities as much as it does the past.

It remains to be seen how many of these young adults will actually do this, and if they do, what this life in *wao öme* will look like. However, in recent years a number of older adults have left their villages to found smaller ones or to live as independent households. Others have abandoned remote villages to live closer to oil roads, in search of employment for cash income. What I want to highlight here is how, even as Waorani engage in cultural and environmental politics, their memories and longings for the future rarely hinge on ideas of 'nature' or 'culture' as distinct domains of permanent loss. In contrast to conventional nostalgic concerns about people 'losing their culture', or the immanent loss of a pristine natural environment, what seems to be at stake for them is the kind of pleasurable and productive socio-natural relations by which they understand their own ability to 'live well' in *wao öme*.

Conclusion: Thinking Beyond Modernist Exo-Nostalgia

What I have described as my Waorani informants' endo-nostalgias are increasingly intertwined with the modernist exo-nostalgias often evident in anthropological writing and conventional representations of Amazonia. Attention to emergent contexts like these matters because, in the very process of divergent ideas of time and loss coming together, key differences can be ignored or conveniently translated into familiar terms, especially in the context of power imbalances.[11] The historical imagination that often frames modernist nostalgia regarding Amazonia construes and values the relationships between past and present in specific ways, such that the past is a scarce resource (Appadurai 1981) ultimately separate from the present. My point here is not to suggest an absolute or generalized contrast between Waorani and 'modern' temporalities of loss, much less reproduce an essentialist image of Amazonian people as antithetical to 'modernity' (Bessire and Bond 2014; Ramos 2012). And yet, when my Waorani interlocutors, both young and old, reflect on what has been lost and gained in recent decades, their ideas of social and ecological change bear little resemblance to conventional ideas of 'tradition' and 'modernity' and the image of loss such ideas tend to imply.

Rather than a teleology of irreversible rupture, their concern is more with the differences between Waorani and *kowori* ways of engaging in *wao öme* and how to 'live well' in the current context. For them, what is under immanent threat of being lost is not 'Waorani culture' or a pristine environment independent of human action, but *wao öme*, a world whose productive potential is inseparable from Waorani engagement. Such ecological nostalgias evoke as much a sense of future potential as they do a concern with loss. In juxtaposing Waorani ideas of change in relation to conventional modernist nostalgia, I hope to have shown more precisely what is at stake for them in the context of social and ecological transformation. Such nostalgias that gesture toward a less permanent sense of loss do not imply an uncritical view of the past or of the present. But they do problematize the tendency in anthropology and beyond to assimilate other nostalgias to conventional Western understandings of rupture so often rooted in concepts of nature, culture and history. Even at a time when both Amazonian and modernist concepts of loss are implicated in indigenous rights and environmental conservation, alternative ecological nostalgias might help push us to think beyond the enduring exo-nostalgia of which our discipline is part.

Acknowledgements

I thank the anonymous reviewers for their comments and suggestions. This chapter is based on several different periods of fieldwork undertaken since the 1990s made possible by several different grants and institutions. I owe thanks in particular to the Wenner-Gren Foundation, the Economic and Social Research Council (ESRC) and the Fulbright Commission for supporting various phases of the research since the early 2000s. I also received support from London School of Economics, Goldsmiths – University of London, and the University of Edinburgh. I am most grateful to the many Waorani individuals and communities who have supported my research and looked after me during fieldwork.

Casey High is Senior Lecturer in Social Anthropology at the University of Edinburgh. His research with Waorani communities in the Ecuadorian Amazon has focused on memory, violence, indigenous politics, language and social transformation in the context of Christian conversion and extractive economies. He is the author of *Victims and Warriors: Violence, History, and Memory in Amazonia* (University of Illinois Press, 2015) and has co-edited *The Anthropology of Ignorance: Ethnographic Approaches* (Palgrave Macmillan, 2012) and *How Do We Know? Evidence, Ethnography, and the Making of Anthropological Knowledge* (Cambridge Scholars Publishing, 2008).

Notes

1. Silver draws a connection between Jean de Léry's sixteenth-century travel writing about Tupian societies in Brazil and Lévi-Strauss's personalized nostalgia in *Tristes Tropiques* four centuries later, noting that the body and imagery of cannibalism are evident in both accounts of loss.
2. Conklin and Graham (1995) described the alliances that emerged between Amazonian peoples and international environmentalists in the 1980s and 1990s, highlighting the fragile and sometimes constraining symbolic politics that situate Amazonian peoples as natural allies to conservation.
3. In contrast to previous concerns with acculturation or cultural loss, in recent years Amazonianist scholarship has reflected a strong emphasis on cultural continuities (High 2015b). This tendency, an example of what Robbins (2007) has described as a preference for 'continuity thinking' in broader anthropology, could also be understood as nostalgic in insisting on indigenous agency and the recuperation of practices previously assumed to be lost.
4. Numerous anthropologists and linguists have written critically about the problems of objectifying language in discourses of language endangerment, preservation and revitalization, especially where such discourses depart in significant ways from local understandings (Errington 2003; Hill 2002; Whiteley 2003). Clifford (1989: 73) makes a similar critique in examining anthropology's older 'salvage' paradigm and its concern with rescuing authentic culture, as a nostalgic understanding of history and culture.
5. The most notable of these conflicts emerged in response to the Maxus Corporation's plans to develop Block 16, an oil concession that opened extensive oil roads into the northeastern part of Waorani territory and the Yasuní National Park. Operation of Block 16 was subsequently taken over by the Repsol-YPF Corporation, placing Waorani communities at the centre of an expanding oil frontier. See Kimerling (2013) for an extensive overview of this case and analysis of the ongoing legal battle on the part of Ecuadorians to seek recognition and compensation for social and environmental damage resulting from past oil drilling by Texaco-Chevron.

6. Most notably, these conflicts have resulted in several killings between Waorani and their neighbours living in relative isolation near oil drilling and logging operations (High 2013).
7. The anthropology of landscape has challenged romanticist views of picturesque painted landscapes as a visual representation, arguing for a concept of landscape as a process rather than a static image (Hirsch and O'Hanlon 1995; Ingold 1993; Tilley 1997). Debates about space and place have also challenged the renaissance rationality that separates people from nature (Low and Lawrence-Zuñiga 2003: 16).
8. In recent decades some Waorani and Kichwa-speaking hunters have used oil roads to transport and sell game meat at a market outside of Waorani territory (see, for example, Finer et al. 2009; and Suárez et al. 2009).
9. The total Waorani population increased from around 500 at the time of initial contact with missionaries in the 1950s (Yost 1981: 679) to around 3000 today, with the establishment of relatively permanent villages since mission settlement.
10. The protests were against the government's decision to sell oil concessions for Block 22, an area in the province of Pastaza where several Waorani communities are located. Many Waorani protested, under the banner of 'Waorani Resistance Pastaza', in part on the basis that their communities were not adequately consulted about planned oil drilling as required in Ecuadorian and international law. See High (2020) for further details.
11. Viveiros de Castro distinguishes between 'uncontrolled equivocations', which he associates with the Western tendency to assume or prioritize similarity in translations, and Amerindian ontologies where translation becomes 'an operation of differentiation' through 'controlled equivocations' (2004: 18–20).

References

Appadurai, A. 1981. 'The Past as a Scarce Resource', *Man* (NS) 16(2): 2012–19.

Århem, K. 1996. 'The Cosmic Food Web: Human-Nature Relatedness in the Northwest Amazon', in P. Descola and G. Pálsson (eds), *Nature and Society: Anthropological Perspectives*. London: Routledge, pp. 185–209.

Berliner, D. 2012. 'Multiple Nostalgias: The Fabric of Heritage in Luang Prabang (Lao PDR)', *Journal of the Royal Anthropological Institute* 18: 769–86.

_____. 2015. 'Are Anthropologists Nostalgist?', in O. Angé and D. Berliner (eds), *Anthropology and Nostalgia*. New York: Berghahn Books, pp. 17–34.

Bessire, L. and D. Bond. 2014. 'Ontological Anthropology and the Deferral of Critique', *American Ethnologist* 41(3): 440–56.

Bissell, W. 2005. 'Engaging Colonial Nostalgia', *Cultural Anthropology* 20(2): 215–48.

Blaser, M. 2009. 'The Threat of Yrmo: The Political Ontology of a Sustainable Hunting Program', *American Anthropologist* 111(1): 10–20.

_____. 2013. 'Ontological Conflicts and the Stories of Peoples in Spite of Europe: Towards a Conversation on Political Ontology', *Current Anthropology* 54(5): 547–68.

Cabodevilla, M.A. 1999. *Los Huaorani en la Historia del Oriente*. Quito: CICAME.

_____. 2013. 'La massacre … qué nunca existió?', in M.A. Cabodevilla and M. Aguirre (eds), *Una tragedia ocultada*. Quito: CICAME, pp. 21–125.

Clifford, J. 1989. '"The Others" Beyond the "Salvage" Paradigm', *Third Text* 3(6): 73–78.

Conklin, B. and L. Graham. 1995. 'The Shifting Middle Ground: Amazonian Indians and Eco-Politics', *American Anthropologist* 97(4): 695–710.

Cormier, L. 2003. *Kinship with Monkeys: The Guajá Foragers of Eastern Amazonia*. New York: Columbia University Press.

Coulthard, G. 2014. *Red Skin, White Masks: Rejecting the Colonial Politics of Recognition*. Minneapolis, MN: University of Minnesota Press.

Davis, S. 1977. *Victims of the Miracle: Development and the Indians of Brazil*. Cambridge: Cambridge University Press.

De la Cadena, M. 2010. 'Indigenous Cosmopolitics in the Andes: Conceptual Reflections Beyond Politics', *Cultural Anthropology* 25(2): 334–70.

Descola, P. 1994. *In the Society of Nature: A Native Ecology in Amazonia*. Cambridge: Cambridge University Press.

_____. 2013. *Beyond Nature and Culture*. Chicago: University of Chicago Press.

Erazo, J. 2013. *Governing Indigenous Territories: Enacting Sovereignty in the Ecuadorian Amazon*. Durham, NC: Duke University Press.

Errington, J. 2003. 'Getting Language Rights: The Rhetorics of Language Endangerment and Loss', *American Anthropologist* 105(4): 723–32.

Escobar, A. 1999. 'After Nature: Steps to an Antiessentialist Political Ecology', *Current Anthropology* 40(1): 1–30.

Fabian, J. 1983. *Time and the Other: How Anthropology Makes Its Object*. New York: Columbia University Press.

Finer, M., V. Vijay, F. Ponce, C.N. Jenkins and T.R. Kahn. 2009. 'Ecuador's Yasuní Biosphere Reserve: A Brief Modern History and Conservation Challenges', *Environmental Research Letters* 4(3): 1–15.

Fisher, W. 1994. 'Megadevelopment, Environmentalism, and Resistance: The Institutional Context of Kayapó Indigenous Politics in Central Brazil', *Human Organization* 53(3): 220–32.

Gilbert, D. 2017. 'Territorialization in a Closing Commodity Frontier: The Yasuní Rainforests of Western Amazonia', *Journal of Agrarian Change* 18(2): 229–48.

'Go Ye and Preach the Gospel: Five Do and Die'. 1956. *Life*, 30 January: 10–19.

Graham, L. 2005. 'Image and Instrumentality in a Xavante Existential Politics of Recognition: The Public Outreach Work of Etenhiritipa Pimental Barbosa', *American Ethnologist* 32(4): 622–41.

High, C. 2009. 'Remembering the Auca: Violence and Generational Memory in Amazonian Ecuador', *Journal of the Royal Anthropological Institute* (N.S.) 15: 719–36.

_____. 2010. 'Warriors, Hunters, and Bruce Lee: Gendered Agency and the Transformation of Amazonian Masculinity', *American Ethnologist* 37(4): 753–70.

_____. 2012. 'Shamans, Animals, and Enemies: Locating the Human and Non-Human in an Amazonian Cosmos of Alterity', in M. Brightman and V. Grotti (eds), *Animism in Rainforest and Tundra: Personhood, Animals, Plants and Things in Contemporary Amazonia and Siberia*. Oxford: Berghahn, pp. 130–45.

_____. 2013. 'Lost and Found: Contesting Isolation and Cultivating Contact in Amazonian Ecuador', *Hau: Journal of Ethnographic Theory* 3(3): 196–221.

_____. 2015a. *Victims and Warriors: Violence, History and Memory in Amazonia*. Urbana: University of Illinois Press.

_____. 2015b. 'Keep on Changing: Recent Trends in Amazonian Anthropology', *Reviews in Anthropology* 44(2): 93–117.

_____. 2015c. 'Ignorant Bodies and the Dangers of Knowledge in Amazonia', in R. Dilley and T. Kirsch (eds), *Regimes of Ignorance: Anthropological Perspectives on the Production and Reproduction of Non-Knowledge*. New York: Berghahn, pp. 91–114.

_____. 2016. '"A Little Bit Christian": Memories of Conversion and Community in Post-Christian Amazonia', *American Anthropologist* 118(2): 270–83.

_____. 2020. 'Our Land Is Not For Sale! Contesting Oil and Translating Environmental Politics in Amazonian Ecuador', *Journal of Latin American and Caribbean Anthropology* 25(2): 301–23.

High, C. and E. Oakley. 2020. 'Conserving and Extracting Nature: Environmental Politics and Livelihoods in the New "Middle Grounds" of Amazonia', *Journal of Latin American and Caribbean Anthropology* 25(2): 236–47.

Hill, J. 2002. '"Expert Rhetorics" in Advocacy for Endangered Languages: Who is Listening, and What Do They Hear?', *Journal of Linguistic Anthropology* 12(2): 119–33.

Hirsch, E. and M. O'Hanlon (eds). 1995. *The Anthropology of Landscape: Perspectives on Space and Place*. Oxford: Oxford University Press.

Hutchins, F. and P. Wilson (eds). 2010. *Editing Eden: A Reconsideration of Identity, Politics, and Place in Amazonia*. Lincoln, NE: University of Nebraska Press.

Ingold, T. 1993. 'The Temporality of the Landscape', *World Archeology* 25(2): 152–74.

Jameson, K. 2011. 'The Indigenous Movement in Ecuador: The Struggle for a Pluricultural State', *Latin American Perspectives* 38(1): 63–73.

Kelly, J. 2011. *State Healthcare and Yanomami Transformations*. Tucson, AZ: University of Arizona Press.

Kimerling, J. 1991. *Amazon Crude*. Washington DC: Natural Resource Defense Council.

_____. 1996. *El derecho del tambor: derechos humanos y ambientales en los campos petroleros de la amazonia ecuatoriana*. Quito: Abya-Yala.

_____. 2013. 'Oil, Contact and Conservation in the Amazon: Indigenous Huaorani, Chevron, and Yasuní', *Colorado Journal of International Environmental Law and Policy* 24(1): 43–115.

Lévi-Strauss. C. 1976 [1955]. *Tristes Tropiques*. Translated by John and Doreen Weightman. New York: Penguin Books.

Low, S. and D. Lawrence-Zuñiga (eds). 2003. *Anthropology of Space and Place: Locating Culture*. Oxford: Wiley Blackwell.

Lu, F. 2001. 'The Common Property Regime of the Huaorani Indians of Ecuador: Implications and Challenges to Conservation', *Human Ecology* 29(4): 425–47.

Lu, F., G. Valdivia and N. Silva. 2017. *Oil, Revolution, and Indigenous Citizenship in Ecuadorian Amazonia*. New York: Palgrave Macmillan.

Oakdale, S. 2004. 'The Culture-Conscious Brazilian Indian: Representing and Re-working Indianness in Kayabi Political Discourse', *American Ethnologist* 31(1): 60–75.

Povinelli, E. 2002. *The Cunning of Recognition: Indigenous Alterities and the Making of Australian Multiculturalism*. Durham, NC: Duke University Press.

Ramos, A.R. 2012. 'The Politics of Perspectivism', *Annual Review of Anthropology* 41: 481–94.

Rival, L. 1992. *Social Transformations and the Impact of Formal Schooling on the Huaorani of Amazonian Ecuador*. PhD thesis, London School of Economics, University of London.

_____. 1993. 'The Growth of Family Trees: Understanding Waorani Perceptions of the Forest', *Man, Journal of the Royal Anthropological Institute* (N.S.) 28: 635–52.

_____. 2000. 'Marginality with a Difference, or How the Huaorani Preserve their Sharing Relations and Naturalize Outside Powers', in P. Schweitzer, M. Biesele and R. Hitchcock (eds), *Hunters and Gatherers in the Modern World: Conflict, Resistance, and Self-Determination*. New York: Berghahn Books, pp. 244–62.

_____. 2002. *Trekking Through History*. New York: Columbia University Press.

_____. 2016. *Huaorani Transformations in Twenty-First-Century Ecuador*. Tucson, AZ: University of Arizona Press.

Robarchek, C. and C. Robarchek. 1998. *Waorani: The Contexts of Violence and War*. Fort Worth, TX: Harcourt Brace.

Robbins, J. 2007. 'Continuity Things and the Problem of Christian Culture: Belief, Time, and the Anthropology of Christianity', *Current Anthropology* 48(1): 5–38.

Sawyer, Suzanne. 2004. *Crude Chronicles: Indigenous Politics, Multinational Oil, and Neoliberalism in Ecuador*. Durham, NC: Duke University Press.

Schmink, M. and C. Wood (eds). 1984. *Frontier Expansion in Amazonia*. Gainesville, FL: University of Florida Press.

Silver, S. 2011. 'Cannibalism, Nudity, and Nostalgia: Léry and Lévi-Strauss Revisit Brazil', *Studies in Travel Writing* 15(2): 117–33.

Slater, C. 2002. *Entangled Edens: Visions of the Amazon*. Berkeley, CA: University of California Press.

Stoll, D. 1982. *Fishers of Men or Founders of Empire? The Wycliffe Bible Translators in Latin America*. London: Zed Books.

Suárez, E.M. Morales, R. Cueva, B.V. Utreras, G. Zapata-Ríos, E. Toral, J. Torres, W. Prado and J.V. Olalla. 2009. 'Oil Industry, Wild Meat Trade and Roads: Indirect Effects of Oil Extraction Activities in a Protected Area in North-Eastern Ecuador', *Animal Conservation* 12: 364–73.

Taylor, C. and A. Gutmann. 1992. *Multiculturalism and the 'Politics of Recognition': An Essay*. Princeton, NJ: Princeton University Press.

Tilley, C. 1997. *A Phenomenology of Landscape: Places, Paths and Monuments*. Oxford: Berg.

Turner, T. 1991. 'Representing, Resisting, Rethinking: Historical Transformations of Kayapó Culture and Anthropological Consciousness', in G. Stocking (ed.), *Colonial Situations: Essays on the Contextualization of Ethnographic Knowledge*. Madison, WI: University of Wisconsin Press, pp. 285–313.

_____. 2002. 'Representation, Politics, and Cultural Imagination in Indigenous Video: General Points and Kayapó Examples', in F. Ginsburg, L. Abu-Lughod and B. Larkin (eds), *Media Worlds: Anthropology on New Terrain*. Berkeley, CA: University of California Press, pp. 75–89.

Viveiros de Castro, E. 1996. 'Images of Nature and Society in Amazonian Ethnology', *Annual Revues of Anthropology* 25: 179–200.

_____. 1998. 'Cosmological Deixis and Amerindian Perspectivism', *Journal of the Royal Anthropological Institute* 4(3): 469–88.

_____. 2004. 'Perspectival Anthropology and the Method of Controlled Equivocation', *Tipití* 2(1): 3–22.

Wallis, E. 1960. *The Dayuma Story: Life Under Auca Spears*. New York: Harper and Brothers.

Walsh, C. 2009. 'The Plurinational and Intercultural State: Decolonization and State Refounding in Ecuador', *Kult 6 Special Issue: Epistemologies of Transformation: The Latin American Decolonial Option and its Ramifications*, pp. 65–84.

Whitehead, N. 2002. 'South America/Amazonia: The Forest of Marvels', in P. Hulme and T. Youngs (eds), *The Cambridge Companion to Travel Writing*. Cambridge: Cambridge University Press, pp. 122–38.

Whiteley, P. 2003. 'Do "Language Rights" Serve Indigenous Interests? Some Hopi and Other Queries', *American Anthropologist* 105(4): 712–22.

Whitten, N. and D.S. Whitten. 2011. *Histories of the Present: People and Power in Ecuador*. Urbana, IL: University of Illinois Press.

Yost, J. 1981. 'Twenty Years of Contact: The Mechanisms of Change in Wao (Auca) Culture', in N. Whitten (ed.), *Cultural Transformations and Ethnicity in Modern Ecuador*. Urbana, IL: University of Illinois Press, pp. 677–704.

Zanotti, L. 2016. *Radical Territories in the Brazilian Amazon: The Kayapó's Fight for Just Livelihoods*. Tucson, AZ: University of Arizona Press.

CHAPTER 5

Ecological Nostalgias and Interspecies Affect in the Highland Potato Fields of Cuzco (Peru)

Olivia angé

Rural societies in the Andean Cordillera are experiencing rapid changes due to increased access to the labour market, formal education, electricity and new means of communication including mobile phones and roads. The people I have met in Cuzco (Peru) are quite satisfied with these changes. Still, there is a recurrent occasion when they yearn for past abundance: that is, when they refer to potato cultivation, the main crop that grows in the harsh ecological conditions of the highlands. Since the turn of the last century, the following Quechua words have become a refrain: 'puchaicunaka manaña ñowpaj jinañachu', meaning that the days are not as they used to be anymore. Others say 'watac manaña ñowpaj jinañachu', meaning that the whole year is not as it used to be anymore. While these words mostly allude to meteorological vagaries, this is more than just a climatic statement because it entails all kinds of living beings, including tubers. Indeed, climatic disruption complicates the cultivators' labour in the field as they must reschedule their tasks according to a highly unpredictable seasonal calendar.

This recurrent statement encapsulates a lamentation for the loss of a past order, an ecological expression of nostalgia theorized in social sciences as 'a longing for what is lacking in a changed present ... a yearning for what is now unattainable' (Pickering and Keightley 2006: 920). Nostalgic tropes and practices have been described by anthropologists in an array of ethnographic contexts (angé and Berliner 2014). While such scholarship focuses on the expression of nostalgia among human beings, the present chapter explores lamentations over the erosion of relations between cultivators and vegetable-beings dwelling in the environment.

More precisely, it documents empirical expressions of longing for idealized aspects of the past unfolding within an interspecies collective, in which the potato stands out as a key protagonist.

Thus, to explore the unfolding of nostalgia in this heterogeneous collective, this chapter focuses on the distribution of affect among human and tuberous beings. Accounting for affective entanglement across species will shed light on growers' consideration for potato emotionality in their quest for agricultural prosperity. This ethnographic lens highlights the importance of *kusisqa* in highland potato cultivation. In the Spanish also spoken in this region of the cordillera, *kusisqa* is expressed as *alegria*, which in turn is best translated into English as 'joy'. The imperative of fostering potato joy is a constant preoccupation of these potato growers. My examination of the distribution of affect and vital impetus in Andean plots draws on Sara Ahmed's (2010) work on the promise of happiness. Ahmed identifies happy objects as those that circulate as social goods, triggering positive affect to whomever comes near. In the conclusion, I shall come back to Ahmed's concerns for the political implication of bringing out happy objects. First, we will see that, in the Cuzco highlands, flourishing potatoes are perceived as happy organisms in themselves. In potato-human relationships, *kusisqa* is not only what follows. Rather, it is a necessary flow in the present of their interaction. Still, potato sadness is another possibility, and increasingly so, as potato joy is unsettled by ongoing climatic upheavals.

A close look at *kusisqa* distribution in the fields outlines an affective agriculture, whereby memories of past ecologies bring out political claims about the future of potato-human companionship. This point will be addressed in the last section concerned with tropes of ecological nostalgias by a local NGO working on potato biodiversity conservation and climate change mitigation. More precisely, I consider the case of the Parque de la Papa (Potato Park), which is widely considered to be one of the most successful initiatives in terms of in situ conservation of biocultural diversity. I will describe the set of actions implemented by the Park in an attempt to foster potato-human reciprocities, despite the fact that 'the days are not as they used to be anymore'.

Potato Flourishing in the Cuzco Highlands

The potato has been vital in Andean economies since archaeological times. In his voluminous *History and Social Influence of the Potato*, Redcliffe Salaman advances the idea that potato consumption was a requisite for Amazonian dwellers to be able to move from the rainforest and establish settlements in the Andean highlands: 'it was the potato which made residence on these plateaux possible' (1985: 11). Apparently, hunter-gatherers started domesticating tubers between 8,000 and 5,000 BC around the Titicaca Lake, at some 4,000 metres above sea level. The *Solanum andigenum* is the most common subspecies cultivated throughout the Andes, comprising a huge gamut of varieties which differ in their morphological and physiological features.

Archaeological data speaks to the importance of the potato in pre-Columbian civilizations. This is attested by ceramics that were excavated in profusion, the oldest ones dating back to the Proto-Chimu period (idem: 15). Potato-human interdependence has been translated into myth in both Quechua and Aymara, wherein potato cultivation stands out as a key feature in the emergence of human societies (Millones 2001: 55). Even though tubers did not receive the same honouring treatment as maize under the Incas, the potato has been crucial to their extensionist project: thanks to its intense nutritional potential and to its resistance to extreme and highly variable highland climates, the potato was crucial in sustaining population growth (Krögel 2010: 20). Stocked in state storehouses throughout the empire, potatoes fed administrators, soldiers and state workers, likewise providing emergency rations in case of a bad harvest. The elaboration of a freeze-dried technique producing *chuño* and *moralla*,[1] particularly suited for the bitter *Stenotomum* species, was also strategic. In these dried forms, potatoes could be stored for years. Their light weight meant they could be easily transported wherever humans needed to be fed.

These stories explain that the domestication of the potato conditioned the congregation of highland collectives including human beings, as well as the need of human care to ensure that the potatoes flourished. In this light, we understand how potato and human became 'companion species' in this mountainous setting. This notion offered by Donna Haraway refers to cross-species intimacy tied by relations of care and usefulness (2008). Such a relationship, whereby humans take care of *Solanum* plants, making them grow in challenging habitats while the tuber fosters human physical and social reproduction, is still tangible today in the highlands of the Pisac Department in Cuzco where I have conducted ethnographic fieldwork since 2015.

Notwithstanding increased integration within the labour market, usually taking the form of temporary migration, the members of these *comunidades campesinas* (peasant communities, as formally acknowledged by the Peruvian state) cultivate potatoes in their *chacras* (agricultural plots). A key ingredient of any proper meal, the production of the potato remains a mainstay of household economies. According to Stephen Brush, up to 70 per cent of the ingested calories of these cultivators come from

Figure 5.1. A meal is made of potatoes from many different varieties. Photograph by the author.

the potato (2004: 102). As daily diet is based on locally produced food, self-sufficiency in potatoes is a priority. This involves the continual culti-vation of a number of varieties that satisfy different economic and social needs (Brush 2004; Zimmerer 1996). In the highest communities where the native potato is the best adapted crop, every household cultivates from ten to several tens of varieties, even reaching a few hundreds in outstand-ing cases. Because most native varieties thrive best in the highest plots at around 4000 metres above sea level, their production requires intense efforts. Growers must climb to the mountain top and work under extreme ecological conditions. These labour-intensive tubers are essentially culti-vated for home consumption. As they can be stocked for months without decaying (even years for desiccated ones), these multiple tuber varieties comprise the basis for a rich and delightful menu until the next harvest.

Commercial endeavours typically involve sowing *papas injertadas* or *mejoradas* (that is, improved varieties), producing bigger and more even tubers that fit market expectations, as compared to smaller and more bumpy native ones. Potato crops intended as commodities are cultivated on lower plots that are close to the road for easy transport. There, land is under the pressure of use. Subsequent shortening of the fallow period drains soil nutrients while propagating disease and pests. In many lowland *chacras*, this is compensated with the use of chemical insecticides and complementary fertilizers to which *papas injertadas* are resistant, though this further erodes the land. Improved varieties were introduced in the Pisac Department in the 1980s as part of an agricultural intensification campaign led by an NGO, now lamented as having provoked a drastic decrease in potato agro-biodiversity. These are widely grown, even sometimes for self-consumption by those striving to reduce the amount of time and energy devoted to potato growing. Most families do eat *papas injertadas* in the lean periods, when long cycled native tubers are still growing in the fields.

Still, if cultivators in the highlands of Cuzco are people of the potato, they are not people of just any potato. They are very critical about the much higher water content in improved varieties as well as their chemical requirements, making them less tasty and less able to nourish the body efficiently. In contrast, native ones are appreciated as enhancing human vitality or *fuerza* (strength). A mature lady from the community of Chahuaytire was definitive as she described the native potato as a medicine that protects human health. She noted that when one eats them, one never needs to go to the hospital. Conversely, growers spend significant amounts of their *fuerza* to foster potato plants' thriving. The next section describes these efforts.

Cultivating Happy Potatoes

The most intense labour periods in the agricultural calendar cluster around seed sowing (early October), digging up plants (January) and harvesting and sorting out the tubers (May-June). At all times, growers regularly 'visit' (*visitar*, in Spanish) their plots, to make sure that their plants are fine. Every two weeks, at the very least, they walk up to several kilometres to reach their remote *chacras* and check that water distribution is balanced, no harmful animals like cows or alpacas have entered the fields, night temperatures have not been low enough to freeze the plants and no hailstorm has shaken them up. The colour and size of the stalk and foliage are the most obvious external signs of potato well-being, as commented by a potato grower in her thirties: 'Rather sad, no? A bit ... It's not ... it doesn't produce leaves thus. It's small, as if thrashed. In that way: weird'. Besides the qualities of soil, water and air, the potato also has affective requirements and their growers' visits to the *chacra* are thus intended to cheer them up. An experienced potato grower in his fifties, Nazario[2] explained that he noticed potato contentment as he reached the *chacra*, mostly by observing the colour and shape of the leaves. As we were chewing coca leaves on the side of the field during a break, he commented: 'when we were arriving [the plants] were a little bit sad. Now, look, their leaves are moving slightly with the wind, they stand up. Look, now they are *kusisqa*. If you don't reach the *chacra*, potatoes get sad'.

Cultivators agree that their plants need to be *kusisqa* to produce beautiful tubers. From the shape, size and colour of the plant, they can predict the volume of the harvest. Conversely, they are concerned that an upset potato can retaliate by deciding to not grow. Instructing me on the importance of loving potatoes, Mariano, another middle-aged potato grower in a highland community, explained that an offended potato 'curses us, the potato hates us, and there is no production in the field. You must respect her [*respetarla*] the most'. The fact that the affected potato[3] can decide not to grow if frustrated indicates a subjectivity involving emotionality and intentionality. Beside the agricultural duties mentioned above, the *kusisqa* imperative is translated into a normative prescription that is constantly verbalized: a cultivator is expected to work *contento* (happily) in his field, if he wishes to cultivate thriving potato plants. Joy is mentioned as an appropriate working affect in Andean ethnographic record (Gose 1994: 111; Revilla 2014: 50, 57, 180; Stobart 1994: 39; Valladolid 1998: 59). I became familiar with this necessity when cultivating potato fields in the Argentinean Cordillera. Here and there, cultivators engage in interactions with their plants that are intended to cheer them up.

Besides ordinary agricultural tasks, the importance of vegetal contentment in the field is enacted in festivities intended to foster potato joy. The Papa T'inkay[4] performed during carnival celebrations provides a striking illustration of the kind of practices which aim at circulating *kusisqa* in the field.[5] In its extended version, this consists of spraying the plots with wine or chicha, burying coca leaves and beer in between furrows, decorating the plants with flower petals, and playing music in the *chacra*. While dancing, musicians give voice to loud and intense whoops through which they share their *alegría* with the potatoes. In Bolivia, Henry Stobart famously reported that potato growing and music 'directly motivate one another and are imbued with enchantment and heartfelt sentiment' (1994: 36). Likewise, in the fields of Pisac, potato growing is enhanced with music and related contentment. For this festivity, a band of dancers wearing Wallatas bird costumes is in charge of the distribution of joy in the *chacra*. As Nazario observed while we were looking at them: 'these white dancers, male Sergentos, that's what they do: "*wuuuuu*", all the time. Because of their *alegría*, always. That's their custom. (This whoop) characterizes them as dancers. Cheerful'. It is noteworthy that these whoops are common to a series of carnival festivities aimed at reproducing the community, thereby epitomizing the entanglement of the reproduction of the humans, the potato and their ecological community. These festivities are jointly addressed to potato plants and earth beings (de la Cadena 2015), like Pachamama and mountainous ancestors called apus. In fact, the latter partake in the daily agricultural work too. Adrian, a father of seven children who makes a living from construction work and infirmary caretaking, as well as potato growing, described these interactions as follows: 'When we give to the Apus, they support us: potatoes produce. For that reason, we always chew coca to start [working in the field], we give it to the Apus. Likewise, to sow the first potato, we drop off a *kintuchi* [coca leaves]. Then, with this, the potatoes produce nicely. It helps us'.

Earth beings' intervention speaks to the heterogeneous collaborations involved in *chacra* agriculture. Sheep and llamas are key protagonists as well, as their faeces provides core *comida* (food) for the potato by fertilizing the soil. Moreover, highland cultivation is enmeshed in a much larger network of communication entailing stellar configuration, a lunar calendar, lekecho birds singing, fox courtship calls or añapanco cactus blooming, to name just a few among an array of other disparate protagonists. Thus, in these Andean lands, the potato-human companionship unfolds at the core of broader a cosmoecology in the sense of Vinciane Despret and Michel Meuret. They introduced this notion to indicate that 'ecology and cosmology are knotted in a common story, forming a cosmoecology of multiple beings, gods, animals, humans, living and dead, each bearing the consequences of the others' ways of living and dying' (2016: 26). The lives of human and potato are indeed enmeshed, and both depend on entanglements with an array of living beings, from birds to spiders, to sheep, Pachamama, the apus and other earth beings. The next section points to recent cosmoecological disturbances that thwart cultivators' efforts to bring forth *kusisqa* in the fields.

Cosmoecological Upheavals

The affective economy of potato cultivation in Pisac indicates that potato plants are happy, in the sense of Ahmed: they are socially constructed through moral estimations that collectively point to them as desirable. As a result, happiness is what normatively follows from proximity to them. Here the promise of happiness is, notably, a promise of food abundance. Yet in these Andean fields, happiness is not only what follows: it is a necessary flow in the moment of the potato-human encounter. If thriving potato plants are a core happy object in these communities, the potato is treated as a subject, imbued with life force, intentionality and emotionality. Henceforth, the potato is not only a happy object triggering positive affect to whomever comes near, but rather, a potato is content in the sense that it experiences *kusisqa*, as a vital resource for its own flourishing.

The vital relevance of *alegría* does not mean that potato growing always brings contentment. The recurrence of joy in potato norms and practices is instead intended to edge sadness out, as their growers are all too aware that affliction is always a possibility. In Andean history, potato growing has been a point of affective conversion. In times of bad harvests or market upheavals the potato also raises negative affect despite growers' joyful orientation to their tuber. Although the potato is acknowledged by archaeologists as a cherished crop to pre-colonial civilizations, its value has been neglected in the colonial economy. It was discarded by the Spanish invaders as a wretched food, or damned subterranean protuberances barely suitable as fodder. The potato's relegation to 'food for the poor' continued through the centuries. Today, although it is a core ingredient in the Peruvian diet, its consumption is nonetheless associated with indigenousness and poverty.[6] While its monetary value fluctuates with market whim and state intervention (Mayer 2002: 215), it never reaches a decent price, actually positioning potato cultivation as an economy of deprivation. This is even more so for smaller highland tubers, that are despised by urban consumers, despite their production being extremely labour intensive. As compared to bigger and more uniform-sized improved varieties of the Peruvian agro-industry, small and uneven native potatoes are viewed by city dwellers as epitomizing highland growers' backwardness and poverty.[7] A happy object in the flourishing fields, the potato agglomerates resentment when circulating beyond its growing place to reach national regimes of appreciation where it is symbolically and economically undermined. Anxiety in the face of a devalued potato economy was fresh in the memory of the cultivators I was working with.[8]

The cosmoecology where the life of potato and human are entangled in the circulation of *kusisqa* is unsettled by significant changes in these highland villages. I have already mentioned that the number of native varieties cultivated by every household has been decreasing with the diffusion of improved varieties.[9] The volume of production is also shrinking. Highland inhabitants observe a decreased interest in potato growing as compared to previous decades. The contemporary domestic economy is not exclusively driven by potato production as people say it used to be until the end of the last century. Potato growers have gained access to the labour market where they intermittently work as craftspeople, construction workers or backpack carriers on tourists' expeditions. As they temporarily sell their labour force to earn money, they have less time to devote to the cultivation of the potato, observing that their elders used to produce higher quantities and diversities of tubers. Whenever possible, a significant part of the money channelled through intermittent participation in the labour market is devoted to fund their children's education until college. Adults now lament that their educated children aspire to an urban life free from field labour which they dislike and despise exhausting and dirty. While young people who stay in the village do work in the fields, many of them would prefer not to.

Their potato labour is compared to that of their elders in terms of a lack of respect. Mariano's words instantiate these widespread tropes of vanishing potato respect: 'This is how my grandfather taught me: you must have quite a lot of respect for the potato. … you must go without sandals, you must enter [the *chacra*] on the side of the potato, with respect, in this way, without your hat. … Before there was so much respect for the potato. But now, nowadays, there isn't that respect anymore'. Walking barefoot and hat in hand is just one example among an array of gestures embodying potato respect that are posited as elders' norms barely practiced today, at the expense of tuber contentment. In fact, growers do not only lament that they are cultivating less, but also that cultivated plants are producing less tubers. As he drove me from Pisac to the highlands, Roberto who combines taxi driving with potato growing, shared his observations in tropes that epitomize a widespread appreciation of past tuber thriving:

> Mostly, varieties are dropping. Before, there used to be more varieties. We are also reducing the quantity. Before, there was more quantities. We were working a lot, now a little. We dedicate ourselves to other jobs on top. Also, it produces few. It is not as it used to be anymore [*Ya no es como antes*]. It's not as usual. [The potato] does not give a lot.

In addition to changes in economic practices, climatic disturbances are pointed out as another reason for the decay of potato flourishing. Among these, rain disorder is devastating to the potato cosmoecology. Growers gauge unexpected rainfall by comparison to what appears to have been the ecological plenty of earlier times. In a conversation from 2017, a young cultivator lamented:

> *Ya no es como antes.* Before the potato was much better. And the climate likewise, it used to be normal. But now, the rain isn't on its right timing anymore. There is drought. Hence, it is not as it used to be. Only with the rain does the potato produce. If there is no rain, its produce, the small potatoes, so small, so they remain. There is no production.

Rain disorder takes two forms. On the one hand, continual soft rains that used to soak the field evenly now take the shape of sudden downpours that erode the surface of the fields without humidifying the roots of the plants. On the other hand, while rains used to start in December and end in April, the first heavy rains now only appear in February, extending to June. The temporality of potato growing has been consequently modified since growers are postponing their sowing due to this late rainy season. This is to avoid baby plants enduring drought while waiting for the first rain to come, or to avoid too much rain after the tubers are formed, which would cause mould. Despite major efforts by humans, potato plants suffer from these climatic calamities. The young cultivator quoted above continued, lamenting: 'the potato is somehow sad with the rain because if there is no rain, its small roots aimed at producing dry out'.

Rain disturbances also impact the proceedings of the harvest. Harvesting is as hard as it is exciting, but doing it under the rain in muddy plots is just painful. In full harvest swing, kin work in each other's fields in order to complete the harvest before it is hit by frost. During this time, lunch takes a festive turn, enhanced by the delicious taste of the *huatia*. *Huatia* is a merry meal made of potatoes baked in a mud oven, built at the edge of the field. A piece of fabric is then laid out on the ground where hot potatoes of all kinds of varieties are spread. Guests taste them all, joyfully comparing their tastes, colours and textures. The particular taste of smoked new potato is thus associated with the satisfaction of harvest time. Several times in May 2015, we had to eat cold potatoes that had been boiled in the morning instead, because the soil was too wet to prepare the *huatia*. This provoked collective disappointment at lunch time, turning the discussion to the unusual weather conditions that prevented us experiencing the pleasures of the missing *huatia*. In 2017, some growers had finished their harvest without having a taste of *huatia* because rains were still falling daily at the beginning of June. The situation was so unusual that my friend Nazario joked about it when we were doing a round of the potato harvest in the community in Paru Paru: 'we came to share your *huatia*', he would ironically announce each time we entered another muddy plot. Although Nazario was making fun of the situation to spread good mood in the field, the culinary loss was rather serious. *Huatia* is an act of sharing with Pachamama: while humans enjoy the taste of fresh smoked potatoes, the Earth is pleased with the smell of the smoke. To thank Mother Earth for being so prolific, on the first day of the harvest cultivators even stuff the *huatia* with guinea pigs, enhancing the smoke with the smell of grease, which is a recurrent ingredient in offerings, considered to be Pachamama's favourite.

Climate disturbances also impact the festive calendar around potato growing. The member of a lower community lamented that his neighbours were not going to celebrate the Papa T'inkay during carnival time in 2016, since the potatoes were not flowering yet. 'Perhaps they might do

Figure 5.2. Papa T'inkay on a barely flowering field, as rains had come very late in the agricultural calendar. Photograph by the author.

it later on, by the end of February', he speculated when I asked if I could attend the festivities.

In the Andean highlands, weather conditions are historically renowned for being particularly harsh: the sun burns, the winds lash and the torrential rains come with fierce thunderbolts. Climatic conditions can even change dramatically from one plot to another according to its niche on the uneven mountain slopes. Climate disturbances are thus far from being unusual. Yet cultivators share the feeling that something unusual is going on, beyond the variable weather conditions common in their highlands. Hence the refrain of estrangement: 'the year is not as it used to be anymore'. Disruption of carnival merry making, *huatia* disappointment, and the sadness of cultivators looking at their potato suffering drought in the midst of the supposedly rainy season, are all examples that point to the impact of climate change on the circulation of *alegría*. It is becoming increasingly laborious for cultivators to craft fields which are favourable for the emergence of the potato *kusisqa*. These situations are points of affective conversion: instead of promising joy, potato-human encounters trigger anxieties pointing to present disappointment and future austerity. Ahmed notes that '"happy objects" can indeed become "unhappy" over time, in the contingency of what happens, which is not to say that their happiness no longer persists as an impression, available as memory' (2010: 44). In the next section, I turn to considering potato contentment in the context of conservation initiatives implemented by growers who collaborate with agronomists, to better care for their tuber companion species in the face of new weather conditions.

Ecological Nostalgias in Conservation Programmes

For its remarkable nutritious and productive qualities, the potato is promoted by international institutions as a strategic crop to cope with rural poverty throughout the world. This is also related to its appreciation as an important reservoir of biodiversity, expected to support human adaptation to extreme environmental conditions. For these reasons, initiatives of potato agro-biodiversity conservation have blossomed across the cordillera (Shepherd 2010). One of these is the Parque de la Papa, covering a territory of more than 9,000 hectares in the Department of Pisac, ranging from 3,800 to 4,300 metres above sea level. In 2017, it counted about 6,000 Quechua inhabitants, spread among five hamlets, which are now cultivating some 1,367 varieties of native potatoes. It was initiated on 30 May 2002 by an agreement between local cultivators heading the association of the Park and ANDES (Association for Nature and Sustainable Development), a Cuzco-based NGO.

The scope of this initiative goes far beyond this local setting, since the constitution of the Park aims at conserving potato resources that could strengthen the food sovereignty of highland dwellers as well as food security all over the world. To achieve these targets, the Park is part of an assemblage of conservation programmes involving international institutions such as the International Potato Center (CIP), Oxfam, Biodiversity International, the European Commission, the International Union for the Conservation of Nature, and universities worldwide. Locally, an experimentation centre, a greenhouse, a museum, a potato tasting restaurant and a storage room were built in the different communities of the Park. Communal land was allotted to the experimental cultivation of a range of mostly *andigenum* varieties which are planted at different altitudes, using different kinds of organic fertilizers and insect repellents. Cultivation, experimentation and conservation tasks are undertaken by a team of eight potato growers acting as 'local technicians'.[10] Their work is supported by agronomists from ANDES, who travel constantly from Cuzco to the Park where they are involved in every activity. More sporadically, technicians collaborate with engineers from the CIP, who visit the Park to follow up on experiments.

Potatoes for experimentation were selected from among the 400 virus-free landraces that were repatriated from the CIP in Lima to support agro-biodiversity in the Park. Repatriation means that these varieties were brought to Lima through CIP's collection expeditions from the 1970s, and now returned to the communities of the Park, although some might not have been originally collected from the Pisac Department. The ambition of these experiments, which merge cultivators' and scientists' agricultural knowledge, is to identify resistant varieties that would thrive in extreme conditions in order to be able to cope with future ecological calamities.

But the investigation has a local purpose as well, as it is aimed to increase productivity on highland plots whose dimensions could become restricted as the lower ones become too warm for native potato thriving. An agronomist from the CIP worried: 'we have a serious problem. The top of the mountain is just here, and we can't put more potatoes up there. This is serious. For how long will we be able to go on?' These concerns are related to the fact that 'potatoes are moving uphill', as growers observe. This means that the latter climb to higher and colder plots to grow their native tubers because warmer temperatures increase the spread of pests and diseases in the fields. In the discourse of international institutions' representatives, global warming is put forward as the announcement of a disaster yet to come. This contrasts with the embodied experience of the growers who lament the extent of emptied fields on the mountain-tops. Those who are involved in the labour market have restricted the number of their *chacras*, giving preference to less fertile but closer plots in the village surroundings, at the expense of those in the remote peaks. For the time being, cultivators experience global warming as a somewhat ambivalent turn, as compared with the calamities of rain disorder. Clearly, warmer temperatures have recently increased the dissemination of pest and diseases at altitudes where native potatoes used to thrive. However, some humans enjoy milder temperatures for themselves, and because they enable an increase in the variety of vegetables they are able to grow at a given altitude. By the end of the last century, the highest communities were producing beans. The mid-height ones are gaining access to fruit production.

The activities of the Park are not only concerned with conserving agro-biodiversity. Their staff are also intent on fostering an ethic of potato care, within member communities and beyond. Alejandro Argumedo, the administrative director of ANDES, explicitly explained to me that the transmission of environmental ethics inspired from Andean cosmology was a key concern to him. During a meeting at the headquarters of the

NGO in Cuzco, he developed his argument by commenting on a 1613 drawing by indigenous chronicler Juan de Santa Cruz Pachacuti, which was used to represent Andean cosmovision at that time. In this vein, ANDES staff conceptualize potato care as an *ayni* relationship between human and other entities in the environment. *Ayni* is a Quechua word describing a long-standing relationship of reciprocity. It is considered by anthropologists as a central feature in the socio-economic organization in the Andes (see for instance Gose 1994; Mayer 2002). In an article co-authored with Michael Pimbert (2010: 343), Argumedo defines *ayni* as 'ethical and spiritual norms that regulate all exchanges between people and their environment, promoting the preservation of the integrity of eco-logical processes, which in turn ensure energy flows and the availability of biodiversity and ecosystem goods and services'. The broader objective of the collaboration between ANDES and cultivators in the Potato Park is to work through the diffusion of *ayni* ethical and spiritual guidelines, where *ayni* relationships are conceived as balanced reciprocities between the three communities entangled in earthly flourishing life. These are the domesticated entities, the wild entities and the spiritual ones, respectively named *runa ayllu*, *sallqa ayllu* and *auki ayllu* in the institutional vocabu-lary. Observing that *ayni* has been severed by agricultural intensification policies and increased participation in the labour market, at the expense of growers' quality of life, participants in the Potato Park work through the strengthening of interspecies reciprocities.They refer to the distur-bances in weather patterns as *Pachamama phiñakuyni*, the Quechua words for 'Mother Earth's anger'. Embedded in global climate change concerns, this expression hints at *auki ayllu* beings' discontent for the overuse of chemicals in the massive culture of improved species for the agroindustry, or for younger generations' disinterest in potato cultivation or in agricul-ture more generally.

As an example of the many initiatives meant to foster reciprocities from across *ayllus*, in January 2016, ANDES provided funding to organize a col-lective Papa T'inkay. Thanks to this material support, the hosting commu-nity was able to perform a widely appreciated celebration, as the money served to buy the offerings to *auki* beings and to hire two local specialists to perform the celebration appropriately. Their presence was appreciated for attracting massive participation from community members and in-creasing the success of the Papa T'inkay. After a team of dancers cheered up the potato plants with petals of flowers and their typical sounds of enjoyment, the spiritual masters gave respect to Mother Earth by burying pleasing ingredients. The attendants then went back to the centre of the community, where we shared a feast and played a football championship match. In so doing, the Park enhanced interspecies flows of *alegría* tying together the potato cosmoecology.

Conclusion

In situ conservation and experimentation within the Potato Park reclaim a pre-Hispanic heritage, in order to cope with present and future ecological damage. In doing so, they also work towards the economic and social appreciation of the native potato in a society where its value has been dismissed by national elites for centuries. Within the Potato Park native varieties are promoted as a promise of happiness. This departs from discourses praising the proliferation of varieties crafted in laboratories. The spread of the *canchan* variety is widely lauded as an agronomic success on the national scene. This improved variety now covering about 40 per cent of the Peruvian potato fields is celebrated for producing big specimens of evenly shaped potatoes fitting with market demand. Such praise links potato cultivators' prosperity to the chemically supported thriving of an improved variety. The latter is posited as a happy object, in the sense of Ahmed, meaning that they circulate as social goods, triggering positive affect to whomever comes near.

In this vein, highly productive *papas injertadas* are contrasted against native varieties despised by the national agro-industry as poorly productive. The native potato's potential to produce healthy people and to foster an outstanding agro-biodiversity is silenced. Ahmed insisted on the political implications of the social construction of the happy object: that a given object should be experienced as happy is a normative statement, raising the question of who decides what is actually good, and for whom. The struggle over which is a happy potato, and under which ecological conditions, reveals a political field in which highland people's livelihood and liveliness are at stake. Still, further political tension around the value of the potato relates to its appreciation as a lively being, a subject of joy who deserves to be respected (Angé et al. 2018).

Shifting affectivities in this potato cosmoecology thus unravel growers' ecological nostalgia as they realize how challenging it has become to foster native potato *kusisqa* in their fields. Longings for past potato bounty emerge in the contact zone of interspecies interdependence, disturbed by the erosion of human and non-human mutualities. Following Hastrup (chapter 2 in this volume; see also High, chapter 4), I should make it clear that highland growers do not long to live back in the past. When cultivators scrutinize their agricultural past, they aim to better engage with present ecologies in ways that will enable them to maintain their highland potato livelihood. This means performing cultivation work that brings forth tuberous contentment, despite the fact that the 'days are not as they used to be'.

As this ethnographic account has shown, the current agricultural harshness is related to the unexpected outcome of interspecies reciprocities, due to shifting socio-economic strategies and, importantly, to changing climatic conditions. The notion of broken reciprocities, expressed by potato growers and custodians, echoes the famous conceptualization of nostalgia by Michael Herzfeld as a trope about 'a mutuality that has been, perhaps irreversibly, ruptured by the self-interest of modern times' (2005: 149). This ethnographic exploration of potato cultivation in the Andes suggests that Herzfeld's treatment of nostalgia should be extended to embrace ruptures in mutualities that also involve beings other than human. The affective agriculture performed by potato growers in the Cuzco highlands invites us to consider not only the human yearning for flourishing fields that are threatened, but also the pain of other living beings who compose with us earthly ecologies, like the potato. While these cultivators continue to spend considerable effort in cultivating a potato cornucopia that offers measly monetary rewards, the bulk of the potato industry draws profit from monoculture unfolding at the dull edge of tuberous extinction (see Van Dooren 2014). Their care for potato *kusisqa* instructs us with admirable forms of responsiveness to non-human suffering, and teaches us embodied acts of consideration for the doom of vegetal beings that are currently striving to find a comfortable home on our 'damaged planet' (Tsing 2015).

Acknowledgements

This chapter is the fruit of a field collaboration with potato growers in several communities of the Potato Park (mostly Pampallacta and Chahuaytire). I am thankful to my hosts who generously shared their expertise with me. In particular, I want to thank Lino Mamani and Nazario Quispe for their care and affection. I am also thankful to ANDES directors, Cesar and Alejandro Argumedo, for their admiring political engagement, and for making my research possible in the first place. This chapter presents ethnographic investigation, initially funded by a Marie Curie Intra European Fellowship (627769, 2014–2017). Professor Alberto Arce was my promotor for this grant at Wageningen University and I am deeply thankful for the rich insight he provided. Later fieldworks were funded by the Belgian Fonds de la Recherche Scientifique.

Olivia Ange is Associate Professor at Université Libre de Bruxelles. She specializes in the study of economic exchanges, agricultures and value creation in the Andes. She is the author of *Barter and Social Regeneration in the Argentinean Andes* (Berghahn, 2018), and co-author of *Anthropology and Nostalgia* (Berghahn, 2014).

Notes

1. *Moralla* and *chuño* are two kinds of dehydrated potato, which production process makes use of the typical winter climatic conditions in the Andean highlands. Potatoes are frozen during the cold nights, and the water is extracted by squeezing them under feet pressure at dawn, before the sun starts shining.
2. Beside growing potatoes for family consumption, Nazario is curator for the Potato Park, as are other potato experts quoted in this chapter.
3. In the Pisac Department, potatoes are mostly feminine, but their gender may shift according to the variety, and the social context in which potato takes existence. However, this is not the place to develop this intriguing and complex question.
4. In Quechua, T'inkay means splashing maize beer or wine around as a form of libation.
5. Libations performed to enliven crops are reported across the Andes (Ange et al. 2018; Arnold and Yapita 1996; Gose 1994; Revilla 2014).
6. According to statistics put forward by Rose et al. (2009: 528), tubers' nutritious supply is indeed more important to rural inhabitants or poor urbanites, than to well-off urban citizens.
7. This attitude has recently been challenged by a call by Peruvian chefs to valorize native ingredients in the national cuisine. But this remains very much restricted to touristic and wealthy gourmet menus.
8. This is also related in the literature. In another department of the Cuzco Province, Allen describes the situation in the 1980s as 'a pervasive sense among Sonqueños that their backbreaking labor is not valued by the nation as a whole' (2002: 2018; see also Arnold and Yapita 1996; Mayer 2002).
9. Despite the Andean potato genetic pool having been maintained at the regional level, the diversity cultivated by every household has decreased. Brush refers to this trend as a shift in landraces' 'population structure' (1992: 148).
10. This apprenticeship involves techniques featuring the tool kit of governmentality in a Foucauldian sense: process of examination, quantitative evaluation, numeration, strict timeframe, hygiene prescriptions, and architectural infrastructure where activities take place (I am borrowing this list from Cepek [2011: 506], who himself quotes Jonathan Xavier Inda). While the disciplined experimentation in breeding and growing gives rise to negotiation between local experts and agronomists, the former very much appreciate the latter's teaching.

References

Ahmed, S. 2010. *The Promise of Happiness*. Durham, NC: Duke University Press.

Allen, C. 2002. *The Hold Life Has: Coca and Cultural Identity in an Andean Community*, 2nd ed. Washington DC: Smithsonian Books.

Angé, O. and D. Berliner, 2014. 'Introduction', in O. Angé and D. Berliner (eds), *Anthropology and Nostalgia*. Oxford: Berghahn, pp. 1–16.

Angé, O. et. al. 2018. 'Interspecies Respect and Potato Conservation in the Peruvian Cradle of Domestication', *Conservation and Society* 16(1): 30–40.

Argumedo, A. and M. Pimbert. 2010. 'Bypassing Globalization: Barter Markets as a New Indigenous Economy in Peru', *Development* 53(3): 343–49.

Arnold, D. and J.D. Yapita. 1996. *Madre Melliza y Sus Crias Ispall Mama Wawampi: Antologia de la Papa*. La Paz: Hisbol Ediciones.

Brush, S. 1992. 'Reconsidering the Green Revolution: Diversity and Stability in Cradle Areas of Crop Domestication', *Human Ecology* 20(2): 145–67.

_____. 2004. *Farmers' Bounty: Locating Crop Diversity in the Contemporary World*. Ann Arbor, MI: Sheridan Books.

Cepek, M. 2011. 'Foucault in the Forest: Questioning Environmentality in Amazonia', *American Ethnologist* 38(3): 501–15.

De la Cadena, M. 2015. *Earth Beings: Ecologies of Practice Across Andean Worlds*. Durham, NC: Duke University Press.

Despret, V. and M. Meuret. 2016. 'Cosmoecological Sheep and the Arts of Living on a Damaged Planet', *Environmental Humanities* 8(1): 24–36.

Gose, P. 1994. *Deathly Waters and Hungry Mountains: Agrarian Ritual and Class Formation in an Andean Town*. Toronto: University of Toronto Press.

Haraway, D. 2008. *When Species Meet*. Minneapolis: University of Minnesota Press.

Herzfeld, M. 2005. *Cultural Intimacy: Social Poetics in the Nation-State*. New York: Routledge.

Krögel, A. 2010. *Food, Power, and Resistance in the Andes: Exploring Quechua Verbal and Visual Narratives*. Lanham, MD: Lexington Books.

Mayer, E. 2002. *The Articulated Peasant: Household Economies in the Andes*. Boulder, CO: Westview Press.

Millones, L. 2001. 'The Inner Realm', in C. Graves (ed.), *The Potato Treasure of the Andes: From Agriculture to Culture*. Lima: International Potato Center, pp. 55–60.

Pickering, M. and E. Keightley. 2006. 'The Modalities of Nostalgia', *Current Sociology* 54: 919–41.

Revilla, L. 2014. *Costumbres de las Papas Nativas*. Cuzco: Centro de Servicios Agropecuarios.

Rose, D. et al. 2009. 'Understanding the Role of Potatoes in the Peruvian Diet: An Approach that Combines Food Composition with Household Expenditure Data', *Journal of Food Composition Analysis* 22: 525–32.

Salaman, R. 1985. *The History and Social Influence of the Potato*, 4th ed. Cambridge: Cambridge University Press.

Shepherd, C. 2010. 'Mobilizing Local Knowledge and Asserting Culture: The Cultural Politics of In Situ Conservation of Agricultural Biodiversity', *Current Anthropology* 51(5): 629–54.

Strobart, H. 1994. 'Flourishing Horns and Enchanted Tubers: Music and Potatoes in Highland Bolivia', *British Journal of Ethnomusicology* 3: 35–48.

Tsing, A. 2015. *The Mushroom at the End of the World: On the Possibility of Life in Capitalist Ruins*. Princeton, NJ: Princeton University Press.

Valladolid Rivera, J. 1998. 'Andean Peasant Agriculture: Nurturing a Diversity of Life in the *Chacra*', in F. Appfel-Marglin (ed.), *The Spirit of Regeneration: Andean Culture. Confronting Western Notions of Development*. London: Zed Books, pp. 51–88.

Van Dooren, T. 2014. *Flight Ways: Life and Loss at the Edge of Extinction*. New York: Columbia University Press.

Zimmerer, K. 1996. *Changing Fortunes: Biodiversity and Peasant Livelihood in the Peruvian Andes*. Berkeley, CA: University of California Press.

CHAPTER 6

The Village and the Hamlet in the Mixe Highlands of Oaxaca, Mexico

Nostalgic Commitments to Working and Living Together

Perig Pitrou

Every year since May 2005, I have travelled to Santa María Tlahuitoltepec to carry out an ethnographic study of this peasant community in Oaxaca State in Mexico. The 10,000 inhabitants who live there are Mixe, an ethno-linguistic group with about 130,000 speakers. When I began my investigation on poultry sacrifices, which I presented in my book *Le chemin et le champ* (Pitrou 2016a), I was impressed by the striking contrasts I observed between lifestyles in the centre and the periphery of the municipality of Santa María Tlahuitoltepec. The 3,000 inhabitants living in the central village, or *pueblo*, have direct access to water, electricity and state services (clinics, schools, high schools), as well as the federal road, which makes Oaxaca, the colonial capital city of the State, accessible by shared taxi within a few hours. Small shops and government jobs provide economic prosperity for many families, whose standards of living have risen considerably over the years. However, after walking for a few minutes or hours of travelling by pickup truck along unpaved roads, the visitor discovers about fifty small hamlets, or *ranchos*,[1] where the other 7,000 inhabitants are scattered, and which present a very different situation. Their social morphology is that of a semi-dispersed habitat, and the farmers who live in these adobe brick houses have a more traditional existence, centred on corn cultivation and self-subsistence agriculture.

I had mixed feelings about the discrepancy I observed between these social realities. At first, I could not get rid of the somewhat ingenuous impression that I had to follow the most remote paths to uncover the most authentic conditions of life. When I stayed in hamlets, in traditional

Figure 6.1. Santa María Tlahuitoltepec. Village. Photograph by the author.

houses where traces of modernity were not really visible, I could not help but think that living conditions there had hardly changed over the previous several decades, if not centuries. Yet I quickly understood that it was in the central *pueblo* that I would collect the most data. In a political structure governed by the cargo system of political-religious offices, it is in this changing space that I have observed the most instructive elements concerning, for example, the ceremonies in which power staffs are handed over, which take place in the central square, and the poultry sacrifices made in the town hall and the prison. On these occasions, inhabitants converge on the central square, just as they do on market days or during festival times. Once a year, on the first of January, when the outgoing municipal team transmits various symbols of power (staffs, flags, the keys to the town hall) to their successors, villagers can hear ritual discourses emphasizing that it is crucial to follow the traditions initiated by their ancestors. On these occasions, representatives explain how important it is not to forget *costumbre* (custom); in the Mixe language, which belongs to the Mixe-Zoque group, this idea is expressed by a phrase meaning to follow 'the way of sitting': *ja tsïnää'yïn* (way of life, tradition).

Figure 6.2. Santa María Tlahuitoltepec. A rancho, outside of the village. Photograph by the author.

In this context, one might be puzzled by a discrepancy between two kinds of relations with the past. On the one hand, there is a claim to maintain and strengthen a 'way of sitting' and to ensure that the teachings of former generations 'come, go up'. On the other hand, all the inhabitants of the village have given up most of what constituted the traditional way of life they knew when they were young. In this context, I would like to show how this ambivalent relation to the past implies a specific relation to nature and to non-human beings (animals, plants and entities such as the Mountain, the Earth, the Rain, and so on).

In the West, when nature is involved in typical nostalgic discourses, it is often through the description of an aesthetic relation. A landscape can be described as a spectacle to contemplate, which triggers specific feelings or representations of the imagination. In this case, the expression of nostalgia is due to the impression that a landscape has changed and, because of urbanization, pollution, contamination, etc., is no longer able to offer the same pleasure. But such an interpretation of the relation to nature implies a Kantian dichotomy that has been challenged by contemporary anthropology in works such as *Beyond Nature and Culture* (Descola 2013). Instead of focusing on disjunction, Descola contends that we should investigate the diversity of relations that human societies establish with non-humans. From this point of view, in order to tackle the issue of ecological nostalgias it is important to complement the aesthetic approach with a more pragmatic approach, in order to better understand the processes that make nostalgia an active engagement with the environment. Thus, we may consider that, beyond transforming perceptions of nature, nostalgia has to do with modifying interactions between humans and non-humans.

This is why I suggest addressing the issue of nostalgia through an analysis of Mixe conceptions of *tunk* (a Mixe word meaning activity, work, rite) and collective activities which are connected with *et näxwii'nyït* ('the Extension, the Surface of the Earth'), the Mixe word used to translate 'nature'. More precisely, I will explore how nostalgia associated with these activities is related to a connection between two different spacetimes: the hamlet (*rancho*) and the mountain. I will show that even if many inhabitants now live in the village, the fact that they continue to frequently return to the *ranchos* where they were born enacts a nostalgic attachment to activities (cooking, sowing, cultivating) and values (cooperation, reciprocity, hospitality) associated with traditional peasant life. The ritual paths connecting the village to the mountain where sacrifices are made constitute another kind of *tunk* that instantiates such values and weaves connections to the past within a context of deep social change. My contention is that in both cases the object of nostalgia is constituted by the various types of *tunk* that the Mixe carry out in interactions with living beings and with entities that 'bring life' or 'make being alive', either in the intermittent activities performed in the *ranchos* or in the ritual activities associated with animal sacrifices. My idea is that this ecological nostalgia is less about elements (objects, landscapes, moments) than about a form of collaboration and exchange that governs relations between humans and with beings in nature.

In previous texts, I have explained how the ritual *tunk* involved in a birth rite (Pitrou 2017) aims both to shape the body of the new-born child and to teach him or her how to act in conformity with custom and with the Mixe way of life. That is to say, I have shown that this formative activity on and with the child can be described as a process involving both (biological) life form and (social) form of life. In the same way, I wish to show that the individual and collective activity of producing and consuming animals and plants goes beyond material and biological dynamics: it is also a way of fostering social rules of co-existence, such as reciprocity, collective work and commensality. It is precisely this strong link between the biological and the sociological that is the object of nostalgic representations. Moreover, since nostalgia also involves the participation of non-human agents such as 'He Who Makes Being Alive' and 'the Extension, the Surface of the Earth', it is also connected to the commitment to perform ritual journeys. Indeed, the villagers consider that the tradition of going to the top of the mountain to sacrifice poultry to these entities should be followed. These collective moments epitomize the nostalgic desire to continue to work and live together, 'in the society of nature', to use Descola's title (1994).

The Village and the Hamlet: Walking Back to the Past, With or Without Pain

I will start with the biographical and personal way in which individuals experience nostalgia through intermittent returns to their hamlets of origin to cultivate their plots and share meals with their families. Comparing past and present conditions of life is an activity of the memory. Nostalgic feelings and sensations are rooted in these facts of consciousness, producing an emotional hiatus between what is perceived and what is remembered. As a social fact, memory of the past is nurtured by stories and collective remembering that maintain the subject of nostalgia in existence. And, above all, it is the very materiality of the world, the texture of places and beings, their flavours, smells, appearances and sounds, that constitute the tangible foundation on which nostalgic feelings build up. For these two reasons, as Olivia Angé and David Berliner point out (see introduction), the temporal essence of nostalgia is articulated with spatialities, and this connection between nostalgia and space must be examined. Two complementary approaches are therefore available to address the nostalgia felt by Amerindian populations: scrutinizing practices of memory-making and mapping geographies of displacements across contrasted livelihoods.

For those who migrated further away, nostalgia for traditional livelihoods usually hints at the harsh life experienced in the metropolises of Mexico and the United States. Even if the financial benefits help individuals to cope with the difficulties they encounter, the memory of their community of origin, either the *rancho* or the *pueblo*, always causes cruel pain to be felt. The food is not as good, the houses are tiny and, even if there are networks of mutual aid and support, everyone experiences loneliness at some point. More surprisingly, negative judgments of this kind are also made about the central village of Santa María Tlahuitoltepec. But in this case, the comparison is between the part of the community engaged in a process of modernization and the hamlets located a few dozen minutes' drive from the central village. To a certain extent, some discourses can give the impression that some inhabitants of the village consider themselves migrants who have left behind their *rancho* to live in the village centre. Hence, the *rancho* represents the ultimate space-time from which nostalgic evaluations are expressed, even against the type of livelihood practised in the village.

Although the name of the village has been identified in colonial documents since the sixteenth century and the church was built in the eighteenth century, the huddling together of villagers around this religious building and the town hall that adjoins it is very recent. The main town as we know it today was actually built when the federal road connected the village centre to the state capital and when primary and secondary schools were built there, beginning in the 1970s. This is why residents over forty years old usually declare that they come from one of the hamlets (Fríjol, Salinas, Flores, Tejas, Guadalupe, Nejapa, and so on) when asked about their place of birth. Just as some inhabitants of Paris claim to be Breton, Corsican or Auvergnat, the inhabitants of Tlahuitoltepec feel deeply attached to their birthplaces. To the latter, this means the houses in which, in accordance with birth rites, their umbilical cords were buried, and the plots of land on which they continue to intermittently grow corn, black beans and squash. As a place of origin, the *rancho* materializes a relation to the past and can be seen as the core of nostalgic representations.

Within a single day, it is possible to observe a radical shift in conditions of life in the same *municipio* (local council). In the village, you find cyber cafes where teenagers dressed in modern clothes are connected to their Facebook pages, watching video clips and sports on their screens. In addition to all the industrial sweets sold in small shops, some of these young people particularly delight in the flavour of *Maruchan* soup (industrially manufactured dry noodles that are consumed after being heated in a microwave). A few kilometres from there, in the *ranchos*, you are more likely to observe peasants engaged in much more traditional activities. For instance, old women, wearing their traditional dresses and blouses, carry wood in their *mecapal* (front bands) and men plough fields with oxen. If you are invited into one of their adobe houses, you may have the pleasure of sharing a family meal prepared in clay pots, which are used to heat corn and beans in the open wood fire.

On a temporal axis, the *rancho* is described as the place of childhood, in which everyone keeps memories of past episodes: the paths they used to take to go to school (previously, the only school was located in the central village) as well as to go to neighbouring villages; the types of meals prepared by their parents; the sites where families would cultivate their *milpa* (plots) or collect firewood. When recalling fragments of past livelihoods, narrators generally seem to enjoy the pleasure of reminiscence triggered by the observation of an artefact (a house, a tool) or a landscape, or by conjuring up certain significant events: a birth, a death, bad weather, and so on. At the same time, the contrast with the current prosperity of the inhabitants of the central village highlights the harshness of traditional living conditions, which are thus recalled with mixed feelings. The pleasure associated with childhood memories does not prevent people from declaring that, at that time, they were 'suffering', especially from hunger. In self-sustaining domestic economies, meat consumption was rare, with daily meals usually consisting of a few tortillas, black beans and wild herb soup.

Nowadays, in the prayers uttered during poultry sacrifices, you can still hear this anxiety of privation. When they ask to be protected from misfortune, the Mixe say *kiti yuuj kiti pä'äm* ('may there not be hunger, may there not be disease'). They repeatedly ask for 'health' (literally the fact of 'being tough', *ja jënts'äjtïn*) and 'strength' (the fact of being 'strong', *ja mëjk'äjtïn*). Strength is the corporal condition required when you want to work (*tunk*), and it depends on the quantity of food consumed. In economies of scarcity, the memory of deprivation is thus associated with bodily pain. The lean season, which comes in mid-summer before the autumn corn harvest, was a particularly difficult time. At the end of July, a ritual meal called *machucado* in Spanish (*määtsy* in Mixe) was organized, using the last grains from the previous harvest. A cooked corn paste with a spicy sauce was placed in a common hot container from which members of a household helped themselves directly by grabbing small balls. The pleasure taken in this moment of commensality was so intense that today, as we will see, the ritual journeys organized in agricultural, political or therapeutic contexts are systematically concluded by such a moment of sharing. However, we must not forget (and the Mixe always remember this fact) that this dish used to symbolize a moment of deprivation that all families had to suffer.

Similarly, memory of the past provokes comments about the hours- or even days-long walks necessary to conduct daily *tunk* such as growing *milpa*, carrying wood or going to a regional market. Narrators insist on the hardships represented by these activities, which required considerable effort to ensure a sometimes very precarious level of subsistence. This was especially the case for women, who had to begin preparing tortillas for meals for the whole family in the early morning. You can actually gauge the weight of this daily burden when you observe women bent over, carrying bulky bundles of wood with headbands or walking through the village at dawn to grind their corn at the municipal millstone. The cars and gas cookers that are now arriving in even the most remote areas of the village are not only changing means of transport and cooking methods but are also profoundly transforming the operational chains that once made days endless. These techniques profoundly transform bodies, which are gradually relieved of part of their workload, thus continuing the multi-millennial movement of outsourcing biological functions to technological devices (Leroi-Gourhan 1970). Yet, even if everyone is happy that they no longer suffer from deprivation and that they have lightened the burden of daily tasks, some ambivalent comments manifest a nostalgia for this bygone time. The goal of such narratives is not to recall the pleasure of a sweet childhood. Rather, narrators long for the pleasure felt when experiencing the vigour of their bodies coping with the harshness of existence. This, at least, is how I interpret a remark often made by my interlocutors when they talk about daily hours-long walks and the painfulness of agricultural work: 'I couldn't do it today!'. Although this expresses relief, as bodies have been freed from burdensome constraints, one can also perceive the lilt of nostalgia for the strength (*mëjk*) of those bodies that were always in tension. On the one hand, strength is the opposite of suffering. On the other, efforts to cope with suffering and hunger condition the emergence of strength. By escaping the suffering of hamlet life, inhabitants also feel that a certain state of self tends to disappear, i.e. a way of being active, of valiantly exercising a *tunk*.

Inhabitants of the central village who are no longer only peasants (in addition to doing farm work, they may also work as teachers or tradesmen for example), and who return to cultivate a plot on a regular basis, explicitly verbalize this form of nostalgia for the vitality and vigour of the body. It is one of the pleasures they enjoy in such activities. While remembrance allows you to return to the past in your imagination, the *rancho* is a place to which you can physically return and sporadically experience former conditions of existence. Extremely laudatory statements describe these periodic visits, during which those who return for one or two days work their fields or participate in a community activity such as opening a road, repairing a chapel or a school building, or cleaning up the territorial boundaries. Unburdened by the pain of hard work and daily efforts, enjoying the dramatic improvement in their living conditions in homes equipped with household appliances, families 'return' to their previous place of life without having to suffer the deprivations related to their past existence. While the improvement of conditions provides undeniable satisfaction, this regular returning reveals, by contrast, the flaws of the proto-urban existence developing in the village. Once, I was with Mauro Delgado Jiménez, former director of the local music school CECAM, and his family, helping to rebuild part of a small house he owns in a *rancho*. He told me: 'in these preserved places, we enjoy more silence, cleaner air, better quality food'. This is quite a common discourse, one which I have heard in many situations during my fieldwork.

By working in their fields occasionally and, for a few hours, enjoying the charms of a partly outdated existence, the villagers experience a purified relationship with the past, of which they retain only the rewarding elements (physical vigour) without having to bear the burden of the daily tasks that overwhelm the families who continue to live in the hamlets. Thus, a very subtle nostalgic pleasure, perhaps coupled with a sense of superiority, is experienced, since the 'suffering' (*algos*) caused by the impossibility of 'returns' (*nostos*) is overcome, but without having to pay the price of 'suffering' actual life in the *rancho*. However, this does not mean that it is only an individual corporal pleasure that is sought: the return also implies a reconnection to collective activity, which in turn implies special bonds with living beings and entities of nature.

Nostalgia for Shared Activities

In addition to an individual nostalgia related to individual *tunk*, a specific corporal state, nostalgia depends on collective activities involved in the production and consumption of corn. What is at stake is a kind of idealized lifestyle; when you walk in the town hall you can see good illustrations of this valorization of the traditional life that still exists in the *ranchos*. Indeed, it is very common for teachers in primary and secondary schools to ask the children to draw or to photograph the traditional agricultural or culinary activities that can still be observed there. Displayed at the centre of the village, on the wall of the place of power, these images can be interpreted as expressions of a nostalgic attachment to a world that is, to a certain extent, about to vanish. Together with the discourses uttered during the ceremony of transmission of power staffs, this visual reflexivity can be interpreted as a way of highlighting what the villagers' 'way of sitting' was like.

The fact that families continue to cultivate a plot of land to grow corn for pleasure and not out of necessity proves that nostalgia is not about establishing a contemplative and idealized contact with nature. Through the *tunk* made during these short stays, it is an active relationship with living beings, and with the vitality of one's own body, that is sought. In fact, this bodily commitment is only a substitute for the real effort that farmers tied to their land still have to make when their resources depend exclusively on *kamtunk* (work in the fields). For families who return from time to time, bountiful harvests depend largely on the employment of day labourers who perform a *mïtunk* (a work at the service of someone else). But, in the end, this does not matter; the objective is by no means a *retour à la nature* as we say in French, that is, a return to rurality whereby families would be forced to re-engage, on a daily basis, in all the activities necessary for survival in isolated hamlets.

Nostalgic attachment emerges from recollection that enables one to isolate and select emotionally charged moments in order to preserve them as time capsules. A sample, a brief experience, is all it takes to immerse yourself in the world you value and miss. Nonetheless, this selection of specific moments of the past, which extracts the most striking or pleasurable ones, would be nothing without the synthetic power of imagination. Strictly speaking, nostalgia is therefore never about places, living beings, artefacts or sensations per se. Rather, it is made up of a set of processes that connect them to each other. Memory is a linking activity *par excellence*, which builds bridges between temporal strata, sometimes relying on synaesthesia, a powerful tool that produces associations between sensations, actions and events. It actively participates in the 'physio-psycho-sociological montages of series of acts' mentioned by Mauss in his essay *Les techniques du corps* (2013 [1934]). However, far from confining itself to the formation of an aesthetic capacity to perceive the world, memory operates in active relationship with it. In this light, we see how technical activities constitute synthetic motions which connect elements of memory with an actual engagement of the body in productive activities learned during childhood. In this case, among the Mixe, it is this commitment to a series of acts connecting the body, technical objects, living beings and social relationships that is valued. This is where ecological nostalgia manifests itself as a connection to transformative processes at work within the same environment. From this point of view, it is not only nostalgia for an individual body state that should be noted: *tunk* performed in working the fields implies collective moments, experienced during productive activities or in situations of commensality, when Mixe people share the products of their work. The expression *tunk pejk*, 'to work, to receive', designates this value of reciprocity which is epitomized in the *kïmuunytyunk* (community *tunk*) performed when the villagers gather to open a road or to clean up the boundaries of the territory. All these collective activities benefit everyone who participates in them. Indeed, they begin with a meal and a drink shared by all participants.

Likewise, visits to the *ranchos* not only provide the satisfaction of working your field properly: they imply the pleasure of consuming your crop. Everyone insists on how much they enjoy having the tortillas that women spend time preparing themselves and cooking on a clay griddle (*comal*), sometimes with help of the flat grinding stone (*metate*) still used by the elderly, even more so when it has become common for villagers to buy tortillas in the shops where they are machine-made. The flavour of traditionally made products is considered a clear mark of authenticity. Like the flavour of Proust's madeleine, a good meal shared in a cottage has a powerful evocative power. But, unlike Proustian anamnesis which affirms the power of aesthetics and the deep perception of the world recombined by the interplay of multidimensional memory, it is an active relationship with the environment which is valued. Longing for homemade tortilla entails a set of relationships and activities and encapsulates an ecological system of vital and technical processes from which human work patiently extracts the sources of food.

In fact, the taste of traditional foods results from the convergence of a three-way combination: the non-human entities who grow the plants, the farmers who take care of the crops, and the cooks who transform corn into food. Nostalgia for this active relationship is not only about the individual pleasure felt in the invigorating exercise of the body's strength and ability. Beyond this individual dimension, *tunk* has a collective value. In the fields and in the kitchen, nothing good is expected to arise if it is not produced by collective work. Therefore, in addition to reconnecting with individual experiences, the nostalgic pleasure of working in *ranchos* activates relationship systems based on mutual exchanges of services and mutual aid. Similarly, the commensality associated with meal-sharing contributes, as much as the unique flavour of food and beverages, to giving a delightful tone to the activities carried out together.

In these circumstances, I would make the following assumption. As much as nostalgia is a phenomenon that affects each individual psychologically and physically, it implies a hybrid whole constituted by the collective techniques that the Mixe develop to interact with living beings, whether plants grown in the field, or poultry, which are also known to have a more delicious taste in the hamlets. To grasp this nostalgia, it is not individual mental states or objects that need to be examined, but complex socio-technical networks in which vital and technical processes are intertwined. These processes combine a biological and a social dimension: the distribution of work and its benefits are strongly structured by the idea of reciprocity. The value attributed to corn and to techniques of preparing the foods for which it is the basis is strongly linked to work, which combines several dynamics: physical and social, individual and collective. In the end, it is as if the flavour of the aliments incorporates all these processes and values. Olivia Angé (2015) analyses a similar dynamic with sourdough bread consumption, although in her case, it is only the 'techniques' of consumption that are experienced, since consumers of these breads do not return to former agricultural activities in order to savour the pleasure of a specific taste. In the case of the Mixe, nostalgia is based on an assemblage of techniques and on the coordination of the work of production. Returning to these collective activities means composing a way of life at the interface between the *pueblo* and the *rancho*, while avoiding the daily efforts and uncertainty of agricultural livelihood.

In this configuration, what is at stake is a specific articulation that technical activities create between biological species (corn, beans, turkey) and a system of rules and values that constitute the background for collective existence. In other words, we can say that through interactions with life forms forms of life are instituted and are the subject of a particular attachment, because they give each society its own identity (Pitrou 2017; see also Helmreich 2009). This co-constitution explains the solidity of the associations created generation after generation between territories, bodies and life forms, as well as the determination with which human beings battle to defend their traditions, which they do with the same intensity as when they defend their physical safety and survival. In this context, nostalgia is ecological because it invites us to think about how interactions with living beings, mediated by technical activities, create a world of social interactions. Through the activities involved, these interactions are inserted into and structure interactions between humans, based on rules organizing the reciprocal exchange of services, hospitality or collective work.

Periodic stays in the *ranchos* thus represent an attempt to preserve ecological bonds despite the process of centralization and urbanization which constitutes a small-scale migration for the villagers. Through these short trips back and forth, a former livelihood is maintained, encapsulated in a new way of life. In the same way, the next section considers nostalgic attachment as enacted through a ritual *tunk* that sublimates technical activities and social relations and stages them for inhabitants to see.

Ritual Journeys as a Nostalgic Experience

With ritual *tunk*, it is not only the activity of human groups which is at stake, for these rituals try to establish what I call co-activity with non-human agents. Thus, it is also the *tunk* of Nature, namely 'He Who Makes Being Alive' and 'the Extension, the Surface of the Earth' which is stimulated. In this way, another dimension of ecological nostalgia appears: nostalgia for engagement with these non-human entities.

In addition to school images, a visit to the town hall offers another point of interest: a mural painting which represents a mythological event and refers to a fundamental ritual activity for the community. First, you can see the representation of the birth of two mythical entities: King Konk Öy hatching out of an egg like Athena, already an adult and carrying a weapon, and of his sister Tajëew, the woman-snake associated with fertility. This apparition is found at the centre of a sort of 'cosmogram' (Tresh

2007) which represents places of power: the town hall, the church, the mountain and above all, the *tun(k)pajt* ('place of activity'), that is, the place where sacrifices are performed, at the top of Zempoaltepetl, a mountain situated above the village. The mural displays a strong attachment to what the ancestors have 'made walk, made go up', as well as the importance of the 'covenant' (to use the expression in the title of John Monaghan's monograph on the Mixtec, another Oaxacan ethnolinguistic group, in *Covenants with Earth and Rain* [1995]) with the non-human entities responsible for fertility.

During staff transmission ceremonies, ritual discourses are made to perpetuate this tradition of establishing such covenants with non-human entities. For instance, you can hear the representatives saying:

ïjyxyäm n'ijyxyïntï najä'wïntï	now we know, we see (= we are witnesses)
ku jatë'n ja tsïnää'yïn	that it is 'the way of sitting' (= our way of life, our tradition)
yääj jatë'n nyïktuu'yë'yïntï	that we are making walk (= we begin our service according to the tradition)
ayuujkjää'yjëëty	within the territory of the Mixe
uk ja wïntsëntëjk nayïtë'n	and the federal authorities [of the State of Mexico]
x'ijyxyïntï xnïjää'wïntï	they see, they know (= they are witnesses)
ku atëm ja ncostumbre	that us, our costumbre (custom)
nka'yïkkutïkëyïntï	we do not forget it

In the Mixe language, in some contexts, the expression 'we sit, we stand' (*tsen tan*) can be translated as 'how we live'. In a shorter form, the expression *ja tsïnää'yïn*, literally 'our way of seating', signifies 'our tradition', which is also mentioned in this fragment, with the Spanish substantive *ja ncostumbre* (our *costumbre*, our custom). The claim of not forgetting the *costumbre* means that the representatives of the village, and more generally, all the members of the community, give high value to the public event of the transmission of power staffs and to the ritual journeys organized before this public event. Under the supervision of the mayor (*alcalde*), the members of the municipal team perform poultry sacrifices in the town hall and at the top of Zempoaltepetl. The aim of these ritual activities is to ask non-human entities such as 'He Who Makes Being Alive' or 'the Earth' to help produce vital processes and to resolve conflicts in the community. With the valorization of a way of life, it is therefore the continual reiteration of an alliance with non-human agents which is at stake. This is why, when they utter ritual discourses during the public ceremony, the participants repeatedly declare that they are following the example of the Ancients and, at the same time, that they are setting an example for the new generations:

meets pujx käjp	you, inhabitants of the village
xäm x'ejxtï xnïjäwïtï	now, you see, you know
sääj nakyë'tëkïyï ëëts	how we have transmitted between ourselves (= the incoming and outgoing teams)
ja nkutujk uk ja ejxpajt	our staff and our flag
sääj ja majää'tyëjk	in the same manner the Ancients
tëëj tyïktsoo'ntä'äktï	have begun to do it
sääj ja majää'tyëjk	in the same manner the Ancients
tëëj xtuk'ijyxyïm	have shown us
xtuknïjää'wïntï ...	have taught us ...
ku yä'ät ja uu'nk ku yä'ät ja unä'äjk	so that the children, the sons (= the new generations)
ntukpa'ijyxyïntï	can be taught by us how to do it

Among the Mixe, each new generation is conceived as a group that 'continues to go up', that is to say, passes on traditions to those who follow in their footsteps and will continue, later on, to act in accordance with the model they have had before them. As evidenced by obedience to the word of ritual specialists and to tradition, the value of ritual sequences is that they repeat actions that are similar to those performed by ancestors. That is why the participants in the ceremony declare that they act 'as the grandfathers and grandmothers began to act, as it has come, as it has gone up (= following the tradition)': *säyam yä'ät ja tety'amëj ja täk'amëj tëëj tyïktsoo'ntä'äktï ku yä'ät jatë'n myiny ku yä'ät jatë'n piety*.

In these circumstances, let us bear in mind that these rules of socialization extend far beyond the sphere of humanity and involve non-human partners with whom bonds are established through ritual journeys and poultry sacrifices (chickens, turkeys). I would now like to demonstrate that these journeys extend and refine a nostalgic logic of selecting fragments of existence that valorize both relationships to the living and social relationships, which involve non-human entities such as 'the Earth' or 'He Who Makes Being Alive'.

The ritual journeys organized by the inhabitants of Tlahuitoltepec, whether in the central village or in the hamlets, involve various stages that I have thoroughly analysed elsewhere (Pitrou 2016a): prayers in the village church, poultry sacrifices, and shared meals in domestic spaces, or in places where power is exercised, such as the town hall, and at the top of the mountain. The translation of ritual discourses shows that this chain of actions aims to ask for favours from entities of nature, and to invite them to come and share a meal to thank them for making the effort to support humans in their activities (agricultural, therapeutic or politico-judicial). This collaboration abides by rules similar to those that organize human relations, such as the exchange of services, hospitality and commensality. The precautions surrounding the ascent to the place of sacrifice are thought of, by analogy, as similar to those that accompany asking favours of any inhabitant of the village. Symmetrically, during the meals served at the end of the journey, the prayers indicate that the entities of nature are invited to have a seat next to the guests and to enter the circle of commensality. The food offered and the drinks poured in libation materially compensate the effort made by these non-human agents who are deemed to exert *tunk*, as any villager does. But they should also be interpreted as sequences taking place within a system of exchanges of services and collaboration.

Therefore, the intention behind the organization of these ritual processes is to solicit a specific *tunk* from nature's entities: to grow corn, to help resolve conflicts, to cause children to develop. Starting from a relatively fixed pragmatic dynamic (setting out to ask for a service and offering a meal as a reward), the ritual journey contains sequences during which participants specify the services expected through the prayers formulated or the composition of the ceremonial deposits accompanying the sacrifices of poultry. When the *kuntunkti* ('those who work for the inhabitants and represent them', or in other words the representatives of the village) make sacrifices in the town hall, they ask 'He Who Makes Being Alive' to become a leader in the hierarchy of the municipal team and to send ideas to the mayor and the judge so that they may resolve conflicts. During agricultural rites, the distribution of handfuls of corn flour on ritual tables, which function as miniaturized fields, establishes a regime of co-activity between humans and non-humans: while farmers sow the grains uniformly in the *milpa*, they urge 'He Who Makes Being Alive' to distribute the rainwater necessary for plants to grow (Pitrou 2016b).

These rituals are highly valued moments for all the inhabitants of the municipality, whether they reside in the central village or in the hamlets. I observed that these ritual ensembles are imbued with an ecological nostalgia related to the systems of relationships that are established with living beings as well as with the entities who are deemed to sustain life. Above all, these moments of collective activity celebrate the cardinal values of community life: exchange, commensality and working together. We could therefore assume that these journeys preserve the quintessence of living techniques (from agriculture and livestock to cooking) and the rules that are established to structure a form of life. For a short period of time, the participants experience the pleasure of making a shared effort (such as walking to the top of the mountain and preparing offerings and meals) and the satisfaction entailed by sharing its fruits during a meal. Episodic trips to hamlets offer an occasion to approach a refined ideal that families seek to preserve without having to endure the suffering of their past existences. With rites, actual engagement with the complications inherent to traditional lifestyles is even less important. Only the privileged moments of collective existence seem to be retained, staged and idealized. For example, the *machucado* (the meal eaten before famine periods, which I discussed above) is shared at the end of all ritual journeys. Thus, what initially symbolized a period of deprivation and suffering is transformed into a moment of pleasure associated with the sharing of food.

Consequently, there exists a kind of disconnection between ritual sequences and references to the real activities and conditions that originally determined ritual morphology. Families share famine meals without really suffering hunger, just as ceremonial deposits depict the distribution of equal amounts of materials, mimicking sowers' actions, even when individuals have stopped cultivating their fields. This discrepancy is sometimes expressed explicitly in certain prayers, as I realized during a birth rite I attended in 2007. Traditionally, after the birth of a child, the parturient and the new-born child take a steam bath called *temazcal* in Spanish, every day for twenty days, to fortify their bodies, to make them *mëjk*. At the end of one such period, a ritual journey was organized to ask 'He Who Makes Being Alive' to help the child grow, develop intellectually and ensure that his or her bodily shell would strengthen (Pitrou 2017). Nowadays, as childbirth most often takes place in the clinic, this practice has disappeared almost entirely. Nevertheless, families continue to make sacrifices at the top of the mountain in front of small corn paste figurines placed near a miniature *temazcal* in order to obtain the help of non-human entities. A fragment of a prayer uttered by the two grandfathers of a new-born indicates that families are aware of the tension linked to asking for a service without participating in a collective *tunk*, thus breaking with the regime of co-activity. They declare: 'we have not done the number of sessions of ritual baths … Please, you, forgive' (*winë'n ëts nkayïkpu'uy nkayïkka'apyxy yä'ät ëëts ja ntsejxk' u'nk … mejts maa'kx*).

Hence, the evolution of conditions of life accentuates the disjunction between ritual morphology and the actual techniques used to act on vital processes, whether they emerge in the human body or in corn fields. To a certain extent, then, these ritual journeys can be interpreted as nostalgic attachment to an ecological and sociological system of relations established either between humans or between humans and non-humans present in the environment. However, it would be inaccurate to consider that these ritual practices are mere relics of a past social structure. Ritual journeys among the Mixe highlight the value of a traditional form of collaboration with non-human entities, but they possess enough plasticity to be used to elaborate new forms of collaboration. We can infer an ecological, even 'cosmo-biopolitical' (Pitrou 2015) nostalgia from attachment to these traditions, that is, a desire to continue to maintain strong bonds with non-human entities present in the environment.

Ritual Journeys as a Project

As Durkheim noted in his *Formes élémentaires de la vie religieuse* (1912), ritual activity is characterized by versatility and relative plasticity: the same rite can be mobilized for various purposes, while distinct rites can achieve the same objective. It is therefore not surprising that poultry sacrifices, once used mainly in agricultural contexts, are also a means of ensuring success at university, safe aircraft travel or the profitability of a commercial enterprise. For the topic at hand, it is remarkable that this ritual plasticity, the ability of rituals to evolve and adapt, explains the continued use of them by both village and hamlet inhabitants. Even if ritual journeys among the Mixe no longer correspond, strictly speaking, to actual situations of collaboration between humans and non-humans, their organization expresses the willingness to keep such a system of relationships alive. They are therefore nostalgic manifestations that value a way of living together, appearing even in situations where participants are not engaged in techniques of living, whether it is to feed themselves or to raise a child. In the face of the profound changes in techniques for obtaining means of subsistence, rites manifest an ecological nostalgia that maintains the presence of links to living beings and to the entities that sustain life.

The ability of rituals to be detached from their primary referent can therefore be thought of as manifesting an ecological nostalgia that endeavours to preserve the values of the past while also embracing social change. This leads to a better understanding of nostalgia, which cannot be reduced to simply preserving a bygone past. The connection between the stability of ritual morphology and the variation in requests formulated during prayers, which today may focus on travelling by aircraft or graduating from university, points to the effectiveness of nostalgia in dealing with value discrepancies. As previous ethnographies have shown, nostalgia is often used as a way of negotiating contemporary changes in ways of life. Ritual journeys organized in the Mixe highlands can be considered abstract forms that continue to highlight rules the group must continue to value (reciprocity, mutual aid and hospitality) even if living conditions have radically changed. This also applies to the *Día de Muertos* (Feast of the Dead), which embodies these same values (Pitrou 2014) and is also the object of strong nostalgic promotion, both in Amerindian communities and in the major cities of the Republic of Mexico. In both cases, rites collectively emphasize the importance of respecting core social rules, even when faced with beings whose existence is uncertain: the dead or entities of nature. With these 'metapersons' (Sahlins 2017), a specific precaution regarding the uncertainty surrounding the power to make beings alive or to cause diseases and death is expressed. From this standpoint, ritual journeys enact both nostalgic attachments to a traditional ecological system of relations and a strategy to affirm the identity of a community engaged in a process of modernization without losing its fundamental values.

Perig Pitrou is an anthropologist and senior researcher in the CNRS. He leads the team Anthropology of Life in the Laboratoire d'Anthropologie Sociale, Collège de France / Université Paris Sciences et Lettres. He is the author of *Le Chemin et le champ: Parcours rituel et sacrifice chez les Mixe de Oaxaca (Mexique)* and the co-editor of the book *La noción de vida en Mesoamérica* (CEMCA-UNAM, 2011). In the framework of several interdisciplinary programmes, he has published ten collective books and special issues, and published more than thirty papers in the field of the Anthropology of Life.

Note

1. Strictly speaking, a *rancho* is a family farm in the countryside, but the word is also used to refer to small hamlets made up of a few dozen farmhouses, which is why I have chosen to translate the Spanish word as 'hamlet' here.

References

Angé, O. 2015. 'Le Goût d'autrefois: Pain au levain et attachements nostalgiques dans la société contemporaine', *Terrain* 65: 34–51.

Angé, O. and D. Berliner. 2015. 'Pourquoi la nostalgie?', *Terrain* 65: 4–11.

Descola, P. 1994. *In the Society of Nature: A Native Ecology in Amazonia*. Cambridge: Cambridge University Press.

———. 2013. *Beyond Nature and Culture*. Chicago: Chicago University Press.

Durkheim, E. 1912. *Les Formes élémentaires de la vie religieuse: le système totémique en Australie*. Paris: Presses Universitaires de France.

Helmreich, S. 2009. *Alien Ocean: Anthropological Voyages in Microbial Seas*. Berkeley, CA: University of California Press.

Leroi-Gourhan, A. 1970. *Le Geste et la parole*. Paris: Albin Michel.

Mauss, M. 2013 [1934]. 'Les techniques du corps', in *Sociologie et anthropologie*. Paris: Presses Universitaires de France, pp. 363–86.

Monaghan, J. 1995. *The Covenants with Earth and Rain: Exchange, Sacrifice, and Revelation in Mixtec Sociality*. Norman: University of Oklahoma Press.

Pitrou, P. 2014. 'Nourrir les morts ou "Celui qui fait vivre" , les différents régimes de commensalité rituelle chez les Mixe (Oaxaca, Mexique)', *Journal de la société des américanistes* 100: 45–71.

———. 2015. 'Life as a Process of Making in the Mixe Highlands (Oaxaca, Mexico): Towards a "General Pragmatics" of Life', *Journal of the Royal Anthropological Institute* 21(1): 86–105.

———. 2016a. *Le Chemin et le champ: Parcours rituel et sacrifice chez les Mixe de Oaxaca, Mexique*. Nanterre: Société d'ethnologie.

———. 2016b. 'Co-activity in Mesoamerica and in the Andes', *Journal of Anthropological Research* 72(4): 465–82.

———. 2017. 'Life Form and Form of Life Within an Agentive Configuration: A Birth Ritual Among the Mixe of Oaxaca, Mexico', *Current Anthropology* 58(7): 360–80.

Sahlins, M. 2017. 'The Original Political Society', *Hau: Journal of Ethnographic Theory* 7(2): 91–128.

Tresch, J. 2007. 'Technological World-Pictures: Cosmic Things and Cosmograms', *Isis* 98(1): 84–99.

CHAPTER 7

Peaceful Countryside

Ecologies of Longing and the Temporality of Flux in Contemporary Mongolia

Richard D.G. Irvine

'May I Always Remember'

In their 2012 recording *Amgalan huduu* ('Peaceful Countryside'), the rappers Panz and Gee evoke a bucolic scene of the Mongolian forest steppe: the grass waving in the breeze, the gentle touch of rain, the sounds of the herds grazing on the hills. They describe the evening sounds of the horsehead fiddle and of the cuckoo, the taste of fresh yoghurt and the smell of burning dung. Gee ends the rap:

> Morning star, clouds clearing, evening frost
> May I always remember the feel of the wind
> Though I am far away from my homeland where the cattle breed
> In my heart I am still a Mongolian man.

What is evoked here? The words are a rich sensory recollection of a particular landscape, and of how the Mongolian countryside acts upon the body situated within it. But crucially, it becomes clear that it is a recollection from a situation 'far away', outside of that landscape, a calling to mind of what it feels like to be there, so as not to forget. And with this calling to mind of place, we also see the evocation of an ideal, a particular mode of interacting with that landscape: herding as a way of life. Here is the exemplary centre of Mongolian identity: what must be remembered in order to remain a Mongolian. The rapping done, we hear the galloping hooves of horses over the backing track.

In this chapter I want to explore the particular temporality of such longing for the 'peaceful countryside' in contemporary Mongolia. I start this chapter with rap, and I will return to it – albeit by a circuitous route – but I first set out with this example precisely because it provides an excellent instance, I would argue, of what could be termed the 'fabric of nostalgia' (Angé and Berliner 2014: 8). Here we see the physicality and materiality of the landscape as a locus of desire for a particular form of life, one which is perceived to be in danger of being left behind by the vector of history, yet retains its potency for precisely this reason. I set out with this example in particular for two reasons. The first is that its depiction of an idealized peaceful countryside is characteristic of Mongolian pop music, a key theme in which is the depiction of the nomadic herding lifestyle and praise for the environment which supports it. Music DVDs played on buses and taxis frequently include exactly these kinds of scenes: horse riding, livestock herding, domestic life around the hearth inside the nomadic *ger* (Mongolian nomadic dwelling). Rap, an apparently 'urban' genre, certainly does not exclude such imagery (Irvine 2018). But secondly, what is interesting is the sense of desire for the countryside which is central to Mongolian identity even in the hearts of those who do not inhabit it. The rap above reflects the economic and environmental transitions that have shaped Mongolia's recent history.

The shift away from communism towards privatized forms of ownership has been dramatic, a process which prompts Humphrey and Sneath (1999) to ask whether we have seen 'the end of Nomadism'. Changes in land use, and reduction in mobility in particular, have been associated with severe pasture degradation (Sneath 1998; Sternberg 2008) and consequently, the loss of herds. This has been a factor accelerating urbanization: the population of the capital has doubled since 1989, with many new arrivals living in semi-permanent nomadic dwellings on the edge of the city (Byambadorj et al. 2011). In addition, the emergence of mining as Mongolia's largest economic sector (see Bulag 2009; Jackson 2015) has brought economic growth at a national level, while at the same time generating widespread concern not only about the ecological impacts of such activity, but also of the loss of resources to the interests of other nations. This contributes to a 'populist' narrative of mining not only as harm to the land, but as harm to the nation. The central importance of the countryside, and of the herding lifestyle associated with the countryside, plays out against the background of a changing Mongolian economy and ecology in which the value and character of the countryside is being reshaped by mining, and the population is increasingly distanced from that countryside – yet their identity remains intimately connected with it.

The idealized 'peaceful countryside' as the site of 'authentic' life which is central to national identity even as (or perhaps especially as) the percentage of the population living in the capital city increases raises a particular question: what does it mean to recall a landscape that you have not directly known? What kind of thinking is made possible by the evocation of a (nostalgic?) ideal beyond experience, and how should we account for this? Casey (1993: 37) remarks that nostalgia 'is not merely a regret for lost times; it is also a pining for lost places'. Along these lines, Albrecht (2005) has coined the term 'Solastalgia' as a way of describing the sense of dislocation people feel in the face of the sheer scale of environmental transformation. The sense of the peaceful countryside as a lost place is certainly an important theme to trace in contemporary Mongolia given the sheer scale of economic change and, in particular, the extent of urban development and centralization. Yet at the same time, an emphasis on loss can create a misleading impression of the inevitability and completeness of the break with the past, the sense that nostalgia can do nothing other than provide psychological respite from an unassailable machinery of progress. This sense of clear directionality in movement through time seems particularly ill-fitting with Mongolia's 'ever-deepening climate of pervasive precarity and uncertainty' (Plueckhahn and Bumochir 2018: 343), a context where promised futures do not arrive (Pedersen 2017).

In a different post-socialist context (that of East Germany), Boyer (2006: 362) proposes using nostalgia as a 'lens through which to examine the problem of the future'. In a situation where, in the face of uncertainty, people are consciously addressing the politics of what kind of society they might become, nostalgia becomes as much about a desire for the future as it is about longing for a lost time. 'Pastness' becomes a medium through which people can think critically about where they are going.

What this chapter explores then is the role of nostalgia as a means of navigating temporality, a mode of expression which does the work of revealing relationships between past, present and future (as per Angé and Berliner 2014: 11). What I am interested in are the ways in which the evocation of an idealized 'peaceful countryside' enables people to critically reflect upon the experience of rapid environmental change. Such images provide a conceptual framework within which it is possible to recognize and comment upon environmental flux.

The central focus of this chapter will be a particular series of encounters: between researchers, children and their landscape, and a writer. Collaborative fieldwork with thirty-nine children in the fourth and fifth grades at the primary school (between ages nine and eleven) in Mungunmorit *sum*, a district which covers over 3,500 square kilometres within Tuv Aimag,[1] offered children the opportunity to share and explore their surroundings, leading the researchers on walks through the landscape. The reflections these walks generated on the countryside within which the children lived, and with which they were connected, led into writing workshops with the poet Mend-Ooyo Gombojav, a writer who had a particular desire to revisit this region. I move between the children's reflections as they moved through the landscape, Mend-Ooyo's own literary evocation of the Mongolian countryside, and the children's written work generated in the writing workshop with Mend-Ooyo. This series of encounters provides us with a number of routes through which we trace not only how the countryside generates a sense of place, but also the way in which this sense of place navigates time.

Moving in the Presence of the Past

The methodological decision to make walking the starting point of the research provided a space in which children were able to articulate experiences, memories and perceptions of change within their dwelling places.[2] This focus on the sensing of place follows Basso (1996) and his phenomenologically inspired emphasis on 'Place-based thoughts'. Taking walking to be a 'relational and textural activity' (Vergunst 2008: 120), we walked, ran and climbed as a group, led along routes that the children had planned out, taking in sites of importance that they themselves had chosen amongst themselves as meaningful in their lives. This offered a rich opportunity for in situ reflection and conversation about the children's relationships with the land through which we were moving.

The route chosen covered about four and a half miles, moving out of the built-up *sum* centre where the school is located and over the hills, with the children revisiting and sharing places that were quite familiar to them. No sooner had we returned than the children insisted they would like to go walking again. Though weather conditions were wet and cold, the children had the energy to run around, explaining the history and myths of the locations, as well as their own direct experience of these places (and as we shall see later in the chapter, their perceptions of how they might be changing).

The children led the way first up a hill from which we could see the whole of the *sum* centre, and the *huduu* (countryside) spreading out around it. This was a particularly well-known site for the children, especially those who lived in the dormitories,[3] who said that they would frequently come up here together to play. Some of the traces of this play could be seen very clearly: the children had used stones to mark out 'play houses'

Figure 7.1. Children at Mungunmorit school lead the way to a vantage point within the landscape, September 2015. Photograph by the author.

(*togloomiin ger*), or more specifically, setting out the round outline of a *ger*, taking care to ensure that the entrance (that is, the gap in the stones) was oriented to the south in the correct way. The *ger* was then furnished with stones and sticks in a manner that mimics the layout of these homes, with a 'stove' at the centre, and an altar in the place of honour in the north.

This hill was the location of a *suvarga* (stupa) erected in 2007 after the death of a regionally well-known race horse trainer, who was said to have raised his children very well. This gave the children an opportunity to share their enthusiasm for horse riding, explaining that several of them had ridden horses in the race at *naadam*, the annual national festival of sports. Near the stupa was an *ovoo* (cairn), visible as a heap of rocks raised at a particular point within the landscape (such as, in this case, at the summit where the hill meets the sky), as a place of recognition and offering to the spirits within the landscape, or 'lords of the land' (*gazryn ezed*; for a discussion of the significance of *ovoos* see Chuluu and Stuart 1995 as well as Lindskog 2016). Here each of the children circumambulated the *ovoo*, tossing stones onto it to build it up in the manner they have learned from family.

Considered as a whole, what this location revealed was a site of play, but one which conveyed a familiarity and engagement with embodiments of mobile pastoralism as an ideal of how to be in the land: the *ger*, horse riding, and the recognition of the sacred landscape by way of the *ovoo*. Evans and Humphrey (2003: 208) write of *ovoo*s as a 'repository of ancestral values'. They are 'symbolic constructions of timelessness' (2003: 195), yet constituted and reconstituted within history, 'in and out of time'. The point I wish to draw from their argument and apply more widely is the potency of such expressions of transcendent timelessness that nevertheless emerge in relation to present-day historical consciousness. This can be seen more generally in the children's relationship with their environment, as condensed in this first location: we see knowledge of enduring ideals that can be placed in dynamic tension with change in the present. This dynamic tension is at the heart of the ecology of longing that I am setting out in this chapter, and which we will later see in the children's own narratives.

As we continued to move across the landscape, the children indicated important sites in the hills around and were at pains to express their significance. *Meem had* (breast rock), a natural feature whose shape communicated a particular symbolism, which the boys in particular felt obliged to explain to me with a certain urgency, was well-known as an *eeltei gazar* (auspicious place) for mothers to visit. Mungunmorit hill was also pointed out by the children, recognized as the site of the legend which gave the *sum* its name:

> One day, a man went out hunting and killed a deer. After this, he and his family suffered misfortune and sickness. He went to a monk for advice, who told him that the deer he had killed was the embodiment of the spirit of the land. The monk told him to gather all the silver he could find and to melt it down to make a horse of silver, which was to be placed as an offering of reparation at the location where the deer had been killed. Having done this, the man and his family regained their health. From that point on the hill was known as Mungunmorit [which literally means 'at the silver horse'].

They also ran to sit under the *gants mod* (lone tree), which had been honoured with prayer scarves and at which they spoke of gathering to greet the rising sun at the *tsagaan sar* (lunar new year). Here again, children offered the story associated with this point in the landscape, as learned from parents and grandparents:

> Once there was a beautiful girl. She was in love with a poor herder, but her family would not let her marry him. They told her: 'we have arranged for you to be married to a wealthy man with a large herd'. So she ran away, and came to the place of the lone tree. The lone tree is where she wept and where she died.

Figure 7.2. The *gants mod* (lone tree) in Mungunmorit *sum*, September 2015. Photograph by the author.

A tree that stands alone is sometimes said to have a powerful spirit that causes the tree to flourish where others have not (Humphrey 1995). Yet it was observed that the tree was not in good health, a point which we will return to later.

What was clear was that a knowledge of the distinctive local features was a strong part of the children's sense of identity and pride in the surrounding landscape, and that they felt it was important to know the stories and their cultural resonances. These accounts were vivid even when the children had not been to a particular place themselves. This became particularly clear in the significance given to Burkhan Khaldun, a sacred mountain on the borders of the *sum*, which in fact only one of the boys in the school had visited,[4] but was given particular honour as a site associated with the life of Chinggis Khan (c.1162–1227), builder of the Mongol empire, who is understood to have retreated here and submitted to the mountain, honouring it as a divine entity before his military campaign to unify the Mongolian people. Given the lack of clear knowledge of Chinggis' birthplace or place of burial, Burkhan Khaldun and its environs are often reputed as a possible site of both.

Here we see especially clearly the way in which cosmological knowledge of the landscape and its significance is entangled with particular notions of Mongolian national heritage (Sneath 2014): to know and honour the land is to know one's place in the nation, an association which has become particularly acute in the revival of state practices honouring mountains and other landscape features in the post-socialist period. Yet the children's sense of historical consciousness also incorporated the socialist period and its initiation, as became clear when they led us to a site where the revolutionary hero Sukhbaatar and his army had stayed and fought during the Mongolian Revolution of 1921. What is of interest here is the children's relationship with the past as immanent in the land around them. Maurice Bloch (1992) describes two ways of 'being in history': history as a transcendent force, and history as an ongoing flow of events. The children's sharing of the landscape here shows it to be precisely a source of enduring values and presences, yet this is not to disconnect it from the flow of time and of historical events. Rather, it grounds this flow.

Back in the school, in conversation with the teachers, we decided to further explore the children's sense of place by means of a writing workshop which would give the children further opportunity to express the narratives they had shared on the walk. We were joined for this workshop by the writer Mend-Ooyo Gombojav, a poet and novelist with whom I had been collaborating, and whose own writing explores legends and stories of the landscape from his place of birth, and who was therefore particularly keen to show the children how literary writing could emerge from such local stories. He had a particular desire to make the trip to Mungunmorit,[5] as it was a place he associated with the memory of a close friend, the late poet Bat-Ochirin Sundu, who had been a fellow member of the secret literary group Gal (which means 'fire') during the late socialist era, a group whose work found particular resonance in the rediscovery of national heritage following the democratic revolution of 1990. Working with young students in Mungunmorit, he expressed a desire to hear the voices of the 'native hearth' of his friend.

In the workshop, children not only recalled received stories heard from parents and grandparents (such as the legend of the *gants mod* and of the Silver Horse), but also expressed their own narrative imagination about the land around them through *magtaalin shuleg*, the poetry of praise. This is from one eleven-year old boy's poem, 'Beloved Mungunmorit' (*Mungumorit hairhan*):

> The land of my birth
> My beloved Mungunmorit
> Eternal land
> Let's sing praise, praise

Hill, water, plants, the spreading flowers
To our vast beautiful land
To where the herds of sheep call
All my people are going joyfully

And from the poem of a girl in the same class, simply titled 'Homeland' (*Nutag*):

With the vast beautiful sky
With the trees reaching high
With the beautiful animals
With the dawn cuckoo
Let's praise our beautiful homeland

What is striking about these poems is the way in which knowledge of the landscape they know, through play, participation in the work of their herding families, and everyday involvement, opens out into a landscape of desire and longing. This is praise for a land not just as it is, but as it should be. The significance of this is clear through the repeated use of the term *nutag* (homeland) by the children. As Sneath (2010) has argued, the development of Mongolian national identity in the twentieth century placed a growing emphasis on the *nutag*, or 'homeland', in which people have their roots, as a constituent feature of the nation-state. This sense of locally anchored belonging therefore plays an important role in the imagination of the national community. To praise the beauty of one's *nutag* is therefore not only to express attachment to a locality, but to a national ideal.

Writing with Longing

In order to explore further the significance of *nutag*, at this point I turn directly to the work of Mend-Ooyo Gombojav (b. 1952), the writer who met with the children for their workshop, a poet whose praise for the Mongolian countryside resonates with the narratives shared above. He is a nationally honoured writer and calligrapher, whose life story reflects the pull of the two magnetic poles of city and countryside life in contemporary Mongolia. Born into a herding family, he was drawn towards Ulaanbaatar, where he studied and developed as a poet. Nevertheless, he writes with longing for the countryside, identifying himself with nomadic life on the steppe, which he treats as the embodiment of the true Mongolian national ideal. (See Simon Wickham-Smith 2013 for a comprehensive account of Mend-Ooyo's life, work and historic context. Wickham-Smith has also translated some of Mend-Ooyo's best-known work into English.)

The work for which Mend-Ooyo is best known is the 1993 poetic novel *Altan Ovoo* (Golden Hill),[6] a meditative reflection on the geography of his native Dariganga, in Sükhbaatar Aimag, Eastern Mongolia. The title refers to a sacred mountain and popular site of pilgrimage, the existence of which is portrayed not just as a backdrop for life, but as an intimate presence within it. At the outset, Mend-Ooyo tells us: 'A stone from Altan Ovoo stood in the place of honour to the north of the ger' (2007: 8). This is the place in the home where guests, or the oldest people present, would be seated as a mark of respect. From the start, then, we are introduced to Altan Ovoo's geology as a social being: spoken to, called upon and inter-acted with as an honoured person. Indeed, elsewhere in the book Altan Ovoo is called upon specifically as a lord of the land.

The rock in the *ger* not only stands for but also contains within itself a greater whole. It is interacted with not just as part of, but as Altan Ovoo. In the same way, Altan Ovoo is seen not just as a part, but as a wider world itself: 'The love of my homeland [*nutag*] and of my motherland [*eh oron*] and of the world itself shone forth from this little stone' (2007: 86). As explained above, it is through a locally anchored sense of belonging to the *nutag* that a wider sense of national belonging emerges. Mend-Ooyo's treatment of the rock reflects this, but takes it to yet another level: 'Altan Ovoo is the world on a reduced scale' (2007: 8). It is thus the whole world taking the place of the guest of honour in his childhood *ger*. He recalls his father telling him: 'my son, please think about Altan Ovoo. Every hill and body of water is contained within it' (2007: 84).

Mend-Ooyo describes vividly the morning his father saddled the horses and took him to Altan Ovoo for the first time, his encounter with it in body and spirit. The encounter with the hill is therefore rooted in the time of his own autobiography. Yet by rooting autobiographical time in the landscape, his own encounter with Altan Ovoo is understood and given meaning through other stories through time. 'Will the flame of my ancestors' wisdom not illuminate us as we discuss the landscape?' (2007: 8), he asks; a question which calls to mind Keith Basso (1996) and his ethnographic account of how, for the Apache he moves with, wisdom sits in places, and how they interweave life histories and stories handed down the generations with current concerns over the course of the journey. Mend-Ooyo writes of Altan Ovoo: 'the thoughts of people have at all times been absorbed into the mountains and water and stones' (2007: 85). And thus the road to the hill which he travelled with his father is a shared road: 'This road is the artery of eternal time which joins me with the universe, tens of thousands of feet are moving, striking out under the pulsing moments of history' (2007: 21).

What is striking here is the manner in which time is nested, and the role topography plays in this. Mend-Ooyo's own life history is grounded and given significance through the history of the *nutag*, recognized in and recalled through the landscape: to speak of the encounter with Altan Ovoo is to speak of one's own autobiography, but also to locate it within the story of one's family, one's ancestry, and through this, of the Mongolian people. These are themselves nested in the timespan of the geological beings upon which we are dependent. Yet in spite of the magnitude of geological time, human life finds a home in the possibility of an intimate relationship with the temporality of the landscape.

This cross-hatching of biographical and deep time (see Irvine 2014) is one way in which Mend-Ooyo's work navigates temporality. Yet, to return to a theme raised earlier, we also see in his work a desire to place the flow of history in dynamic tension with the 'timelessness' of life on the steppe. It is here that his nostalgic register becomes most apparent, not simply as a longing for the past, but as a means of critiquing the present and questioning the kind of future Mongolians might seek.

A year before our workshop with Mungonmorit school, Mend-Ooyo had published a collection of his writing, *The Time When River Water Runs Clear* (*Gol us tungalagshih tsag*). The collection took its title from a poem of 1995, included in the collection (Mend-Ooyo 2015: 150–51). The poem describes the River Tuul at autumn, when 'there are birds in every branch of the willow on the riverbank/ Light between its leaves', a time of year when the poet might return to drink from the clear-running river and so renew himself. Yet in the current historic moment, the poem's desire for a time when river water runs clear takes on an additional resonance, given the impact of massive development in the capital city through which the Tuul runs, and the effect of mining activity on the river's water quality (Stubblefield et al. 2005). This desire is reflected in the ecological sensitivity of much of the writing collected within the book.

This is perhaps clearest in the series of *Letters from the Wild Mongolian Steppe* (*Mongolin heer talaas bichsen zahidluud*) in which the ideal of mobile pastoralism is juxtaposed with contemporary economic development in Mongolia and its associated ecological degradation. 'Below the earth on this broad wild steppe there is gold and coal and uranium and oil. From deep in the earth they extract these fine riches and build towns, and they refer to the life which the nomadic herders live, and which they call "backward", as being like something from a storybook' (Mend-Ooyo 2015: 333). He then cuts from this scene of rapid and intensive economic development to the stillness of the night in the steppe, but not of a storybook past, but of an expression of an ideal in the present: 'right now it's midnight…

Figure 7.3. G. Mend-Ooyo running a creative writing workshop in Mungunmorit school, March 2016. Photograph by the author.

the dungfires are blazing and we are joined with the world by computer, powered by an electric generator charged by the sun. This original power supply of the sun and the wind will never be exhausted' (2015: 334).

Here the nomad on the steppe is not placed outside the flow of time, but rather is portrayed as a symbol of stability calling 'progress' into question: 'war brings disaster, the Earth shakes, tall buildings collapse, the oceans pulse with storms… and meanwhile the nomads move on, transporting their gers on their camels. For thousands and thousands of years, small nomadic gers have moved through windstorms and floods and freezing cold and fierce heat' (2015: 332). On the one hand, we might see in this evocation of life on the wild steppe a 'solastalgia' (Albrecht 2005), a longing for a landscape and its associated way of life that is being swept aside by major social and environmental transformation. Yet this would be to overlook the political significance of such 'nostalgic' appeals to scenes that call developments in the present into question. Indeed, as we noted above, in the context of post-socialism, such a revival is itself at the heart of national identity:

By plundering the world, humans are also plundering themselves, and by
waging war against the earth, humans are aggressively harming themselves.
During the socialist period, the wisdom of the early Mongols was expunged
from the national consciousness, but at the present time the shamanic spirits
which have a deep connection with nature… are awakening and returning
to give advice to the human world. This advice is of particular importance.
(Mend-Ooyo 2015: 345)

He ends these letters by sharing the words of *Delhii Eej* (Mother Earth),
a well-known pop song whose lyrics he wrote in 1980, under the existential shadow of the cold war and nuclear threat, explaining that its refrain
finds new urgency and resonance in the face of the present existential
threat of greed (*shunal*):

From your womb all humans were born
Your children have held you in their hearts
I love you Mother Earth

After the children had written and shared their work at the workshop in
Mungunmorit school, Mend-Ooyo chose to end the session by playing a
recording of this song while the children sang along. The work of lyrical
reflection upon the beauty of the *nutag* was linked to the urgent moral
imperative of ecological care.

Witnessing Change

At this point I want to return once more to the Mungunmorit children's
sense of place, reflecting on their relationship with the temporality of the
landscape, focusing now on the striking time depth of their experience. As
touched upon above, the children's knowledge of their landscape encom-
passed multiple registers of time. Memories of personal experiences and
play with friends sat in relation to activities with parents and grandparents
that marked out particular places as being closely associated with family
histories. These in turn were located in relation to shared representations
of the deeper temporality of the environment. In addition to the sense of
the historic landscape associated with the making of the Mongolian nation
as described above, there was an attentiveness to the legends associated
with particular geographical features, which the children placed in an
unspecified distant past.

Hastrup (1992: 115) uses the term 'uchronia' (coined as a temporal
equivalent to the spatial term 'utopia') to explain how in early modern
Iceland an unchanging mythical past of the sagas, the uchronia, existed
alongside the continuous history of a changing society: '"History" itself
was split in two: an externally induced and uncontrolled succession of

changes and an internally emphasized repetition of traditional values'. While in many respects this sense of an enduring uchronia is in clear evidence in narrations of the idealized Mongolian countryside, what I want to emphasize is the dynamic interaction between these apparently distinct 'ways of being in history' (Bloch 1992). Crucially, the Mungunmorit children's sense of the time-depth of the landscape did not place the enduring landscape outside the flow of ongoing history, but enabled a narration of those environments as changing. Their sense of place was open to a recognition of flux.

So along the route of our walk, the children noted the drying out of grass along the way, commenting that they believed the grass was no longer as green as it had been in past years. Such a recollection not only recalled the children's own direct experience of seasonal change year after year, but reached further into a past troubled by developments in the present. Similarly, children's accounts of the seasonality of fruit picking, which featured as a particularly important activity with family and with friends, led to a reflection on how seasons themselves were changing in character. They remarked on the early arrival of fruit, and their difficulties finding wild strawberries in particular, seeing this as an indication of global warming (*delhiin dulaaral*).

At the *gants mod*, discussion of the drying out of the land arose once again, as it was remarked that the tree did not seem to be in good health compared to previous years. As noted above, a tree which stands alone is said to have a particular spirit: what, then, is indicated when the tree appears to be weakening due to changes in the land around?[7]

The clearest sense of the children's recognition of flux was in their insistent descriptions of rivers drying up. There was a strong sense of the importance of the rivers for peoples' livelihood as well as their being a pleasant place to go and play; the children were therefore keen observers of changes in the river, remarking on seasonal changes as the river froze and thawed, and also remarking on reduced flow during the summer months. Children joined up their own observations with what they had heard from family members about rivers drying up, expressing vicarious memories[8] evoking a time of flowing rivers that the teachers remarked must have been many years before their own birth. The children connected the drying out of the land with a lack of rain, and worried about how livestock would survive. As Marin (2010: 174) has observed, 'the nomadic herders of Mongolia demonstrate a detailed understanding of weather and climate and provide an account of climatic change that integrates multiple indicators', including observations about the frequency, quantity and intensity of rainfall. Such observations are present as part of the child's family life. Significantly, children spoke of this not only as a local problem that they themselves had observed, but also as a problem on the national level, affecting not just their own *sum*, but threatening Mongolia as a whole. Several children referred to this directly as being caused by global warming, attributing their knowledge of climate change to television, as well as to lessons in school.

For the children, there seemed to be a clear sense of the significance of rural lives and of their own locality for a Mongolian national identity. Yet children's sense of their *nutag* was also outward looking. Hence, they were able to articulate their own local observations with what they perceived as national issues: aridification, pasture land degradation and mining. Evoking a sense of the changing landscape under their feet, and a desire for an idealized vision of the countryside as it existed in a past they know vividly, the children had a keen sense that the health of the countryside – their countryside – was diagnostic of the health of the nation, and in this way their close observation of local changes against the backdrop of the temporality of the environment gave them a vantage point to comment on politically salient environmental issues facing Mongolia's future.

In this sense, the expression of desire for an ecological ideal beyond, and yet intimately connected with, one's own experience reveals something about what it means to live within and to know the temporality of a landscape in flux. 'Nostalgic' praise for one's idealized homeland is not simply hankering for a past, but a potent way of speaking about a desired present in the face of major environmental challenges.

Nostalgia and the Desire for a Future

Tacking back and forth between national and local contexts, and between literary representations and the narratives of schoolchildren, my goal in this chapter has been to explore contemporary Mongolian ecologies of longing: the way in which ideals of the 'peaceful countryside' are expressed not only as a yearning for the past, but as an active consideration of how the land should be. I argue that such apparent 'nostalgia' is the grounding which makes it possible to recognize and comment upon environmental flux. This dynamic engagement between the enduring history of the lived landscape and the ongoing experience of change is an arena in which the impact of forces of progress, and thus the way the Mongolian nation is navigating its own history in the present, can be called into question. I therefore also argue that nostalgia is as much a means of grappling with the future as it is a desire to recapture a lost past (see Boyer 2006).

I said I would return to rap, and I want to do so now in order to draw attention to lyrics which contrast sharply with those that featured in the introduction and with the poetry of praise written by the children, but which nevertheless rely productively on the same narrative frame of the idealized (perhaps nostalgically imagined) *nutag*.

> I'm the owner of this land
> Left to me by my parents and ancestors
> At least I didn't lose that to others

These are the first words we hear from the Mongolian rapper Gee in his 2011 video 'Leave Me My Homeland' (*Minii nutgiig nadad üldee*). The sound of the horsehead fiddle rising over the looped bassline comes as no surprise given the frequent incorporation of traditional motifs and musical styles into contemporary Mongolian pop music (Dovchin 2011). Neither is there anything surprising about an urban rapper being filmed out in the countryside; as I have already said, in common with the literary traditions highlighted above, Mongolian rap frequently offers praise to the homeland, and images of life in the Mongolian countryside, often including horse riding and herding animals, are commonplace. In fact, given the ubiquity of such bucolic scenes, it is the kind of countryside that shocks: a future vision of a countryside that is dust (*toos shoroo*).

Delaplace (2014) argues that authenticity is a central concern of Mongolian rap, exploring what it means to be a 'real' Mongol. He suggests that the central question posed by much Mongolian rap is 'how to be Mongolian today', or rather 'what is preventing us from being Mongolian nowadays?' Nationalistic themes are prominent, as is the invocation of national history, and specifically the figure of Chinggis Khan, unifier of the Mongolian people and builder of empire. The countryside as the site of 'authentic' life is central to this identity, and so the glorification of the natural environment is a key theme, as seen in the rap *Amgalan huduu* ('Peaceful Countryside') which I discussed at the outset of this chapter. However, in parallel with this glorification of nature, rappers frequently turn to the condemnation of the moral failure of this generation as custodians of that nature (Irvine 2018).

Returning to Gee's 'Leave Me My Homeland', this sense of how moral failure marks time is explicit: 'I fear that we see the future where Mongolia will be called a desert.' The chorus calls from this imagined future to the ancestors (that is, contemporary Mongolians), urging them: 'don't live only for yourselves'. The damage that is described is harm done to Mongolia's natural history as well as its national history:

> Real wealth isn't what's under you …
> Real wealth comes with the growing plants

Gold, silver, people can't eat money
It seems we don't know that herds eat grass, people eat the herds

What we see, then, is a depiction of slow violence (Nixon 2011), or harm whose full extent is displaced in time. The rap looks back and forward in time by way of genealogy: back to the ancestors (in whose number it includes those alive today) and forward to descendants. But this capacity to see generations through time is dependent on ecology, and the disquiet of a future time of dust is that the destruction of the land's fertility is the destruction of a people's fertility. 'I've seen our offspring traded for money', Gee continues, weaving a thread of descent through Mongolian history, invoking the figure of Chinggis, calling to mind those who fought for the motherland. But this descent can only be traced and sustained in the presence of the fertile land:

Can we live without rivers and streams?
What will our descendants depend on after my time?
The future will curse us

The device of speaking from a future of dust makes starkly visible the presence of the present generation as a mark in geological time, and as a mark which leaves what remains of human time in doubt. 'I'm an unlucky man, I'm a man without destiny [*zayagui*]'.

As we saw above, to know physical geography as *nutag* is to read autobiography, kinship and history into the temporal depth of a living environment (and vice versa). Environmental degradation is a rupture which makes this knowledge in time impossible, leaving the individual stranded in the face of an uninhabitable deep time. Central to the treatment of environmental degradation in these raps is a concern about continuity of descent through time. To quote Gee, 'our fathers never abandoned us/but we have forgotten our own children'. This is what shocks in the image of a future homeland that has become dust – and indeed in the children of Mungunmorit's description of rivers that now run dry. They confront us with a vision of severance.

The video of 'Leave Me My Homeland' shows Mongolians of the future left wandering through a barren geology trying to piece together a history from what they find buried in the dust: a portrait of Chinggis Khan, a sign pointing the way to a mine, a photograph of trees by a lake, a dribble of water in a plastic bottle. In the context of such a potential rupture in time, ecological nostalgia is not simply the depiction of a timeless ideal, but a temporal grounding for the recognition of flux. In this way, it is a powerful tool in this process of piecing together not only a history, but also a desired future in the face of contemporary challenges.

Acknowledgements

My thanks go above all to the children and teachers at Mungunmorit school for their enthusiastic participation in this research. I am also grateful to my collaborator in the field D. Amarbayasgalan, and to Mend-Ooyo Gombojav and Munkhnaran Mugi for their eagerness to come to Mungunmorit to offer the writing workshop. David Sneath and Libby Peachey laid the groundwork that made this research possible, and G. Munkherdene and Gregory Delaplace offered essential advice and assistance. This work was supported by the Arts and Humanities Research Council (AHRC) project grant 'Pathways to understanding the changing climate: time and place in cultural learning about the environment' (AH/K006282/1).

Richard D.G. Irvine is Lecturer in Social Anthropology at the University of St Andrews. In his research across three ethnographic fieldsites – Orkney and East Anglia in the UK, and Tuv aimag in Mongolia – he focuses on moral relationships with the changing landscape and the deep time of geological formation. He is the author of *An Anthropology of Deep Time: Geological Temporality and Social Life* (Cambridge University Press, 2020).

Notes

1. A *sum* is an administrative district within a larger *aimag*, or administrative region.
2. This research was part of a comparative multi-researcher study of children's perceptions of environmental change across several regions, taking broadly the same methodological approach in each location; see Irvine et al. (2019) for a discussion of the overall project and its findings. Work with schools in Mongolia was carried out in collaboration with D. Amarbayasgalan; see Amarbayasgalan and Dashdeleg (2017) for an account of the project's work in Mungunmorit and its context.
3. Due to the large land area that the school serves, and the herding background of many of the children's families, around a third of the children stay in dormitories at the school during term-time because the *sum* centre is too far from where their family is based. For many parents, this is not a desirable situation. As might be expected, the need for children to be at school from the age of six places particular pressures on mobile pastoralist families to live closer to the *sum* centre (Ahearn and Bumochir 2016), sometimes causing the mother to move to the *sum* centre with the children, leaving the father alone to tend to the herds.
4. Many of the children in the class were particularly eager that we should visit Burkhan Khaldun, but this was ruled out by the teacher as impossible on a

number of scores: not only was it a considerable distance from the *sum* centre, there are also restrictions on females climbing the sacred mountain (due to its martial associations), and also on foreigners entering the site due its place of national honour.

5. Mend-Ooyo describes the trip made as part of the project in a chapter within the book *Orshihuin gerelt hureen dotor* (Mend-Ooyo 2018: 192).

6. I have referred to the second edition of the text (Mend-Ooyo 2002); however all quotations in the paragraphs to follow are taken from Simon Wickham-Smith's beautiful and scholarly English translation (Mend-Ooyo 2007).

7. Susan Crate, agreeing with Basso (1996) that 'wisdom sits in places', argues that anthropology needs 'to grapple with the extent to which global climate change is transforming these spaces, symbolic forms, and places' (Crate 2008: 573). The children's speculations about the impact of these changes at the *gants mod* demonstrates the extent to which they are themselves reflecting on such transformations.

8. I use the term vicarious memory here to refer to recollections that are beyond the personal experience of the person sharing them, yet are communicated as a personal memory. See Berliner (2005) for a discussion of such phenomena in a different context.

References

Ahearn, A and D. Bumochir. 2016. 'Contradictions in Schooling Children Among Mongolian Pastoralists', *Human Organization* 75(1): 87–96.

Albrecht, Glenn. 2005. '"Solastalgia": A New Concept in Health and Identity', *PAN: Philosophy, Activism, Nature* 3: 41–55.

Amarbayasgalan, D. and N. Dashdeleg. 2017. 'Exploring the Environmental Aspects of Locality as a Response to Curriculum Change in Mongolia', *Environmental Education* 114: 20–21.

Angé, O. and D. Berliner. 2014. 'Anthropology of Nostalgia – Anthropology as Nostalgia', in O. Angé and D. Berliner (eds), *Anthropology and Nostalgia*. Oxford: Berghahn, pp. 1–14.

Basso, K.H. 1996. *Wisdom Sits in Places: Landscape and Language Among the Western Apache*. Albuquerque, NM: University of New Mexico Press.

Berliner, D. 2005. 'An "Impossible" Transmission: Youth Religious Memories in Guinea-Conakry', *American Ethnologist* 32(4): 576–92.

Bloch, M. 1992. 'Internal and External Memory: Different Ways of Being in History', *Suomen Antropologi* 1: 3–15.

Boyer, D. 2006. 'Ostalgie and the Politics of the Future in Eastern Germany', *Public Culture* 18(2): 361–81.

Bulag, U.E. 2009. 'Mongolia in 2008: From Mongolia to Mine-golia', *Asian Survey* 49(1): 129–34.

Byambadorj, T., M. Amati and K.J. Ruming. 2011. 'Twenty-first Century Nomadic City: Ger Districts and Barriers to the Implementation of the Ulaanbaatar City Master Plan', *Asia Pacific Viewpoint* 52(2): 165–77.

Casey, E.S. 1993. *Getting Back into Place: Toward a Renewed Understanding of the Place-world*. Bloomington, IN: Indiana University Press.

Chuluu, Ü. and K. Stuart. 1995. 'Rethinking the Mongol Oboo', *Anthropos* 90: 544–54.

Crate, S.A. 2008. 'Gone the Bull of Winter? Grappling with the Cultural Implications of and Anthropology's Role(s) in Global Climate Change', *Current Anthropology* 49(4): 569–95.

Delaplace, G. 2014. 'The Ethics and Esthetics of Mongolian Hip-hop', in Y. Konogaya and A. Maekawa (eds), *Understanding Contemporary Mongolia in 50 Chapters*. Tokyo: Akashi Shoten, pp. 296–302.

Dovchin, S. 2011. 'Performing Identity Through Language: The Local Practices of Urban Youth Populations in Post-Socialist Mongolia', *Inner Asia* 13(2): 315–33.

Evans, C. and C. Humphrey. 2003. 'History, Timelessness and the Monumental: the Oboos of the Mergen Environs, Inner Mongolia', *Cambridge Archaeological Journal* 13(2): 195–211.

Hastrup, K. 1992. 'Uchronia and the Two Histories of Iceland, 1400-1800', in K. Hastrup (ed.), *Other Histories*. London: Routledge, pp. 102–20.

Humphrey, C. 1995. 'Chiefly and Shamanist Landscapes in Mongolia', in E. Hirsch and M. O'Hanlon (eds), *The Anthropology of Landscape*. Oxford: Oxford University Press, pp. 135–62.

Humphrey, C. and D. Sneath. 1999. *The End of Nomadism? Society, State, and the Environment in Inner Asia*. Durham, NC: Duke University Press.

Irvine, R.D.G. 2014. 'Deep Time: An Anthropological Problem', *Social Anthropology* 22(2): 157–72.

_____. 2018. 'Seeing Environmental Violence in Deep Time: Perspectives from Contemporary Mongolian Literature and Music', *Environmental Humanities* 10(1): 257–72.

Irvine, R.D.G., B. Bodenhorn, E. Lee and D. Amarbayasgalan. 2019. 'Learning to See Climate Change: Children's Perceptions of Environmental Transformation in Mongolia, Mexico, Arctic Alaska, and the UK', *Current Anthropology* 60(6): 723–740.

Jackson, S.L. 2015. 'Imagining the Mineral Nation: Contested Nation-building in Mongolia', *Nationalities Papers* 43(3): 437–56.

Lindskog, B.V. 2016. 'Ritual Offerings to Ovoos Among Nomadic Halh Herders of West-Central Mongolia', *Etudes mongoles et sibériennes, centrasiatiques et tibétaines* 47. Retrieved 24 June 2020 from https://journals.openedition.org/emscat/2740.

Marin, A. 2010. 'Riders Under Storms: Contributions of Nomadic Herders' Observations to Analysing Climate Change in Mongolia', *Global Environmental Change* 20(1): 162–76.

Mend-Ooyo, G. 2002. *Altan Ovoo*, 2nd edn. Ulaanbaatar: Botibileg.

_____. 2007. *Altan Ovoo*, trans. S. Wickham-Smith. Ulaanbaatar: Mongolian Academy of Culture and Poetry.

_____. 2015. *Gol us tungalagshih tsag*. Ulaanbaatar: Munheen.

_____. 2018. *Orshihuin gerelt hureen dotor*. Ulaanbaatar: Munheen.

Nixon, R. 2011. *Slow Violence and the Environmentalism of the Poor*. Cambridge, MA: Harvard University Press.

Pedersen, M.A. 2017. 'The Vanishing Power Plant: Infrastructure and Ignorance in Peri-urban Ulaanbaatar', *Cambridge Journal of Anthropology* 35(2): 79–95.

Plueckhahn, R. and D. Bumochir. 2018. 'Capitalism in Mongolia – Ideology, Practice and Ambiguity', *Central Asian Survey* 37(3): 341–56.

Sneath, D. 1998. 'State Policy and Pasture Degradation in Inner Asia', *Science* 281(5380): 1147–48.

_____. 2010. 'Political Mobilization and the Construction of Collective Identity in Mongolia', *Central Asian Survey* 29(3): 251–67.

_____. 2014. 'Nationalising Civilisational Resources: Sacred Mountains and Cosmopolitical Ritual in Mongolia', *Asian Ethnicity* 15(4): 458–72.

Sternberg, T. 2008. 'Environmental Challenges in Mongolia's Dryland Pastoral Landscape', *Journal of Arid Environments* 72(7): 1294–304.

Stubblefield, A., S. Chandra, S. Eagan et al. 2005. 'Impacts of Gold Mining and Land Use Alterations on the Water Quality of Central Mongolian Rivers', *Integrated Environmental Assessment and Management* 1(4): 365–73.

Vergunst, J.L. 2008. 'Taking a Trip and Taking Care in Everyday Life', in T. Ingold and J.L. Vergunst (eds), *Ways of Walking: Ethnography and Practice on Foot*. Aldershot: Ashgate, pp. 105–21.

Wickham-Smith, S. 2013. *The Interrelationship of Humans and the Mongol Landscape in G. Mend-Ooyo's Altan Ovoo*. Lewiston, NY: Edwin Mellen.

CHAPTER 8

Melt in the Future Subjunctive

Cymene Howe

In recent years ice has become a climatological gauge: a substance that renders visible rising temperatures.[1] It can be measured, its retreats photographed, its depths plumbed and its lifespan calculated. And it is melting: nowhere faster, and faster than expected, in the Arctic region.[2] An IPCC report released in September 2019 details that global sea levels are set to rise much more quickly than previously thought and that the melting of land ice is the greatest contributor to global sea level rise. Ice's physical changes and the geohydrological implications associated with it are now regular media features as news of catastrophic melt continues to mark our times.

In this chapter, I focus upon human and other-than-human encounters in and around frozen hydrospheres. Ethnographically, my research is sited primarily in Iceland, a place that has experienced some of the most dramatic glacial retreat on earth. About 10 per cent of the island's surface area is covered with approximately 400 glaciers, which are losing an estimated 11 billion tons of ice per year.[3] In this project, which I began in summer of 2016, I have been seeking out points of transformation where ice's material form is changing, moving and presencing differently. What I have found are the liminal qualities of ice's materiality: as object, as resource, and as vessel of environmental and social history. I have come to see ice as an index of an aesthetic both sublimated and conditioned by ecological and economic inputs. I also see ice as a nostalgic prosthetic in at least two ways. First, ice contains, literally, an archive of material history in the form of sediments, pollen and atmospheric chemistry that is captured in the layers of glaciers and ice sheets. Cryoforms thus demonstrate a condition of 'nature' and times past, which were less troubled by human impacts. Secondly, ice, both in its frozen state or as it is turned to liquid, speaks to a nostalgia in the future subjunctive. Its melting or its remaining solid portends a future that might, or might not, be; it is a site of prognostication and subjunctive, ecohuman futures.

Figure 8.1. Glacier. Sveitarfélagið Hornafjörð, East Iceland. Photograph by the author.

Rapid changes to cryoforms, such as glaciers, sea ice and ice sheets, are indicative not only of icy morphologies, but allegorical to the ways that human history has become enacted upon 'nature'. Thus, ice can be taken as illustrative of a particular set of nostalgic attachments, both biophysically in its containment of minerals, isotopes or atmospheric materials, as well as 'socially' in its containment of those same materials, and more. The minor time of human existence and its period of colonial industrialization has carved out signals and indexes, curving in particular ways both the ontology of ecological systems and human social life. Here, Michel Serres's (2008) concepts of 'the hard' and 'the soft' may be useful. The former is the adjective associated with the physical sciences, and thus nature, while the latter is a diagnostic of a socio-anthropological domain, where the seemingly mutable truths of culture live in contrast to the experimentally inscribed 'facts' that populate material sciences. For Serres, 'hard' is given, while 'soft' is made. In the analytics of this chapter, I take the coordinates of hard and soft quite literally by examining how hard ice is made soft through human contact.

In the Anthropocene condition, the hard or soft qualities of the natural and social sciences have become further destabilized and unsure, while still surely affecting one another, just as surely as human habit has come to bite deeply into planet-wide systems and ecological spheres. The material world is being made soft by resolutely social and political human behaviour. The hard and the soft no longer hold (if they ever did). We are in a place much stickier than that. In thinking through the present ecological moment, we may be compelled to recognize that 'stickiness' has probably always epitomized the relationship between natural and social worlds and their sciences. And one wonders if there is not nostalgia here too. If nostalgia is a 'longing for what is lacking in a changed present' (Pickering and Keightley 2006: 920) or 'a reaction against the irreversible' (Jankélévitch 1983: 299, quoted in Angé and Berliner 2016), then present environmental conditions would seem to cry out for a nostalgic reckoning for the forms of 'nature' that were.

Bears

I began with the proposition that ice has become a signal for rapidly transforming environmental systems, an index of an earthly irreversibility and passed past. But before receding glaciers or melting ice sheets came to occupy much of the popular imagination around climate change, there was another charismatic figure of demise: the polar bear. Indeed, dead bears are one way of interpreting lost ice.

Egill Bjarnason was the first to spot the bear in the northern Icelandic town of Sauðárkrókur in the summer of 2016. He was in no doubt that it needed to be killed immediately, as it was close to a farm where children had been playing. This was the first polar bear to have come ashore in Iceland since 2010. The bears are not native to the island, but drift over on sea ice or swim from Greenland as their own cryoscapes elapse. After the bear's carcass was dissected it became clear that the female bear had been swimming for many miles as well as floating on drift ice. The shortest distance between Greenland and Iceland, is 300 km (or 186 miles). But the distance between Greenland and the shore where this polar bear was first seen is considerably longer, about 600 km (or 373 miles). The bear was also a mother who was still lactating, so it could not have been long since she was accompanied by her cubs.

It is national policy in Iceland to kill polar bears on sight as they are inevitably hungry after their sea voyage and therefore considered a danger to residents and livestock. Throughout recorded history there have only been a few hundred recorded sightings of polar bears in Iceland. The oldest of these was in 890, sixteen years after the first settlers arrived on the island. During the Middle Ages, polar bears were frequently tamed; but since that time, no bear has been captured alive in the country.

The shooting of the mother bear induced a passionate outpouring of affect across the country in the days that followed, seen especially on social media sites like Facebook. Reactions were divided along two general lines. From one perspective, Icelanders needed to protect themselves and their livestock and, given that the bears invariably come ashore in remote parts of the island, it would be up to local farmers or marksmen to ensure the safety of local residents. From another point of view, Icelanders were encouraged to revisit the kill-on-sight policy and put into place more humane responses to bear landings given that they will probably increase with the continuation of climate induced melting. Jón Gnarr, the former mayor of Reykjavík, who had campaigned, albeit partly facetiously, on a platform that included hosting a polar bear at the Reykjavík zoo, saw future bear migrations as a potential boon for the country. 'Why not make a tourist attraction of a polar bear haven?'[4] he asked. Jón Gunnar Ottósson, head of the Icelandic Institute of Natural History, along with many others, decried the shooting of the bear, saying that it could have been shot with a tranquillizer rather than killed. (Officials contended that it would have taken an hour by plane to get the tranquilizers to the site and that it would have been impossible to keep track and control over the animal for that long.) A spokesman for PolarWorld, a German group dedicated to the preservation of the polar regions and the creatures that inhabit it, called the bear's death 'an avoidable tragedy', adding, in full irony, 'this is another great day for mankind'.

Sea ice, which forms and melts each year, has declined more than 30 per cent in the past twenty-five years. In November 2016, ice levels hit a record low, with one scientist describing Arctic sea ice loss equal to 'an area of ice larger than Denmark' at a time when sea ice is usually growing (Milman 2016). Another scientist proclaimed that Arctic temperatures 'are literally off the charts for where they should be this time of year' (Vidal 2016). Unprecedented rates of melt appear to continue unabated, with new record lows occurring regularly, if not annually, as the floating cryospheres of the Arctic disintegrate into the sea.

Unlike on the Antarctic continent, melting sea ice in the Arctic exposes dark, open ocean beneath, absorbing more sunlight and thus warming seas and ice faster. Dark waters absorb heat. The reflective 'albedo' effect, which bounces sunlight off the surface of white ice sheets and glaciers, is also reduced with each phase of melt. This, in addition to weather patterning, is why the Arctic is heating much faster than the rest of the planet, about twice the rate[5] of temperate latitudes, or by some estimates, as much as four times the average in the Northern Hemisphere.

Helga Eymundsdóttir remembers the sea ice from when she was a girl growing up in a little village in the northwest of Iceland. It terrified her at night. Ghostly moans were emitted as floating mountains of ice rubbed up against each other, aching out a frictional chorus. That is heard much, much less now. Early explorers to the Arctic remarked extensively on the sound of sea ice as their ships plucked their way through massive tracts of ice in concert. This is what many of them called 'the Devil's Symphony'.

Lost ice, dead bears and fading sounds are fragments of the irrecuperable. Their absence harmonizes like a requiem in the future subjunctive. Like extinction narratives that may take the form of elegiac repetition, reprising the names of the deceased in mantra-like form, sensory and vital experiences of ice seem to drum on endlessly about a time coming to an end. In these encounters of the cryohuman we find the conjunction of elegiac mourning – for bears not yet dead or ice not yet disappeared – along with a worry tied to the future subjunctive, the impending conditions of the might-be.

Living at the End of the Glacier

Guðni Gunnarsson and his wife Hulda Magnúsdóttir have lived their entire lives near the village of Höfn in southeast Iceland. They are sheep farmers, with a home at the foot of a glacial tongue at Fláajökull. They have an old dog and grown children and Hulda is quick to bring cakes and coffee. She has never left Höfn, literally having never travelled further than the next two villages over.

Guðni is very clear that he has always found the glacier to do more harm than good. He explained in detail its dangers, the way it would crawl over the land and 'destroy' it. People knew the glacier as an imminent threat; it was hard to live with, but one had to learn how. The glacier could become monstrous, sometimes toppling and uprooting structures and homes. More terrifying than the groaning and growing ice however, were the threats of *jökulhlaups* (glacial outburst floods), when melted water would pool and seep beneath the surface, causing instability at the

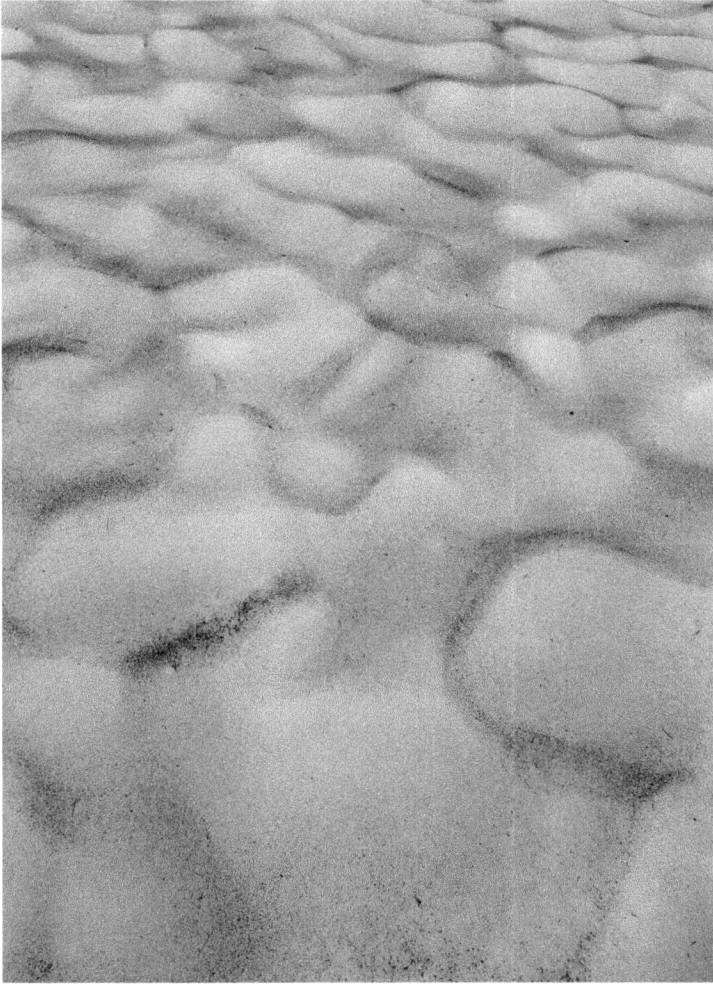

Figure 8.2. Ice. Borgarbyggð, Western Iceland. Photograph by the author.

juncture between water and ice. For a time, the ice dam might hold but it could just as easily burst without warning, sending crashing floods to all below it. This is why, Guðni explained, houses are placed higher up on the hillsides to avoid being whisked away and swept out to sea.

Guðni had to think for a while to come up with anything positive to say about the glacier nested in the mountain near his home. Proximity is not easy. He conceded that they used to utilize the glacier for ice in the 1930s and 1940s. Prior to refrigeration the glacier could provide adequate ice to keep freshly caught fish cold. Perhaps it was doing some good in retaining water over the year for what would later become waterfalls. He remembered too teams of scientists coming to the glacier in the 1940s, but he was unclear what precisely they were looking for.

What Guðni returned to several times is that the glacier is in fact a part of 'nature'. Glaciers are a part of the mountain, he insisted, not distinct from it. It seemed that speaking about the glacier in the singular was awkward or even illogical. For Guðni, glaciers are folded into the world. After we had eaten through several dishes of cakes washed down with dark coffee, Guðni did agree that he finds the glaciers beautiful, but only at times.

Glaciers may have sublime beauty. But they have also been menacing, threatening life with their mass and watery outbursts. So how might we take this ice? As ominous threat or thing of wondrous beauty? As that to be avoided, or that to which we should direct our care and concern (Latour 2004)?

Responding

Jóhanna Jónsdóttir has just returned from Sólheimajökull, a glacial tongue about two hours southeast of Reykjavík. Johanna teaches a glaciology class for exchange students in addition to her regular research and teaching as a professor at the University of Iceland. Each year she takes a group of students to Sólheim glacier where they use a steam drill, which she describes as acting like a pressure cooker, a mechanism that bores through the glacial ice like a hot knife through butter. Down the drill tube is placed a wire line, dipping ten metres into the glacier. As the ice on the surface of the glacier melts away, the line will show more of itself. It is a simple, low-impact technology of measurement.

Johanna explains that glaciers are anything but static. In fact, she says, they are best understood as operating like a conveyor belt. They move, and they move material. Snow and ice accumulate in the higher altitudes of the glacier and are depleted in the lower reaches. There is a circulation of material from high to low and from solid to liquid. Johanna also describes glaciers in economic terms. They are like a bank account, she explains. In the winter, positive accumulation fills up the bank. Deposits are made at higher elevations, while at lower ones, withdrawals occur. And just as you would with your accounts, Johanna adds, you want to keep it in a healthy balance. But we know that balance is not being achieved of late and that deposits have not kept up with expenditures.

Icelandic glaciers are especially well documented compared to many others in the world. Since the Middle Ages, and arguably over the last 1,200 years (since the first known human settlement of the island), Icelanders have been attuned to the glaciers that occupy their homeland. Historically, the country's ice cover has varied. For Sólheim glacier, Johanna explains that they have excellent records going back to the 1930s. In the 1930s, temperatures had risen and glaciers retreated. In the 1960s and 1970s it became cooler and they grew. Since the mid-1990s however, they have only gone in one direction, and that is toward 'ablation'.

Ablation is the technical term for ice loss. In English the word denotes, in the first instance, 'the surgical removal' of bodily tissue.[6] Coincidentally, the first person to thoroughly document Icelandic glaciers systematically was, by trade, a surgeon. In the second definition, ablation denotes the melting or loss of snow and ice. About half of ablation events occur through calving (cracking off of ice forms) and the other half through melting. While there have always been advances and retreats of glaciers in Iceland, Johanna notes that the country's glaciers have now withdrawn further than in the warm 1930s. She describes that in the West Fjords, on the northwestern peninsula, they are finding vegetation growth indicating newly exposed surfaces that have been ice covered for at least 2,000 to 3,000 years. This is effectively 'new land' now uncovered by melt.

Johanna and I talk for some time about what she terms 'glacial response'. She notes that Earth systems have only accumulated about 150 years of intensive fossil fuel use. 'The atmosphere and the glaciers', she says, 'haven't managed to respond to it yet. Not fully. It is a slow system'. And it is a very 'stochastic' system, having a random probability or pattern that may be analysed statistically but that will not be predicted precisely: 'If you push it that way, you can expect a dramatic effect'. She adds, however, that:

> The climate models are not really managing to consider all of the physics. We have weather forecast models that are similar and they simulate the physics six or seven days into the future. This is a model that can tell you that about short-term weather, but not how the weather will be in December! And with climate models we are really asking them to tell us what the weather will be in 100 years' time...

It is telling that Johanna turns to weather prediction as she speaks of glacial response. For her, and for several other glaciologists with whom I spoke, their role as scientists was changing. Historically, glaciologists have been trained as geologists who might then specialize in cryoforms and their interactions. Glaciology, as Helgi Björnsson, a prominent Icelandic glaciologist, put it to me, 'has always been closer to geology: observing what is happening, the forces and movements and cracks'. Helgi himself began his studies and career in the 'slow science' of geology. In the present, both Helgi and Johanna are convinced glaciology has become an

Figure 8.3. Glacial lagoon. Sveitarfélagið Hornafjörð, East Iceland. Photograph by the author.

exercise in understanding how ice and melt respond to larger systemic changes, including atmospheric conditions and weather. Glaciological expertise, like the cryoforms of glaciers themselves, is changing, now being actively shaped by meteorology and the patterning of weather. If it began as a slow science, glaciology would now appear to be speeding up and becoming attuned to new inputs of unprecedented weather events.

Before the 2007 4th Assessment Report of the IPCC, Johanna explained, glaciers and ice sheets appeared in diagnostic modelling as 'white mountains'. Greenland and Antarctica, for example, were represented as white, slightly protruding outlines in most past models (and in some now). But of course, ice sheets and glaciers are not inert, whitewashed and static, but instead dynamic and contributing to sea level rise and changing weather. Reflecting on how glaciology was itself moving in more meteorological directions and aware that models have been insufficient, Johanna quite plainly stated her estimation of the present: 'this is the largest uncontrolled experiment that we have ever done. What we are doing now is we are pushing Earth systems into a regime that we have not been in, ever, naturally before'.

Figure 8.4. Glacial melt beach. Sveitarfélagið Hornafjörð, East Iceland. Photograph by the author.

Time in Ice

On the streets of Paris in December 2015, while the COP 21 climate negotiations took place inside meeting rooms, massive boulders of glacial ice had been set to melt. Arranged in a circle to mimic a watch, a clock face, a compass and a point of navigation, the installation Ice Watch was intended to draw attention from multiple directions. Developed as a collaboration between the Icelandic artist Ólafur Elíasson and the geologist

Minik Rosing, the impetus behind Ice Watch was twofold. First, the ice was arranged like a watch, or the face of a clock, to indicate the passing of time. In real time, observers were able to watch the ice melt. Elíasson explained: 'a circle is like a compass. It leaves navigation to the people who are inside it. It is a mistake to think that the work of art is the circle of ice – it is, in fact, the space it invents' (Zarin 2015).

In an epoch defined by human effects and bracketed by ominous consequences, one wonders about time on ice. Glaciers, ice sheets and other cryoforms are a matter of deep, compacted, illustrative time. They are what the geoscientist Richard Alley (2014) calls 'a two-mile time machine'. Particulate matter like pollen gets stored there, and atmospheric histories get revealed, as do radioactive isotopes, the deep genaeology of climate, carbon and species. Ice can also be a breath of the time it contains. If one were to put her mouth up to the bursting air bubbles that crackled across the icy surface of the art installation in Paris, she could have breathed in utterly pristine, 15,000-year-old air: time captured in a boulder of water.

The great melting at the top of the world, and the bottom as well, may have us wondering about the cool, ancient time that is being washed away and the future to come. Earth's cryosphere is sloughing off as we watch in real time, turned from hard to soft, from durable to mutable, from solid ice to torrents of fresh water. Here we might get a sense of a growing nostalgia for the deep history ice holds. For, while ice has always told a past, it now portends a future as well. It figures as both nostalgic coda to time passed as well as proleptic signal of more to come.

Cymene Howe is Professor of Anthropology at Rice University. Her books include *Intimate Activism* (Duke University Press, 2013) and *Ecologics: Wind and Power in the Anthropocene* (Duke University Press, 2019), which follows the human and more-than-human lives intertwined with renewable energy futures. She is co-editor of the *The Johns Hopkins Guide to Theory* and the *Anthropocene Unseen: A Lexicon* (Punctum, 2020) and has published widely in transdisciplinary journals and volumes. Her current research on cryohuman relations examines the changing dynamics between human populations and bodies of ice in the Arctic region and sea level adaptation in lower latitude coastal cities around the world.

Notes

1. In fact, the Intergovernmental Panel on Climate Change (IPCC) considers glacial diminishment to be the 'highest confidence temperature indicator in the climate system' (Figure 2.39a in Houghton et al. 2001).

2. http://www.independent.co.uk/environment/arctic-warming-twice-rate-rest-of-planet-global-warming-snow-water-ice-permafrost-arctic-monitoring-a7710701.html, retrieved 15 September 2018.
3. https://www.scientificamerican.com/article/what-is-iceland-without-ice/, retrieved 15 September 2018.
4. Personal communication, 24 July 2016; also shared on Facebook in Icelandic.
5. http://www.independent.co.uk/environment/arctic-warming-twice-rate-rest-of-planet-global-warming-snow-water-ice-permafrost-arctic-monitor ing-a7710701.html, retrieved 1 July 2018.
6. See the definition of 'ablation' in Merriam-Webster, https://www.merriam-webster.com/dictionary/ablation, retrieved 7 February 2020.

References

Alley, R.B. 2014. *The Two-Mile Time Machine: Ice Cores, Abrupt Climate Change, and Our Future*. Updated edition. Princeton, NJ: Princeton University Press.
Angé, O. and D. Berliner (eds). 2016. *Anthropology and Nostalgia*. Oxford: Berghahn.
Arctic Monitoring and Assessment Programme (AMAP). 2017. *Snow, Water, Ice and Permafrost. Summary for Policy-Makers*. Oslo, Norway.
Houghton, J.T., Y. Ding, D.J. Griggs, M. Noguer, P.J. van der Linden, X. Dai, K. Maskell and C.A. Johnson (eds). 2001. *Climate Change 2001: The Scientific Basis. Contribution of Working Group I to the Third Assessment Report of the Intergovernmental Panel on Climate Change*. Cambridge and New York: Cambridge University Press.
Latour, B. 2004. 'Why Has Critique Run out of Steam? From Matters of Fact to Matters of Concern', *Critical Inquiry* 30(Winter): 225–48.
Milman, O. 2016. 'Sea Ice Extent in Arctic and Antarctic Reached Record Lows in November', *The Guardian*, 6 December, retrieved February 2020, https://www.theguardian.com/environment/2016/dec/06/arctic-antarctic-ice-melt-november-record.
Pickering, M. and E. Keightley. 2006. 'The Modalities of Nostalgia', *Current Sociology* 54: 919–41.
Serres, M. 2008. *The Five Senses: A Philosophy of Mingled Bodies (I)*, trans. M. Sankey and P. Cowley. London: Continuum.
Vidal, J. 2016. 'Extraordinarily Hot Arctic Temperatures Alarm Scientists', *The Guardian*, 22 November 2016, retrieved 7 February 2020, https://www.theguardian.com/environment/2016/nov/22/extraordinarily-hot-arctic-temperatures-alarm-scientists.
Zarin, C. 2015. 'The Artist Who is Bringing Icebergs to Paris', *The New Yorker*, 5 December 2015, retrieved 7 February 2020, https://www.newyorker.com/culture/culture-desk/the-artist-who-is-bringing-icebergs-to-paris.

Afterword

Dominic Boyer

If you seek to study nostalgia, always be alert for its mania. The 'longing for home' that has been nostalgia's reputation since its first appearance in a Swiss medical dissertation in 1688 has always been more, or less, than it appears to be (Boyer 2006). Johannes Hofer who first coined the term was looking for a way to capture the powerful sentiments of homesickness that seemed to paralyse young people who had been forced by circumstance to spend long periods of time away from their natal villages, often as soldiers or indentured servants. It was an affliction wrapped up with what Raymond Williams (1974) termed the 'mobile privatization' of European modernity. Increasing numbers of young persons were on the move because of war, commerce, studies and work in the seventeenth century. And yet it was still common for Europeans to die not many kilometres away from where they were born.

I have always imagined that Hofer empathized closely with the subjects of his case studies, like the country girl probably working as a servant in a foreign town who deliriously shouted *Ich will Heim* ('I want to go home!') until she seemed on the verge of death. Only when she was allowed to return home did her symptoms disappear. Hofer was himself a student living in Basel many kilometres from his native Mühlhausen when he was working on his dissertation. He must have felt the urge to shout from time to time. His own ability to return home was far from guaranteed, caught somewhere between his professional ambitions, his educational possibilities and the peregrinations of an increasingly translocalized Europe.

Hofer sought to medicalize homesickness (*Heimweh*) more than one way. He considered *nostomania* (an obsession with the return home) and *philopatridomania* (an obsessive love of the fatherland) before settling on 'nostalgia' (pain/sorrow for the return home). I have always found it interesting to consider 'mania' as part of the semantic terroir of nostalgia (Boyer 2010). It suggests a hallucinatory pursuit in which the story of 'the return' operates more as pretext than as honest ambition. Return to where and when? Mania excessively occupies the now.

Hofer seems to have been at least intuitively aware of this. He concludes his text with a remarkable story:

> Thus not long since it was told me by a Parisian that he himself had an Helvetian bound servant who was sad and melancholy at all times so that he began to work with lessened desire; finally, he came to him and sought dismissal with insistent entreaties, of which he could have no hope beyond him. When the merchant granted this immediately, the servant changed from sudden joy, excused from his mind these phantasma for several days, and after a while remained in Paris, broken up no longer by this disease. (1934: 390)

What Hofer offered as a sort of anecdotal remainder to his thesis contains the key to rethinking the whole phenomenon. The freed Helvetian longed not for a return to his place of origin, even though this is what both he and his master were convinced afflicted him, but for the right to determine his own future. Having won that right, he surprised all parties, including the good Dr Hofer, by remaining just where he was. An insistence upon freedom too belongs to the *terroir* of nostalgia.

So with this in mind, what should we make of 'ecological nostalgia'? In what respect is it genuine *Heimweh*, in what respect the pursuit of self-determination, and in what respect pure mania? The introduction to this collection of chapters frames its intervention in terms of engaging pervasive instances of ecological nostalgia 'in modern societies upset by climate change and ecosystem destructions'. *Heimweh* is surely a powerful Anthropocene affect. But Anthropocene grief has a distinctively future anterior character in its focus on how we (in the north) will feel for what we have lost once the Holocene oikos is fully unravelled. There is typically little consideration, let alone grief, expressed for the losses already suffered by those from whom the north expropriated labour, land, materials and life to build its magnificent modern palaces. Moreover, if it were a sincerely presentist grief there would be less focus on the ten or twenty years still remaining to undertake radical civilizational change. But the content of that 'change' often seems as evacuated as the meaning of a term like 'sustainability' which is set forward in countless policy documents as the antidote to the current trajectory. For every sincere effort to imagine alternative ethics, politics and economy (e.g. Kallis 2018), there are hundreds more that seem to wish to preserve contemporary modernity apart from perhaps to change its sources of fuel or distribution of income. Anthropocene *Heimweh* thus offers a politics of the future that frequently aspires to change as little as possible. Again, our introduction: 'in a world that is changing fast, it is no surprise that a world shaped by unexpected ecological turns proves propitious to triggering attachment to forms of life that are jeopardized, or already gone'. Claire Colebrook considers this mode of attachment the 'Anthropocene state of emergency' (2017: 406) and worries that it will ultimately be leveraged to legitimate further non-deliberative technoscientific and military interventions in the name of preserving certain ways of being human, very likely at the expense of others.

A geo-engineered future is no more guaranteed than any future. But I think Colebrook is right to sense the mania that ripples within Anthropocene grief. That mania may sometimes appear to be about the restoration of imperial splendour ('Making the Anthropocene Great Again'). And it may sometimes seem obsessed with achieving new designs for human-environmental balance and futurity. Yet mania, as noted above, is more often about the now, often lividly so. Anthropocene grief does a fairly poor job of recollecting histories and imagining other futures all things considered. We might take that as a sign that its true stakes are the preservation and extension of the contemporary, the time before collapse.

What does it mean to wish to preserve the now? Let us not forget that 'ecology' was the neologism of another German medical doctor, Ernst Haeckel. Dr Haeckel, much like Dr Hofer, was very much a child of his time. Although perhaps not the proto-Nazi he is often characterized as, racism, imperialism and economism richly informed the Social Darwinism that he helped to spread throughout Germany in the last decades of the nineteenth century (Weikart 1993). If Haeckel meant 'ecology' to define a new area of science devoted to the study of creaturely relations with their creaturely neighbours in their immediate environments, it should not be supposed he had in mind the investigation of zones of mutual prosperity and thriving. No; instead, he had in mind spectacles of the Hobbesian-Malthusian agon in which:

> everywhere you find an unsparing, highly embittered bellum omnium contra omnes [*Kampf Aller gegen Alle*]. Nowhere in nature, wherever you may look, does that idyllic peace exist, about which the poets sing … rather everywhere there is struggle and striving to destroy one's neighbor and competitor. Passion and selfishness, conscious or unconscious, is everywhere the motive force of life … Man in this respect is no exception to the rest of the animal world. (1868: 16)

Naturalizing the 'war of all against all' has always been one of the most convenient alibis for European colonialism and empire. Likewise, as Hannah Arendt so aptly put it: 'imperialism would have necessitated the invention of racism as the only possible "explanation" and excuse for its deeds, even if no race-thinking had ever existed in the civilized world' (2004: 241). Racism helped to position European campaigns of extermination and occupation as being in the greater interest of human ecology.

The introduction to the volume closes by considering 'imperialist ecological nostalgias' and, with Haeckel's legacy in mind, there has probably never been another kind. But the trouble here seems less with the politically suspect origins of scientific ecology than with the perpetuation of ecological affects and designs that wishfully ignore the forms of violence and dispossession that contributed to the formation and acceleration of *androleukoheteropetromodernity* (a term I prefer to both 'Anthropocene' and 'Capitalocene'). This is where I think anthropology should shine its spotlight and this collection of chapters is an excellent contribution to that critical trajectory.

Dominic Boyer is Professor of Anthropology at Rice University and Founding Director of the Center for Energy and Environmental Research in the Human Sciences (CENHS), the first research centre in the world designed specifically to promote research on the energy/environment nexus in the arts, humanities and social sciences. He recently led the editorial collective of the journal *Cultural Anthropology* (2015–2018) and edits the *Expertise* book series for Cornell University Press. He is currently pursuing ethnographic research with flood victims in Houston, Texas, and on electric futures across the world. His most recent book is *Energopolitics* (Duke University Press, 2019), which studies the politics of wind power development in Southern Mexico.

References

Arendt, H. 2004. *The Origins of Totalitarianism*. New York: Schocken.

Boyer, D. 2006. '*Ostalgie* and the Politics of the Future in Eastern Germany', *Public Culture* 18(2): 361–81.

———. 2010. 'From Algos to Autonomos: Nostalgic Eastern Europe as Postimperial Mania', in M. Todorova and Z. Gille (eds), *Postcommunist Nostalgia*. Oxford: Berghahn, pp. 17–28.

Colebrook, C. 2017. 'We Have Always Been Post-Anthropocene: The Anthropocene Counter-Factual', in I. Szeman and D. Boyer (eds), *Energy Humanities: An Anthropology*. Baltimore, MD: Johns Hopkins University Press, pp. 399–414.

Haeckel, E. 1868. *Natürliche Schöpfungsgeschichte*. Berlin: Reimer.

Hofer, J. 1934. 'Medical Dissertation on Nostalgia', trans. C.K. Ansprach, *Bulletin of the History of Medicine* 2: 376–91.

Kallis, G. 2018. *Degrowth*. New York: Agenda.

Weikart, R. 1993. 'The Origins of Social Darwinism in Germany, 1859-1895', *Journal of the History of Ideas* 54(3): 469–88.

Williams, R. 1974. *Television*. Hanover, NH: Wesleyan University Press.

Index

ablation, 173, 177n6. *See also* Arctic; climate change; ice melt

acceleration, 4, 12n6, 181

acculturation, 86, 101n3. *See also* loss, cultural

activism, 8, 65–69, 88, 96–98. *See also* NGO

Africa, 10, 32, 42. *See also* colonialism

agon, 180. *See also* war

agriculture, 1–9, 60–83, 107–144; and capitalism, 63–65, 74–75, 84–85; colonial, 91; decline, 74; fertilizers, 65, 70, 111–3; organic, 118; in France, 60–83; history, 4, 13n7, 20, 61, 121–22; modernization, 6, 12n2, 64, 78n3, 111, 119; organic, 69–70, 77; peasant, 61, 65; primitive, 2, 20, 70–71; prohibition of, 76; sustainable, 65; traditional, 9, 20, 62–71, 77, 111–13, 126, 132–34, 137–42. *See also* ancestral seeds; animal traction; biodiversity; collectivism; food; fruit; loss; modernization; peasantry; potato; ritual; sustainability

agri-food industry, 64–65

Ahmed, Sara, 108, 113, 117, 121

Aistara, Guntra, 8

Albrecht, Glenn, 5, 147

Amazonia, 9–11, 84–106, 108–9; animism, 89; anthropology of, 86–87, 99, 101n3; Brazil, 85–86, 101n1; culture, 85, 88–90, 96; development, 85–86; imagination, 85; nature, 85, 94–95; people, 86–87, 96, 101n1; population expansion, 86, 90, 102n9. *See also* anthropology; Christianity; colonialism; deforestation; extraction; indigenous; loss; modernization; oil; politics; preservation; rainforest; Waorani

Amerindian peoples, 85, 102n11, 130, 143

Anarchists, 62–63, 66, 69

ancestors, 5, 11, 91, 95, 98–99, 113, 138–39, 150, 155, 160–61; ancestral lands, 88, 91, 127, 160

ancestral seeds, 1, 68–77; banks, 1; and biodiversity, 70, 76; and neo-peasant values, 70–76; and sustainability, 68–69

Ancien Régime, 63

Andes, 107–25. *See also* agriculture, potato, rainforest

androleukoheteropetromodernity, 181

Angé, Olivia, 10–11, 77, 130, 136

animal, 5–7, 13n10–n11, 28, 42, 45–46, 53, 67, 111, 113, 153, 180; death, 169; horses, 145–6, 149–50, 154, 160; silver, 152; narwhal, 6, 44, 46, 52–54; poaching, 7, 91–94; polar bears, 168–70; traction, 69–72, 76–77. *See also* agriculture; herding; hunting; migration, animal; non-human beings; ritual sacrifice; tourism, wildlife

Anthropocene, 10, 55, 168, 179–81. *See also* emotion; memory; pain

anthropology, 46, 78, 85, 100; of Amazonia, 86–87, 101n3–n4; and climate change, 163n7; colonial, 41; ecological, 181; and the environment, 17–18; of landscape,